SOURCES OF UNOFFICIAL UK STATISTICS

Third Edition

Sources of
Unofficial
UK
Statistics
Third Edition

Compiled by
David Mort

INFORMATION RESEARCH NETWORK

Gower

Published by
Gower Publishing Limited
Gower House
Croft Road
Aldershot
Hampshire GU11 3HR
England

Gower
Old Post Road
Brookfield
Vermont 05036
USA

David Mort has asserted his right under the Copyright, Designs and Patents Act 1988 to be identified as the author of this work.

British Library Cataloguing in Publication Data

Mort, D. (David), 1952–
    Sources of unofficial UK statistics. – 3rd ed.
    1.Great Britain – Statistical services
    I.Title
    314.1'07

ISBN 0 566 07672 1

Library of Congress Cataloging-in-Publication Data

Mort, D.
    Sources of unofficial UK statistics / compiled by David Mort. --
3rd ed.
        p. cm.
    Includes indexes.
    ISBN 0-566-07672-1 (cloth)
    1. Great Britain--Statistical services--Directories. I.Title
HA37.G7M665 1997
016.3141--dc21   96-51905
                                        CIP

Typeset in Palatino by Midland Graphic Services
Printed in Great Britain by Biddles Ltd, Guildford.

Contents

Introduction

Published statistical series and marketing data play an important role in the provision of information for business, industry, economic analysis and academic and other research. In the United Kingdom, Central Government is the main supplier of statistical information. These statistics are usually referred to as 'official statistics' and details of the range of official statistics available can be obtained from the Office for National Statistics (ONS). However, there are many other organizations involved in compiling and disseminating statistics and these include trade associations, professional bodies, market research organizations, stockbrokers, banks, chambers of commerce, economic research and forecasting organizations, consultants, academic institutions, limited companies and PLCs particularly in consumer markets, and commercial publishers. Sources from these publishers form the basis of the entries in this directory, and these resources are usually referred to as 'non-official statistics' or sometimes 'non-governmental statistics'. Traditionally, these two areas of statistical publishing – official and non-official – have been largely separate from each other, although some trade association data has been used in selected official series and various non-governmental bodies often lobby and advise government statisticians on statistical matters. In recent years, however, the line between official and non-official sources has become increasingly blurred with more and more official series distributed and sold through private sector agents. These agents are included in this guide alongside more conventional non-official publishers.

This third edition of *Sources of Unofficial UK Statistics* (previous editions published in 1985 and 1990) provides details of almost 900 non-official statistical titles and services and is a unique source of information on an important area of business information.

Non-official statistics

Central Government may be the major producer of statistics but, for various reasons, these statistics do not always provide sufficient detail on specific markets, sectors and products. Non-official sources can cover product areas and sectors excluded from Central Government data and also different types of data not usually included in official sources: for example, end-user statistics, salary surveys, opinion surveys, product price information and forecasts. In some cases, non-official sources simply repackage and comment on official data but these commentaries often provide a useful analysis of the major trends in official statistics. Many of the private sector agents now selling detailed time series from Central Government are also adding value to the data with commentaries, ratios and calculations from the original figures.

Prices of non-official statistics vary from a few pounds to thousands of pounds for detailed market research, but a considerable proportion of the UK titles are still available free of charge.

One disadvantage of non-official statistics is that, in many cases, the material is not available generally. Many trade associations and professional bodies, for example, only circulate material to members while other organizations limit access to clients, survey participants and so on. However, the percentage of the total non-official output restricted to only a limited group of users is relatively small and, even where detailed statistics are confidential, an executive summary or synopsis of data may be available generally. Another problem is that the reliability and accuracy of the data can vary considerably from one non-official source to another. The amount of resources devoted to statistical activity, and the level of statistical expertise, can vary from one organization to the next and this is likely to have an effect on the statistics produced. Few sources give any details on how the figures have been compiled and the specific methodologies used.

As well as the traditional type of statistical publications consisting of tables and graphs, a surprisingly large number of regular statistics appear in other non-statistical sources such as journals, yearbooks, annual reports, directories, press releases, newspapers, reports, monographs, conference proceedings and machine-readable databanks. Examples of these sources are included in the directory.

Sources included in the guide

Some 870 statistical titles and services produced by around 500 organizations are included in this guide, based largely on information supplied by the publishing organizations at the end of 1995 and early 1996. The number of sources covered in this third edition is slightly less than in the second edition because a decision was taken to exclude local authority publications and other sources which deal with specific local areas. Local authority sources have been excluded because they are really official sources. The coverage of these sources in previous editions has also been patchy and it was felt that it was better to concentrate on other sources which are likely to be more central to the needs of business and industry.

Statistics of interest to business and industry which are produced regularly are included. For a source to be considered as regular it must be produced at least once every six years. Most publications included are either annual, monthly, quarterly or biennial (once every two years), and one-off surveys or market reports do not qualify.

Only sources issued in, and concerning, the United Kingdom or Great Britain are covered. Material with international coverage has generally been excluded. Some regional sources, relating to Scotland and Wales, and some local material covering the capital city, London, have been included but other local statistics on very specific local areas have been excluded.

Sources are included even if they have a restricted circulation but, in some cases, the publishers have asked to be excluded from the guide and we have agreed to this request. As well as the standard time series statistics, forecasts, trend surveys and opinion surveys are included, but data dealing with only one corporate body, such as company annual reports, has generally been excluded. Most of the items included are clearly statistical publications but non-statistical sources listed in the previous section are included if they contain a regular statistical series or feature.

Finally, the sources listed cover a range of physical formats including the standard book form, those which are produced on one or two sheets of paper such as press releases and pamphlets, through to electronic data available on-line, on CD-ROM or on diskette or tape.

The format of the guide

The main part of this guide comprises 870 entries arranged alphabetically by publishing organization and numbered consecutively. The entries have been based on responses from the publishing bodies themselves supplemented, where possible, by a scanning of the source document. Usually if an organization publishes more than one title each has a separate entry. The exceptions are regularly produced market research surveys produced by one publisher on various topics. As most of these surveys follow the same format they are included in one general entry rather than listed separately.

Each entry contains the following information, where available:

Name of the publishing body

Title of source

General description of contents including details of any commentary, analysis accompanying the statistics and the sources of the statistics

Frequency of source

Availability of source and any restrictions on use

Cost per annum and/or per issue

Address of publisher

Telephone and fax number of publisher

Other comments, including availability of data in machine-readable and other publications

The range of information noted above represents the 'ideal' entry where information is available for each category. In some cases, some information is not available or is not applicable to that particular source.

Supporting the main sequence of entries are two indexes:

A *subject index* with references to the relevant entry number in the main sequence

A *title index* where each published title or service is listed alphabetically.

Part I

The Statistics

1 — 3I PLC

Title	**Enterprise Barometer**
Coverage	Based on an opinion survey of its companies, 3I produces a regular report on likely trends in turnover, profit, investment, employment etc. A commentary supports the statistics.
Frequency	Regular
Availability	General
Cost	On application
Comments	Published by Graham Bannock & Partners Ltd at the address below.
Address	53 Clarewood Court, Crawford Street, London W1H 5DF
Telephone	0171 723 1845
Fax	0171 706 1040

2 — ABACUS DATA SERVICES (UK) LTD

Title	**UK Import and Export Statistics**
Coverage	Import and export data, from 1987 onwards, for any traded product with basic data available by value, volume, month or year to date, country of origin, country of destination, port of entry or departure, flag or carrier used. Abacus is an officially appointed agent of HM Customs and Excise.
Frequency	Monthly
Availability	General
Cost	Depends on information required
Comments	Data available in various machine readable formats.
Address	Challenge House, 616 Mitcham Road, Croydon, Surrey CR9 3AU
Telephone	0181 683 6444
Fax	0181 683 6445

3 — ACCOUNTANCY PERSONNEL LTD

Title	**Guide to Salaries in Accountancy**
Coverage	Covers accountancy salaries and merchant and international banking salaries. Information based on surveys carried out in various regional centres in England and Wales. A general commentary accompanies the data.
Frequency	Twice per annum
Availability	General
Cost	£55
Comments	
Address	70 Watling Street, London EC4 9DD
Telephone	0171 329 8895
Fax	

4   ADAMS, JAMES R & ASSOCIATES

Title	**Report on the Housing Market**
Coverage	An analytical review of the housing market with data on performance, building, transactions, prices, attitudes etc. Based on original research and published material.
Frequency	Quarterly
Availability	General
Cost	£650
Comments	
Address	36 King Street, London WC2E 8JS
Telephone	0171 836 5012
Fax	0171 240 9460

5   ADAMS, JAMES R & ASSOCIATES

Title	**Report on the Estate Agency Market**
Coverage	An analytical review of the estates agents market with data on performance, market trends, housing sales, etc. Based on a combination of original research and published sources.
Frequency	Quarterly
Availability	General
Cost	£650
Comments	Data available in various machine readable formats.
Address	36 King Street, London WC2E 8JS
Telephone	0171 836 5012
Fax	0171 240 9460

6   ADAMS, JAMES R & ASSOCIATES

Title	**Residential Property Index**
Coverage	Analysis of prices, transactions, mortgages broken down by property types and geographical areas. Based on a combination of original research and published sources.
Frequency	Quarterly
Availability	General
Cost	£1,850
Comments	
Address	36 King Street, London WC2E 8JS
Telephone	0171 836 5012
Fax	0171 240 9460

7	ADMAP
Title	**Adstats**
Coverage	Statistics on various aspects of advertising and the media including total expenditure, expenditure by media, expenditure in selected product categories. Most of the data is from Advertising Association surveys.
Frequency	Monthly in a monthly journal
Availability	General
Cost	£180
Comments	
Address	NTC Publications Ltd, Farm Road, Henley-on-Thames, Oxfordshire RG9 1EJ
Telephone	01491 574671
Fax	01491 571188

8	ADMAP
Title	**Advertising Business Indicators**
Coverage	Summary data on economic trends plus general information on advertising and media trends.
Frequency	Monthly in a monthly journal
Availability	General
Cost	£180
Comments	
Address	NTC Publications Ltd, Farm Road, Henley-on-Thames, Oxfordshire RG9 1EJ
Telephone	01491 574671
Fax	01491 571188

9	ADVERTISING ASSOCIATION
Title	**The Advertising Forecast**
Coverage	Forecasts for the main media categories – TV, radio, newspapers, colour supplements, magazines, classifieds, display advertising and posters. Also forecasts of expenditure in the main product sectors, eg retail, industrial, financial, government, services, durables, and consumables. Historical data is also included.
Frequency	Quarterly
Availability	General
Cost	£825, £495 for members
Comments	
Address	NTC Publications Ltd, Farm Road, Henley-on-Thames, Oxfordshire RG9 1EJ
Telephone	01491 574671
Fax	01491 571188

10		ADVERTISING ASSOCIATION
	Title	**Advertising Statistics Yearbook**
	Coverage	General trends in advertising and the annual Advertising Association survey. Statistics by type of advertising, eg cinema, direct mail, poster, newspapers, magazines, directories, radio, TV. Also statistics on prices, expenditure by product sector, top advertisers, agencies, complaints, attitudes, and international trends. Data for earlier years and based on various sources.
	Frequency	Annual
	Availability	General
	Cost	£95 (plus £1.50 p+p)
	Comments	
	Address	NTC Publications Ltd, Farm Road, Henley-on-Thames, Oxfordshire RG9 1EJ
	Telephone	01491 574671
	Fax	01491 571188

11		ADVERTISING ASSOCIATION
	Title	**Quarterly Survey of Advertising Expenditure**
	Coverage	Summary tables on advertising trends by main media followed by specific sections on the total press, national newspapers, regional newspapers, consumer magazines, business and professional magazines, and all magazines. A final section looks at trends in specific industry sectors.
	Frequency	Quarterly
	Availability	General
	Cost	£595, £395 for members of the Advertising Asociation
	Comments	
	Address	NTC Publications Ltd, Farm Road, Henley-on-Thames, Oxfordshire RG9 1EJ
	Telephone	01491 574671
	Fax	01491 571188

12		ADVERTISING STANDARDS AUTHORITY
	Title	**ASA Annual Report**
	Coverage	Gives a summary of complaints received by media and by type. Based on complaints received by the ASA.
	Frequency	Annual
	Availability	General
	Cost	On request
	Comments	
	Address	2 Torrington Place, London WC1E 7HW
	Telephone	0171 580 5555
	Fax	0171 631 3051

13 AGB

Title	**AGB Superpanel**
Coverage	A consumer panel comprising approximately 8,500 homes regularly surveyed by AGB. Data on consumer spending and purchases of various goods and services.
Frequency	Continuous
Availability	General
Cost	On request
Comments	Various other consumer panels also carried out by AGB.
Address	AGB House, West Gate, London W5 1UA
Telephone	0181 967 0007
Fax	0181 967 4060

14 AGRICULTURAL ENGINEERS' ASSOCIATION

Title	**Trade Statistics**
Coverage	Import and export data for agricultural products and machinery based on Central Government trade statistics.
Frequency	Quarterly
Availability	Members
Cost	On request
Comments	
Address	Samuelson House, Orton Centre, Peterborough PE2 0LT
Telephone	01733 371381
Fax	01733 370664

15 ALFRED MARKS

Title	**Survey of Secretarial and Clerical Salaries**
Coverage	A survey of salaries based on 11 job categories and covering over 6,000 specific jobs in industrial and service sectors. Based on data collected by the company.
Frequency	Annual
Availability	General
Cost	Free to clients, price to others on request
Comments	
Address	Adia House, Box 311, Borehamwood, Hertfordshire WD6 1WD
Telephone	0181 207 5000
Fax	0181 207 4686

16

ALUMINIUM FEDERATION LTD

Title | **Aluminium Statistics Press Release**

Coverage Production, imports and despatches of primary aluminium, secondary aluminium and wrought and cast products. Based mainly on a survey of members and usually published 4-6 weeks after the date to which the statistics refer.

Frequency Monthly

Availability General

Cost Free

Comments More detailed statistics available to members who participate in the survey.

Address Broadway House, Calthorpe Road, Five Ways, Birmingham B15 1TN

Telephone 0121 456 1103

Fax 0121 456 2274

17

APPAREL KNITTING AND TEXTILES ALLIANCE

Title **Trends in Textile and Clothing Trade**

Coverage Detailed import and export statistics for textiles and clothing based on Central Government trade data.

Frequency Quarterly

Availability General

Cost £85, free to members

Comments

Address 5 Portland Place, London W1N 3AA

Telephone 0171 636 7788

Fax 0171 636 7515

18

APPLIED MARKET INFORMATION LTD

Title **199– UK Plastic Industry Handbook**

Coverage An analysis of trends in the polymer industry and key polymer markets with statistics on production, consumption, capacity, and end user markets.

Frequency Annual

Availability General

Cost £130

Comments

Address 45-47 Stokes Croft, Bristol BS1 3QP

Telephone 0117 9249442

Fax 0117 9241598

19

ARCHITECTS' JOURNAL

Title	**Industry Forecast**
Coverage	Commentary and statistics on likely trends in the architecture sector in the coming 12 months.
Frequency	Annual
Availability	General
Cost	£65
Comments	
Address	33-39 Bowling Green Lane, London EC1R 6DA
Telephone	0171 505 8273
Fax	0171 833 8079

20

ARCHITECTS' JOURNAL

Title	**Workload Survey**
Coverage	Workload trends for the latest quarter compared to the previous quarter and the corresponding quarter in the previous year. Includes data on the value of new commissions, staffing levels, and sector trends. Based on a survey by the journal.
Frequency	Quarterly in a weekly journal
Availability	General
Cost	£65
Comments	
Address	33-39 Bowling Green Lane, London EC1R 6DA
Telephone	0171 505 8273
Fax	0171 833 8079

21

ASDIA

Title	**Personal Pension Statistics**
Coverage	Aggregate details on the personal pensions sector plus data on specific schemes.
Frequency	Annual
Availability	General
Cost	£5
Comments	
Address	Room B2715, Long Benton, Newcastle-upon-Tyne NE98 1YX
Telephone	0191 225 5449
Fax	

22	ASSOCIATION FOR PAYMENT CLEARING SERVICES (APACS)
Title	**Yearbook of Payment Statistics**
Coverage	Statistics on the turnover of inter-bank clearings, automated clearings, inter-branch clearings, Scottish clearings, and London currency dealings. Based on figures collected by APACS from its members.
Frequency	Annual
Availability	General
Cost	£30
Comments	
Address	Mercury House, Triton Court, 14 Finsbury Square, London EC2A 1BR
Telephone	0171 628 7080
Fax	0171 256 5527

23	ASSOCIATION FOR PAYMENT CLEARING SERVICES (APACS)
Title	**Clearing Statistics**
Coverage	Statistics on the turnover of inter-bank clearings through the clearing house and automated clearings. Based on figures collected by APACS from its members.
Frequency	Monthly
Availability	General
Cost	Free
Comments	An annual release provides cumulative data for the year.
Address	Mercury House, Triton Court, 14 Finsbury Square, London EC2A 1BR
Telephone	0171 628 7080
Fax	0171 256 5527

24	ASSOCIATION OF BRITISH INSURERS
Title	**Sources of New Premium Income**
Coverage	A brief report showing the percentage of new premium income for long-term business sold through various distribution channels. Based on the association's own survey and published in March, June, September, and December.
Frequency	Quarterly
Availability	General
Cost	£15 per issue, annual subscription to all the association's titles - £250
Comments	
Address	51 Gresham Street, London EC2V 7HQ
Telephone	0171 600 3333
Fax	0171 696 8999

25	ASSOCIATION OF BRITISH INSURERS
Title	**Insurance Earnings Overseas**
Coverage	Figures showing the contribution of insurance to overall balance of payments results. Based on official data and published in November.
Frequency	Annually
Availability	General
Cost	£15 per issue, annual subscription to all the association's titles - £250
Comments	
Address	51 Gresham Street, London EC2V 7HQ
Telephone	0171 600 3333
Fax	0171 696 8999

26	ASSOCIATION OF BRITISH INSURERS
Title	**Family Spending**
Coverage	Using figures from the Office for National Statistics (ONS), the report shows average expenditure on different types of insurance per households, along with percentage of households with expenditure. Also broken down by type of tenure, region, occupation, and age.
Frequency	Annual
Availability	General
Cost	£15 per issue, annual subscription to all the association's titles – £250
Comments	
Address	51 Gresham Street, London EC2V 7HQ
Telephone	0171 600 3333
Fax	0171 696 8999

27	ASSOCIATION OF BRITISH INSURERS
Title	**General Insurance Statistics: Sources of Premium Income**
Coverage	A brief report showing the percentage of general business premiums received through different distribution channels. Figures split between commercial and personal lines. Based on the association's own survey and produced in October.
Frequency	Annual
Availability	General
Cost	£15 per issue, annual subscription to all the association's titles – £250
Comments	
Address	51 Gresham Street, London EC2V 7HQ
Telephone	0171 600 3333
Fax	0171 696 8999

28 ASSOCIATION OF BRITISH INSURERS

Title	**Long-term Insurance: New Business Results**
Coverage	Detailed figures on new life and pensions business written during the quarter. Brief comments on major influences. Split between whole life, endowment, temporary life policies, personal pensions, and sponsored business. Figures given for last eight quarters and five years for annual figures. Based on the association's own survey.
Frequency	Quarterly
Availability	General
Cost	£15 per issue, annual subscription to all the association's titles – £250
Comments	
Address	51 Gresham Street, London EC2V 7HQ
Telephone	0171 600 3333
Fax	0171 696 8999

29 ASSOCIATION OF BRITISH INSURERS

Title	**AGM Statistics**
Coverage	A press release and leaflet giving key industry statistics, and including the first provisional figures on the industry's performance in the preceding year. Issued in June.
Frequency	Annual
Availability	General
Cost	Free
Comments	
Address	51 Gresham Street, London EC2V 7HQ
Telephone	0171 600 3333
Fax	0171 696 8999

30 ASSOCIATION OF BRITISH INSURERS

Title	**Insurance Trends**
Coverage	Includes articles on current trends and issues plus 27 statistical tables based mainly on the association's own surveys. Produced in January, April, July, and October.
Frequency	Quarterly
Availability	General
Cost	£25 per copy, or £80 per year, annual subscription to all the association's titles – £250
Comments	
Address	51 Gresham Street, London EC2V 7HQ
Telephone	0171 600 3333
Fax	0171 696 8999

31

ASSOCIATION OF BRITISH INSURERS

Title **Insurance Statistics Yearbook**

Coverage Detailed figures on all classes of long-term and general insurance and most statistics cover a ten year period. For long-term business, the information includes sources of new business, long-term business revenue accounts, and investment of funds. For general business, the data given includes revenue account figures by class and for UK and overseas business. Based on the association's own survey and usually published in October.

Frequency Annual

Availability General

Cost £50. Annual subscription to all the association's titles – £250

Comments

Address 51 Gresham Street, London EC2V 7HQ

Telephone 0171 600 3333

Fax 0171 696 8999

32

ASSOCIATION OF BRITISH INSURERS

Title **Insurance Review**

Coverage Provides a review of the developments of the key industry statistics over the preceding five years. With 30 statistical tables, commentary, and graphs. Produced annually in September.

Frequency Annual

Availability General

Cost Free

Comments

Address 51 Gresham Street, London EC2V 7HQ

Telephone 0171 600 3333

Fax 0171 696 8999

33

ASSOCIATION OF BRITISH INSURERS

Title **Quarterly General Business Claims**

Coverage Figures on claims paid split between fire, theft, and weather damage claims for both commercial and domestic business. Figures for business interruption and domestic subsidence are also included. Based on the association's own survey and published in February, May, August, and November.

Frequency Quarterly

Availability General

Cost £15 per issue, annual subscription to all the association's titles – £250

Comments

Address 51 Gresham Street, London EC2V 7HQ

Telephone 0171 600 3333

Fax 0171 696 8999

34 ASSOCIATION OF CATERING EQUIPMENT MANUFACTURERS AND IMPORTERS (CESA)

Title	**UK Catering Equipment Market**
Coverage	Based on returns from member companies, and estimates of sales by non-members, the association produces statistics for sales, imports, and exports broken down by type of catering equipment.
Frequency	Annual
Availability	Usually only available to members but some summary data may be made available to bona-fide researchers.
Cost	Free
Comments	
Address	235-237 Vauxhall Bridge Road, London SW1V 1EJ
Telephone	0171 233 7724
Fax	0171 828 0667

35 ASSOCIATION OF CONTACT LENS MANUFACTURERS

Title	**Annual Statistics**
Coverage	Annual statistics relating to the sales of contact lenses and contact lens solutions. Based on a survey of members' sales by the Association.
Frequency	Annual
Availability	General
Cost	
Comments	Published in the association's journal.
Address	Chartham, Branksome Park Road, Camberley GU15 2AU
Telephone	01276 28964
Fax	01276 686404

36 ASSOCIATION OF INSURERS AND RISK MANAGERS IN INDUSTRY AND COMMERCE LTD

Title	**Status and Salaries Report**
Coverage	A twice-yearly survey covering salary and working conditions trends for insurers and risk managers. Based on a survey by the association.
Frequency	Twice per annum
Availability	General
Cost	£25, free to members
Comments	Also publishes various research reports.
Address	6 Lloyds Avenue, London EC3N 3AR
Telephone	0171 480 7610
Fax	0171 702 3782

37 ASSOCIATION OF MANUFACTURERS OF DOMESTIC ELECTRICAL APPLIANCES (AMDEA)

Title **AMDEA Statistical Yearbook**

Coverage Deliveries by UK manufacturers and imports by country of origin for various appliances including fridges, freezers, dryers, washing machines, cookers, vacuum cleaners, heaters, electric blankets etc. Additional data on prices and employment. Based primarily on AMDEA data supported by some official statistics.

Frequency Annual

Availability General

Cost £600, or £750 combined subscription with AMDEA Quarterly Statistics (see next entry)

Comments

Address Rapier House, 40-46 Lambs Conduit Street, London WC1N 3NW

Telephone 0171 405 0666

Fax 0171 405 6609

38 ASSOCIATION OF MANUFACTURERS OF DOMESTIC ELECTRICAL APPLIANCES (AMDEA)

Title **AMDEA Quarterly Statistics**

Coverage Deliveries and imports of various electrical appliances covering over 25 product headings. Similar data to that contained in the AMDEA Statistical Yearbook (see entry above) with statistics for the latest quarter and summary data for the earlier quarter. Based primarily on AMDEA data supported by some official statistics.

Frequency Quarterly

Availability General

Cost £750, combined subscription with AMDEA Statistical Yearbook.

Comments

Address Rapier House, 40-46 Lambs Conduit Street, London WC1N 3NW

Telephone 0171 405 0666

Fax 0171 405 6609

39 ASSOCIATION OF MARKET SURVEY ORGANISATIONS (AMSO)

Title	**Research Industry Annual Turnover Data**
Coverage	Total turnover of AMSO members analysed by client type, data collection type, and research technique. Also details of overseas earnings. Based on a survey of members with a large amount of supporting text.
Frequency	Annual
Availability	General
Cost	Free
Comments	Issued as a press release in early Spring.
Address	c/o the Research Business Group, Helford Mews, Cruikshank Street, London WC1X 9HD
Telephone	0171 837 1242
Fax	0171 837 9445

40 ASSOCIATION OF UNIT TRUSTS AND INVESTMENT TRUSTS

Title	**Unit Trust and PEP Sales**
Coverage	Sales of units trusts and PEPs in the previous month, comparisons with earlier months, and cumulative data. Based on the association's own survey and accompanied by a commentary.
Frequency	Monthly
Availability	General
Cost	Free
Comments	Previously called the Unit Trust Association.
Address	65 Kingsway, London WC2B 6TD
Telephone	0171 831 0898
Fax	0171 831 9975

41 AUDIENCE SELECTION

Title	**Phonebus**
Coverage	A general omnibus survey carried out every weekend with a sample size of around 1,000. Questions can be agreed up to the Friday and results are available on the Monday.
Frequency	Weekly
Availability	General
Cost	Varies according to amount and nature of data required
Comments	Results available on disc. Other packages and special analysis available.
Address	14-17 St John's Square, London EC1M 4HE
Telephone	0171 608 3618
Fax	0171 608 3286

42	AUDIENCE SELECTION
Title	**Key Directors Omnibus**
Coverage	200 managing directors and 200 finance directors from the top 10% of UK companies are interviewed each quarter. Results cover purchasing trends, brand awareness, advertising awareness, readership trends etc.
Frequency	Quarterly
Availability	General
Cost	Varies according to amount and nature of data required
Comments	Results available on disc. Other packages and special analysis available.
Address	14-17 St John's Square, London EC1M 4HE
Telephone	0171 608 3618
Fax	0171 608 3286

43	AUDIT BUREAU OF CIRCULATIONS LTD (ABC)
Title	**ABC Circulation Review**
Coverage	A well-established report on audited certified net sales, circulation, and distribution data for over 2,000 publications. Covers journals, magazines, and newspapers. Based on a survey by the company.
Frequency	Twice per annum
Availability	Members
Cost	Free
Comments	The data is held on a computerised database and various packages and searches are available.
Address	Black Prince Yard, 207-209 High Street, Berkhamstead, Hertfordshire HP4 1AD
Telephone	01442 870800
Fax	01422 877407

44	AUSTIN INTELLIGENCE SERVICES
Title	**Austintel 199– Annual Insolvencies Report**
Coverage	A review of insolvencies in England and Wales with details of the numbers, reasons for insolvencies, directors disqualified, and a regional breakdown. Based on surveys by the company.
Frequency	Annual
Availability	General
Cost	On request
Comments	
Address	23 Farncombe Road, Worthing, West Sussex BN11 2AY
Telephone	01903 206007
Fax	01903 821604

45

AUTOMATIC VENDING ASSOCIATION OF GREAT BRITAIN (AVAB)

Title **Vendinform Census**

Coverage In 1994, the association carried out its first detailed census of the beverage and snack foods vending sector. The association commissioned an external agency to carry out the census on its behalf.

Frequency Regular

Availability General

Cost £375 to non-members

Comments It is intended to repeat the census at regular intervals.

Address Bassett House, High Street, Banstead, Surrey SM7 2LZ

Telephone 01737 357211

Fax 01737 370501

46

BAA PLC

Title **Patterns of Traffic**

Coverage Based on traffic counts at BAA airports, an annual report on passenger movements in the United Kingdom.

Frequency Annual

Availability General

Cost £10

Comments More detailed statistics available to members who participate in the survey.

Address Jubilee House, Furlong Way, North Terminal, Gatwick Airport, West Sussex RH6 0JN

Telephone 01293 595070

Fax 01293 595200

47

BAA PLC

Title **BAA Airport Traffic Data**

Coverage Based on an ongoing survey of passenger, freight and aircraft movements at BAA airports, this regular publication has statistics on UK traffic.

Frequency Regular

Availability General

Cost Varies according to the amount of data required

Comments

Address Jubilee House, Furlong Way, North Terminal, Gatwick Airport, West Sussex RH6 0JN

Telephone 01293 595070

Fax 01293 595200

48 BAA PLC

Title	**BAA Monthly Traffic Summary**
Coverage	Based on traffic counts of freight, passengers and aircraft at BAA airports, this monthly report is a traffic summary for the UK.
Frequency	Monthly
Availability	General
Cost	On application
Comments	
Address	Jubilee House, Furlong Way, North Terminal, Gatwick Airport, West Sussex RH6 0JN
Telephone	01293 595070
Fax	01293 595200

49 BANK CONSULTANCY GROUP

Title	**Bank Relationship Survey**
Coverage	Survey covering the characteristics of banks, switching behaviour, banks as credit providers, banks as advisers and service providers, differentiation in banking services. Based on original research.
Frequency	Annual
Availability	General
Cost	£550
Comments	
Address	93 Wardour Street, London W1V 3TE
Telephone	0171 287 0422
Fax	0171 494 2695

50 BANK OF ENGLAND

Title	**Inflation Report**
Coverage	A review of current price trends in the economy and the outlook for prices in the short term.
Frequency	Monthly
Availability	General
Cost	£16, or £24 with a combined subscription to Bank of England Quarterly Bulletin
Comments	
Address	Monetary and Financial Statistics Division, Threadneedle Street, London EC2R 8AH
Telephone	0171 601 4030
Fax	0171 601 4771

51 BANK OF ENGLAND

Title	**Bank of England Statistical Release**
Coverage	Summary statistics on monetary and financial trends based largely on the bank's own figures.
Frequency	Monthly
Availability	General
Cost	On request
Comments	Usually published in the first week of the month.
Address	Monetary and Financial Statistics Division, Threadneedle Street, London EC2R 8AH
Telephone	0171 601 4030
Fax	0171 601 4771

52 BANK OF ENGLAND

Title	**Bank of England Quarterly Bulletin**
Coverage	Articles, comment and a statistical annex covering UK and international banking, money stock, official market operations, government finance, reserves and official borrowing, exchange rates, interest rates and national financial accounts. Mainly the bank's own figures.
Frequency	Quarterly
Availability	General
Cost	£24, combined subscription with Inflation Report
Comments	
Address	Monetary and Financial Statistics Division, Threadneedle Street, London EC2R 8AH
Telephone	0171 601 4030
Fax	0171 601 4771

53 BANK OF ENGLAND

Title	**Bank of England Statistical Abstract**
Coverage	Detailed monetary and banking statistics with historical data. Published in two volumes. Volume 1 covers banking, capital markets, government debt and related statistics, interest, and exchange rates. Volume 2 covers monetary statistics with long runs of data.
Frequency	Annual
Availability	General
Cost	£15
Comments	Also available on IBM compatable discs for £25 (plus VAT).
Address	Monetary and Financial Statistics Division, Threadneedle Street, London EC2R 8AH
Telephone	0171 601 4030
Fax	0171 601 4771

54 BANK RELATIONSHIP CONSULTANCY

Title	**Corporate Banking Survey**
Coverage	In its third year in 1994, the corporate banking survey examines the bank supply of corporate credit and compares this with the demand for credit from the UK's top 400 companies. Based on original research.
Frequency	Annual
Availability	General
Cost	£550
Comments	Produced in association with the Association of Corporate Treasurers.
Address	2-8 Victoria Avenue, Bishopsgate, London EC2M 4NS
Telephone	0171 283 5454
Fax	0171 626 1660

55 BANKING INFORMATION SERVICE

Title	**Press Release**
Coverage	Text and statistics usually giving details of advances, balances etc.
Frequency	Regular
Availability	General
Cost	Free
Comments	
Address	10 Lombard Street, London EC3V 9AR
Telephone	0171 626 8486
Fax	0171 283 7037

56 BAR ASSOCIATION FOR COMMERCE, FINANCE AND INDUSTRY

Title	**Remuneration Survey**
Coverage	A survey of members' salaries in all sectors of industry divided into various legal categories. Analysis by age and job and information on fringe benefits.
Frequency	Every 2 or 3 years
Availability	General
Cost	On application
Comments	
Address	2 Plowden Buildings, Middle Temple Lane, London EC4Y 9AT
Telephone	0171 583 4937
Fax	0171 936 3384

57 BARCLAYS BANK

Title	**Barclays Economic Review**
Coverage	A general commentary on the UK and international economy and a statistical appendix with data on exchange rates, interest rates, money market. Text covers 50% of the report.
Frequency	Quarterly
Availability	General
Cost	Free
Comments	Also publishes various short pamphlets on specific UK markets and sectors.
Address	1 Wimborne Road, Poole, Dorset BH15 2BB
Telephone	01202 671212
Fax	01202 344014

58 BARCLAYS BANK

Title	**UK Construction Survey**
Coverage	Commentary, graphs, and statistical tables covering trends in the UK construction industry. Based on various official and non-official sources.
Frequency	Regular
Availability	General
Cost	Free
Comments	Also publishes various short pamphlets on specific UK markets and sectors.
Address	1 Wimborne Road, Poole, Dorset BH15 2BB
Telephone	01202 671212
Fax	01202 344014

59 BARCLAYS BANK

Title	**Small Business Bulletin**
Coverage	Analysis and data on forthcoming trends in the small business sector and developments over the previous few months.
Frequency	Regular
Availability	General
Cost	On request
Comments	Also publishes various short pamphlets on specific UK markets and sectors.
Address	1 Wimbourne Road, Poole, Dorset BH15 2BB
Telephone	01202 671212
Fax	01202 344014

60 · BARCLAYS DE ZOETE WEDD SECURITIES LTD

Title	**BZW Equity-Gilt Study: Investment in the London Market Since 1918**
Coverage	Comparison of returns on equity and fixed interest investment, adjusted for inflation, for any period since 1918. Also investment history since 1918 and the impact of taxation on investment returns. A large amount of text supports the data which is based mainly on BZW's information.
Frequency	Annual
Availability	Primarily clients but available to others if stocks available.
Cost	£100
Comments	
Address	4th Floor, Ebgate House, 2 Swan Lane, London EC4B 3TS
Telephone	0171 623 2323
Fax	0171 956 4615

61 · BEAUFORT RESEARCH LTD

Title	**Welsh Omnibus Survey**
Coverage	A quarterly survey of a sample of 1,000 adults resident in Wales. Data on opinions, attitudes, advertising and product recall and awareness, purchase and usage, image and perception. Analysis available by sex, age, gender, social class, region, Welsh speaking.
Frequency	Quarterly
Availability	General
Cost	On application
Comments	Also carries out a regular omnibus survey of Welsh speakers.
Address	18 Park Grove, Cardiff CF1 3PP
Telephone	01222 378565
Fax	01222 382872

62 · BIRDS EYE WALL'S LTD

Title	**Pocket Money Monitor**
Coverage	A commissioned research survey of pocket money given to 5 to 16 year olds in the UK. Covers average weekly pocket money by age, region, and sex plus earnings from jobs and friends and relatives.
Frequency	Annual
Availability	General
Cost	Free
Comments	
Address	Station Avenue, Walton-on-Thames, Surrey KT12 1NT
Telephone	01932 228888
Fax	01932 244109

63   BISCUIT, CAKE, CHOCOLATE & CONFECTIONERY ALLIANCE (BCCCA)

Title	**Statistical Yearbook**
Coverage	Statistics on the deliveries to the home and export markets of biscuits, cakes, and confectionery. Historical trends and data on specific product areas. Based largely on surveys of members with supporting data from other sources.
Frequency	Annual
Availability	General
Cost	Free to members, £200 to others
Comments	
Address	37-41 Bedford Row, London WC1R 4JH
Telephone	0171 404 9111
Fax	0171 404 9110

64   BISCUIT, CAKE, CHOCOLATE & CONFECTIONERY ALLIANCE (BCCCA)

Title	**Four-Weekly Summaries Services**
Coverage	Monthly data on the deliveries of products with individual reports on biscuits, chocolate confectionery, and sugar confectionery. Detailed breakdowns in each report by type of product. Based on returns from members.
Frequency	Monthly
Availability	General
Cost	Free to members, prices for others on request
Comments	
Address	37-41 Bedford Row, London WC1R 4JH
Telephone	0171 404 9111
Fax	0171 404 9110

65   BOOK MARKETING LTD

Title	**Books and the Consumer**
Coverage	Based on research by BMRB International, a report on the book market covering buying, book types purchased, reading habits, prices, retailing of books, postal buying of books, library usage.
Frequency	Annual
Availability	A summary report from the research is available to anyone. Full survey results and tabulations are only available to survey subscribers.
Cost	On application
Comments	
Address	7a Bedford Square, London WC1B 3RA
Telephone	0171 580 7282
Fax	0171 580 7236

66 BOOKSELLER

Title	**Book Prices/Publishers' Output/Libraries**
Coverage	Various surveys appear throughout the year including surveys of book prices, number of titles published, public and academic library expenditure, salary surveys.
Frequency	Regular in a weekly journal
Availability	General
Cost	£108, £1.70 for a single issue
Comments	
Address	J. Whitaker & Sons Ltd, 12 Dyott Street, London WC1A 1DF
Telephone	0171 836 8911
Fax	0171 836 6381

67 BORTHWICK FLAVOURS LTD

Title	**Flavours Reports**
Coverage	A series of reports on the flavoured food and drink market with reports on adult food and drink and childrens' food and drink markets. The reports include data on flavourings, market factors, changing lifestyles, manufacturers, retailers, and future prospects.
Frequency	Regular
Availability	General
Cost	On request
Comments	
Address	Deningham Road, Wellingborough, Northamptonshire NN8 2QJ
Telephone	01933 440022
Fax	01933 440053

68 BREWERS' AND LICENSED RETAILERS' ASSOCIATION

Title	**UK Statistical Handbook**
Coverage	Production and consumption of beer and other alcoholic drinks, brewing materials, prices, incomes, duties, licensing data, structure of the industry, and drunkenness. Based largely on Central Government data with additional data from the association and other sources. A small amount of supporting text.
Frequency	Annual
Availability	General
Cost	£21.50 (members), £31.50 (non-members)
Comments	The association was previously known as the Brewers Society. Also publishes an annual report with some statistics.
Address	42 Portman Square, London W1H 0BB
Telephone	0171 486 4831
Fax	0171 935 3991

69 BREWING AND DISTILLING INTERNATIONAL

Title	**Crop Commentary**
Coverage	Details of the UK barley crop and hop output based on BDI's European Malting Barley Survey.
Frequency	Regular in a weekly journal
Availability	General
Cost	£44
Comments	UK beer production figures and surveys of specific areas of the brewing trade are also included in the journal at regular intervals.
Address	52 Glenhouse Road, Eltham, London SE9 1JQ
Telephone	0181 859 4300
Fax	0181 859 5813

70 BRICK DEVELOPMENT ASSOCIATION

Title	**Brick Usage and Deliveries**
Coverage	Analysis of brick deliveries by member firms into the various construction sectors. Based on a survey of the Association's members and the association claims to have 95% of the industry as members.
Frequency	Quarterly
Availability	Members
Cost	Free
Comments	
Address	Woodside House, Winkfield, Windsor SL4 2DX
Telephone	01344 885651
Fax	01344 890129

71 BRITISH ADHESIVES AND SEALANTS ASSOCIATION

Title	**Sales of Sealants**
Coverage	Sales in value terms of various types of sealants plus value and volume sales split by chemical type. Based on a survey of members.
Frequency	Bi-annual
Availability	Members only
Cost	Free
Comments	
Address	33 Fellowes Way, Stevenage SG2 8BW
Telephone	01438 358514
Fax	

72

BRITISH AEROSOL MANUFACTURERS' ASSOCIATION

Title	**BAMA Annual Report**
Coverage	Gives details of aerosol filling statistics by various product categories. Based on a survey of members.
Frequency	Annual
Availability	General
Cost	Free
Comments	
Address	King's Building, Smith Square, London SW1P 3JJ
Telephone	0171 828 5111
Fax	0171 834 4469

73

BRITISH AGGREGATE CONSTRUCTION MATERIALS INDUSTRIES (BACMI)

Title	**BACMI Statistical Yearbook**
Coverage	Statistics on the number and location of quarries, pits, and plants with additional information on the use of various types of construction materials. Based primarily on returns from members.
Frequency	Annual
Availability	General
Cost	£20
Comments	More detailed statistics are available to members.
Address	156 Buckingham Palace Road, London SW1 9TR
Telephone	0171 730 8194
Fax	0171 730 4355

74

BRITISH AGRICULTURAL AND GARDEN MACHINERY ASSOCIATION

Title	**Market Guide**
Coverage	A guide to the used tractors and farm machinery market based on a survey by the association.
Frequency	Regular
Availability	General
Cost	£86, £64 to members
Comments	
Address	14-16 Church Street, Rickmansworth, Hertfordshire WD3 1RQ
Telephone	01923 720241
Fax	01923 896063

75 BRITISH AGROCHEMICALS ASSOCIATION

Title   **BAA Annual Review and Handbook**

Coverage   Contains a section on industry sales and pesticide usage in the UK plus data on the world agrochemicals market. Sales data is based on a survey of members with a time series covering the last seven years. Sales data broken down into herbicides, insecticides, fungicides, and others.

Frequency   Annual

Availability   General

Cost   Free

Comments

Address   4 Lincoln Court, Lincoln Road, Peterborough PE1 2RP

Telephone   01733 349225

Fax   01733 62523

76 BRITISH ALCAN CONSUMER PRODUCTS LTD

Title   **Wraps Market Household and Catering Review**

Coverage   Graphs and commentary on aluminium foil, bin liners, greaseproof paper, plastic wraps, cooking bags, food and freezer bags. Based primarily on Nielsen data.

Frequency   Regular

Availability   General

Cost   Free

Comments

Address   Raans Road, Amersham, Buckinghamshire HP6 6JY

Telephone   01753 887373

Fax   01753 889667

77 BRITISH APPAREL AND TEXTILE CONFEDERATION

Title   **Quarterly Statistical Review**

Coverage   Statistics on production, imports, exports, and apparent consumption particularly for cotton and allied fibres. Based on a mixture of official and non-official sources.

Frequency   Quarterly

Availability   General

Cost   £120 per annum

Comments

Address   5 Portland Place, London W1N 3AA

Telephone   0171 636 7788

Fax   0171 636 7515

78 BRITISH APPAREL AND TEXTILE FEDERATION

Title	**Trendata**
Coverage	Statistics covering production, exports, imports, balance of trade, consumer expenditure, employment for the UK apparel and textile industry. Based on both official and non-official sources.
Frequency	Quarterly
Availability	General
Cost	£95 per annum (members), £195 for non-members
Comments	
Address	5 Portland Place, London W1N 3AA
Telephone	0171 636 7788
Fax	0171 636 7515

79 BRITISH BANKERS' ASSOCIATION

Title	**Sterling Lending**
Coverage	Trends in sterling lending with data for the latest available month and cumulative statistics. Based on data supplied by members.
Frequency	Monthly
Availability	General
Cost	On request
Comments	
Address	10 Lombard Street, London EC3V 9AP
Telephone	0171 623 4001
Fax	0171 283 7037

80 BRITISH BANKERS' ASSOCIATION

Title	**Abstract of Banking Statistics**
Coverage	Detailed statistics on the banks and banking with sections on bank groups, clearing statistics, credit card statistics, branches, and financial data. Based on various sources, including data from the association. Many tables have ten-year statistical series.
Frequency	Annual
Availability	General
Cost	On request
Comments	
Address	10 Lombard Street, London EC3V 9AP
Telephone	0171 623 4001
Fax	0171 283 7037

81 BRITISH BANKERS' ASSOCIATION

Title	**Major British Banking Groups' Mortgage Lending**
Coverage	Trends in mortgage advances by UK banks with figures for the latest month and cumulative data. Based on returns from members.
Frequency	Monthly
Availability	General
Cost	On request
Comments	
Address	10 Lombard Street, London EC3V 9AP
Telephone	0171 623 4001
Fax	0171 283 7037

82 BRITISH BANKERS' ASSOCIATION

Title	**Monthly Statement**
Coverage	General statistics covering the activities of the major UK banks. Based largely on data from members.
Frequency	Monthly
Availability	General
Cost	On request
Comments	
Address	10 Lombard Street, London EC3V 9AP
Telephone	0171 623 4001
Fax	0171 283 7037

83 BRITISH CARPET MANUFACTURERS' ASSOCIATION

Title	**Annual Report**
Coverage	A statistical section gives carpet sales by type of construction, trade, and fibres used in carpet surface yarns. Various tables contain figures for the last five years. Based mainly on Central Government data with a large amount of supporting text.
Frequency	Annual
Availability	General
Cost	Free
Comments	
Address	Royalty House, 4th Floor, 72 Dean Trench Street, London W1V 5HB
Telephone	0171 734 9853
Fax	0171 734 9856

84	BRITISH CERAMIC CONFEDERATION
Title	**Production Statistics**
Coverage	Summary of the total production and sales of the ceramic industry, plus overseas trade data. Based largely on government statistics.
Frequency	Annual
Availability	Usually only available to members.
Cost	Free
Comments	
Address	Federation House, Station Road, Stoke-on-Trent ST4 2SA
Telephone	01782 744631
Fax	01782 744102

85	BRITISH CERAMIC CONFEDERATION
Title	**Summary of Trade Statistics**
Coverage	Details of imports and exports of ceramic products, by value and volume. Additional data on main trading partners. Based on government statistics.
Frequency	Monthly
Availability	Usually only available to members.
Cost	Free
Comments	
Address	Federation House, Station Road, Stoke-on-Trent ST4 2SA
Telephone	01782 744631
Fax	01782 744102

86	BRITISH CERAMIC FEDERATION
Title	**Quarterly Trade Statistics**
Coverage	Details of the imports and exports of ceramic products broken down into various industry sub-sectors. Based on government statistics.
Frequency	Quarterly
Availability	Usually only available to members.
Cost	Free
Comments	
Address	Federation House, Station Road, Stoke-on-Trent ST4 2SA
Telephone	01782 744631
Fax	01782 744102

87 BRITISH CHAMBERS OF COMMERCE

Title	**Quarterly Economic Survey**
Coverage	A quarterly review of business and economic conditions based on returns from a sample of members of a selection of the major regional chambers.
Frequency	Quarterly
Availability	General
Cost	£200 per annum, £60 each
Comments	
Address	9 Tufton Street, London SW1P 3QB
Telephone	0171 222 1555
Fax	0171 799 2202

88 BRITISH CHAMBERS OF COMMERCE

Title	**Small Firms Survey**
Coverage	A review of small firms trends with each issue devoted to a specific topic, eg the environment, finance etc.
Frequency	Quarterly
Availability	General
Cost	£200 per annum, £60 each
Comments	
Address	9 Tufton Street, London SW1P 3QB
Telephone	0171 222 1555
Fax	0171 799 2202

89 BRITISH CHICKEN INFORMATION SERVICE

Title	**199– Market Review**
Coverage	Commentary and statistics covering trends in the UK chicken market with data on value and volume sales by types of chicken, prices, retail distribution, and the future outlook. Based on data collected by the British Chicken Information Service.
Frequency	Annual
Availability	General
Cost	On request
Comments	
Address	126-128 Cromwell Road, London SW7 4ET
Telephone	0171 373 7757
Fax	0171 373 3926

90 BRITISH CONSULTANTS BUREAU

Title	**Annual Survey of the British Consultants Bureau**
Coverage	The survey includes details of trends in the consultants' sector with data broken down by work area, in terms of both job categories and geographical area. Based on data obtained by the Bureau.
Frequency	Annual
Availability	General
Cost	On request
Comments	
Address	1 Westminster Palace Gardens, London SW1
Telephone	0171 222 3652
Fax	

91 BRITISH EDUCATIONAL EQUIPMENT ASSOCIATION

Title	**Expenditure on Teaching Materials**
Coverage	Expenditure in England and Wales by counties, districts, and metropolitan boroughs on books, equipment, and stationery. Historical data over a ten-year period with some supporting text. Based on a combination of Central Government and non-official sources.
Frequency	Annual
Availability	General
Cost	Free
Comments	Sponsored by the Publishers Association.
Address	20 Beaufort Court, Admirals Way, London E14 9XL
Telephone	0171 537 4997
Fax	0171 537 4846

92 BRITISH EGG PRODUCTS ASSOCIATION

Title	**Breaking and Production**
Coverage	Includes data on egg production and breakages.
Frequency	Ten issues per annum
Availability	General
Cost	On request
Comments	
Address	Suite 101, Albany House, 324-326 Regent Street, London W1R 5AA
Telephone	0171 580 7172
Fax	0171 580 7082

93 BRITISH EGG PRODUCTS ASSOCIATION

Title	**Import and Export Statistics**
Coverage	Overseas trade statistics for eggs and egg products based on data obtained from Central Government sources.
Frequency	Ten issues per annum
Availability	General
Cost	On request
Comments	
Address	Suite 101, Albany House, 324-326 Regent Street, London W1R 5AA
Telephone	0171 580 7172
Fax	0171 580 7082

94 BRITISH ENERGY ASSOCIATION

Title	**British Annual Energy Review**
Coverage	A review of trends in the British energy industry, broken down by sector, and based on a combination of sources.
Frequency	Annual
Availability	General
Cost	On request
Comments	
Address	34 St James's Street, London SW1A 1HD
Telephone	0171 930 1211
Fax	0171 925 0452

95 BRITISH FIBREBOARD PACKAGING ASSOCIATION

Title	**Annual Production Statistics**
Coverage	Production by weight and area and the sales invoice value of solid and corrugated fibreboard produced in the UK. Based on a survey of members.
Frequency	Annual
Availability	Members
Cost	Free
Comments	
Address	2 Saxon Court, Freeschool Street, Northampton NN1 1ST
Telephone	01604 21002
Fax	01604 20636

96 BRITISH FLUID POWER ASSOCIATION

Title	**Distributor Annual Survey**
Coverage	A survey of distributors providing information on sales, market trends, end users, and companies. Also includes salary structure data and some official statistics.
Frequency	Annual
Availability	Members
Cost	On application
Comments	Established in 1994 to replace the Distributor Profiles.
Address	Cheriton House, Cromwell Business Park, Banbury Road, Chipping Norton, Oxfordshire OX7 5SR
Telephone	01608 644114
Fax	01608 643738

97 BRITISH FLUID POWER ASSOCIATION

Title	**Statistics Newsletter**
Coverage	Summary data and news on the industry plus details of new statistical developments relevant to the industry.
Frequency	Regular
Availability	Members
Cost	On application
Comments	
Address	Cheriton House, Cromwell Business Park, Banbury Road, Chipping Norton, Oxfordshire OX7 5SR
Telephone	01608 644114
Fax	01608 643738

98 BRITISH FLUID POWER ASSOCIATION

Title	**Pneumatic Control Equipment Monthly UK Orders and Sales Index**
Coverage	Orders and sales trends based on returns from member companies.
Frequency	Monthly
Availability	Members
Cost	On application
Comments	
Address	Cheriton House, Cromwell Business Park, Banbury Road, Chipping Norton, Oxfordshire OX7 5SR
Telephone	01608 644114
Fax	01608 643738

99 BRITISH FLUID POWER ASSOCIATION

Title	**Annual Salary Survey**
Coverage	Based on a survey of members, it includes data on remuneration, company cars, working hours, holiday entitlements.
Frequency	Annual
Availability	Members
Cost	On application
Comments	
Address	Cheriton House, Cromwell Business Park, Banbury Road, Chipping Norton, Oxfordshire OX7 5SR
Telephone	01608 644114
Fax	01608 643738

100 BRITISH FLUID POWER ASSOCIATION

Title	**BFPA Hose and Fittings Survey**
Coverage	A survey of a sample of member and non-member companies (the only BFPA survey to cover non-members), with information on market trends. Supplemented by some official statistics and international data.
Frequency	Annual
Availability	Members
Cost	On application
Comments	
Address	Cheriton House, Cromwell Business Park, Banbury Road, Chipping Norton, Oxfordshire OX7 5SR
Telephone	01608 644114
Fax	01608 643738

101 BRITISH FLUID POWER ASSOCIATION

Title	**BFPA Pneumatic Control Equipment Survey**
Coverage	A survey of a sample of member companies providing information on market trends. Also includes some official statistics and international data.
Frequency	Annual
Availability	Members
Cost	On application
Comments	
Address	Cheriton House, Cromwell Business Park, Banbury Road, Chipping Norton, Oxfordshire OX7 5SR
Telephone	01608 644114
Fax	01608 643738

102	BRITISH FLUID POWER ASSOCIATION
Title	**BFPA Annual Hydraulic Equipment Survey**
Coverage	A survey of a sample of member companies providing information on market trends and characteristics. The survey is supplemented by some official statistics and international data.
Frequency	Annual
Availability	Members
Cost	On application
Comments	
Address	Cheriton House, Cromwell Business Park, Banbury Road, Chipping Norton, Oxfordshire OX7 5SR
Telephone	01608 644114
Fax	01608 643738

103	BRITISH FLUID POWER ASSOCIATION
Title	**Hydraulic Equipment Monthly UK Orders and Sales Index**
Coverage	Orders and sales trends based on returns from member companies.
Frequency	Monthly
Availability	Members
Cost	On application
Comments	
Address	Cheriton House, Cromwell Business Park, Banbury Road, Chipping Norton, Oxfordshire OX7 5SR
Telephone	01608 644114
Fax	01608 643738

104	BRITISH FLUID POWER ASSOCIATION
Title	**Hydraulic Equipment/Pneumatic Control Equipment: Short Term Trends Survey**
Coverage	Commentary and statistics on short term trends based on returns from member companies.
Frequency	Quarterly
Availability	Members
Cost	On application
Comments	
Address	Cheriton House, Cromwell Business Park, Banbury Road, Chipping Norton, Oxfordshire OX7 5SR
Telephone	01608 644114
Fax	01608 643738

105	BRITISH FOOTWEAR MANUFACTURERS' FEDERATION
Title	**Quarterly Statistics**
Coverage	Detailed production, imports and exports, and consumption data for specific sectors of the footwear industry. Based mainly on Central Government data.
Frequency	Quarterly
Availability	General
Cost	£110 with the monthly publication
Comments	
Address	Royalty House, 72 Dean Street, London W1V 5HB
Telephone	0171 437 5573
Fax	0171 494 1300

106	BRITISH FOOTWEAR MANUFACTURERS' FEDERATION
Title	**Footwear Industry Statistical Review**
Coverage	Statistics on the industry structure, materials, production, profitability, employment and earnings, prices, supplies to the home market, expenditure, retailing, imports and exports. Based mainly on Central Government sources.
Frequency	Annual
Availability	General
Cost	£50
Comments	
Address	Royalty House, 72 Dean Street, London W1V 5HB
Telephone	0171 437 5573
Fax	0171 494 1300

107	BRITISH FOOTWEAR MANUFACTURERS' FEDERATION
Title	**Monthly Statistics**
Coverage	Short-term economic indicators for the industry with a brief commentary. Data covers deliveries, employment, prices, retail sales, imports, exports.
Frequency	Monthly
Availability	General
Cost	£110 with quarterly publication
Comments	
Address	Royalty House, 72 Dean Street, London W1V 5HB
Telephone	0171 437 5573
Fax	0171 494 1300

108

	BRITISH FORGING INDUSTRY ASSOCIATION
Title	**End of Year Statistics**
Coverage	Annual statistics on the forging industry including market developments, prices, deliveries. Based on the association's own survey.
Frequency	Annual
Availability	General
Cost	£10, free to members
Comments	
Address	245 Grove Lane, Handsworth, Birmingham B20 2HB
Telephone	0121 554 3311
Fax	0121 523 0761

109

	BRITISH FORGING INDUSTRY ASSOCIATION
Title	**BFIA Annual Report**
Coverage	Contains some statistics on the economic performance of the forging industry.
Frequency	Annual
Availability	General
Cost	On request
Comments	
Address	245 Grove Lane, Handsworth, Birmingham B20 2HB
Telephone	0121 554 3311
Fax	0121 523 0761

110

	BRITISH FRANCHISE ASSOCIATION
Title	**BFA/NAT West Survey**
Coverage	Statistics and commentary on the number of franchisees, types, sectors, sales, employment with the latest year's data compared to the previous year. Based on original research by the association. Commentary supports the text.
Frequency	Annual
Availability	General
Cost	£75 plus p+p
Comments	Produced in association with the National Westminster Bank.
Address	Thames View, Newtown Road, Henley-on-Thames RG9 1HG
Telephone	01491 578050
Fax	01491 573517

111 BRITISH FROZEN FOOD FEDERATION

Title	**Monthly Bulletin**
Coverage	Includes statistics on the UK frozen food market with data on consumption, expenditure, and markets for specific frozen foods. Based on various sources.
Frequency	Regular
Availability	General
Cost	£40
Comments	The federation also publishes a yearbook with statistics but this has not appeared in 1994 and 1995. However, it will be re-launched shortly.
Address	55 High Street, Grantham, Lincolnshire NG31 6NE
Telephone	01476 590194
Fax	01476 590152

112 BRITISH GLASS MANUFACTURERS' CONFEDERATION

Title	**Recycling Statistics**
Coverage	Statistics on the recycling of glass bottles and other glass products based on data collected by the confederation.
Frequency	Regular
Availability	General
Cost	On request
Comments	
Address	Northumberland Road, Sheffield S10 2UA
Telephone	01742 686201
Fax	01742 681073

113 BRITISH HARDWARE AND HOUSEWARES MANUFACTURERS' ASSOCIATION

Title	**Business Trends Survey**
Coverage	Based on a survey of members with data on sales, stocks, margins, and business expectations.
Frequency	Quarterly
Availability	General
Cost	£50, £25 members, £5 participants
Comments	Produced in association with DIY Week and summary data from the survey is included in the journal.
Address	35 Billing Road, Northampton NN1 5DD
Telephone	01604 22023
Fax	01604 31252

114

BRITISH HOSPITALITY ASSOCIATION

Title **UK Contract Catering Industry**

Coverage A detailed annual review of the UK contract catering industry with commentary and statistics on the number of businesses, turnover, costs, number of meals served, summary data on the international contract catering industry, and future trends. The report is based on a survey by the association.

Frequency Annual

Availability General

Cost £50

Comments Leaflets summarising the research are available free.

Address Queen's House, 55-56 Lincoln's Inn Fields, London WC2A 3BH

Telephone 0171 499 6641

Fax 0171 355 4596

115

BRITISH IRON AND STEEL PRODUCERS' ASSOCIATION

Title **BISPA Annual Report**

Coverage A review, with statistics, of the UK steel market and UK trade based on a combination of official and non-official sources. Includes details of the key consuming sectors, producer deliveries, and some forecasts.

Frequency Annual

Availability General

Cost Free

Comments

Address 5 Cromwell Road, London SW7 2HX

Telephone 0171 581 0231

Fax 0171 589 4009

116

BRITISH IRON AND STEEL PRODUCERS' ASSOCIATION

Title **Key Statistics Leaflet**

Coverage Basic data on steel consumption, production, deliveries, raw materials, and productivity. Statistics based on industry sources and trade data.

Frequency Twice per annum

Availability General

Cost Free

Comments

Address 5 Cromwell Road, London SW7 2HX

Telephone 0171 581 0231

Fax 0171 589 4009

117

BRITISH IRON AND STEEL PRODUCERS' ASSOCIATION

Title	**SI News**
Coverage	Regular bulletin with data from the UK Steel Information Service on various sectors of the steel industry. Statistics based on industry sources and trade data.
Frequency	Quarterly
Availability	General
Cost	Free
Comments	
Address	5 Cromwell Road, London SW7 2HX
Telephone	0171 581 0231
Fax	0171 589 4009

118

BRITISH JEWELLER

Title	**Market Reports**
Coverage	Mainly news and features on the jewellery trade but it includes a monthly market reports section with data on precious metal prices for the previous month and fine gold prices.
Frequency	Monthly in a monthly journal
Availability	General
Cost	£55, or £3 for a single issue
Comments	
Address	EMAP Fashion, 67 Clerkenwell Road, London EC1R 5BH
Telephone	0171 417 2800
Fax	0171 417 2862

119

BRITISH JEWELLER

Title	**British Jewellery Yearbook**
Coverage	A directory and handbook for the industry which includes statistics on fine gold prices for the last 15 years, including highs and lows.
Frequency	Annual
Availability	General
Cost	£30
Comments	
Address	EMAP Fashion, 67 Clerkenwell Road, London EC1R 5BH
Telephone	0171 417 2800
Fax	0171 417 2862

120 BRITISH MARINE INDUSTRIES FEDERATION

Title	**National Survey of Boating and Watersports Participation**
Coverage	A review of the percentage of the population participating, expenditure, equipment and services, training, craft ownership by type, frequency of visits to water, attitudes to watersports, and consumer profiles. Based largely on original research.
Frequency	Annual
Availability	General
Cost	£395, £50 for the executive summary
Comments	Also produces a BMIF Handbook and an occasional statistical review for members only.
Address	Meadlale Place, Thorpe Lea Road, Egham, Surrey TW20 8HE
Telephone	01784 473377
Fax	01784 439678

121 BRITISH MARKET RESEARCH BUREAU (BMRB) INTERNATIONAL

Title	**Access Face-to-Face/Access by Telephone**
Coverage	The first is a weekly omnibus survey of 2,000 adults above the age of 14 with face-to-face interviews carried out in the home. The telephone survey is carried out every weekend and uses a sample of 1,000 adults.
Frequency	Weekly
Availability	General
Cost	On application
Comments	
Address	Hadley House, 79-81 Uxbridge Road, Ealing W5 5SU
Telephone	0181 566 5000
Fax	0181 579 7280

122 BRITISH MARKET RESEARCH BUREAU (BMRB) LTD

Title	**Youth TGI**
Coverage	TGI data specifically for children and youths aged between 7 and 19. Includes data on purchases and consumption of key products.
Frequency	Annual
Availability	General
Cost	Varies according to the range and nature of the information required. Standard results published in 2 volumes
Comments	Also available online.
Address	Hadley House, 79-81 Uxbridge Road, Ealing W5 5SU
Telephone	0181 566 5000
Fax	0181 579 9809

123	BRITISH MARKET RESEARCH BUREAU (BMRB) LTD
Title	**Premier: The Upmarket TGI**
Coverage	TGI data specifically for consumers in the AB social grades with data covering holidays, leisure, sports, travel, clothing, personal possessions, cosmetics, gifts, household goods, home and car, drinks, and food.
Frequency	Annual
Availability	General
Cost	Varies according to the range and nature of the information required. Standard results published in 8 volumes
Comments	Also available online.
Address	Hadley House, 79-81 Uxbridge Road, Ealing W5 5SU
Telephone	0181 566 5000
Fax	0181 579 9809

124	BRITISH MARKET RESEARCH BUREAU (BMRB) LTD
Title	**Target Group Index (TGI)**
Coverage	A national product and media survey based on information from 24,000 adults. The results are published in 34 volumes: volumes 1 and 2 give general demographic information while volumes 3 to 34 cover individual consumer product areas. Detailed consumer profiles and penetration data for each product. A separate volume also provides a general description of the survey.
Frequency	Annual
Availability	General
Cost	£4,250 per volume
Comments	Specific prices available for reports on individual brands or specific consumer fields. Also available online.
Address	Hadley House, 79-81 Uxbridge Road, Ealing W5 5SU
Telephone	0181 566 5000
Fax	0181 579 9809

125 BRITISH MEDIA RESEARCH COMMITTEE

Title	**British Business Survey**
Coverage	A survey, sponsored by the media owners, examining readership patterns of business managers and executives. Includes data on readership by key demographic group, by occupation, by industry, and by decision making involvement. Further information on the use of services and profiles of British business.
Frequency	Annual
Availability	General
Cost	£300
Comments	Produced for the Business Media Research Committee by RSL Research Services at the address below. The survey is also available in electronic form from Donovan Data Systems, HRS, IMS (UK) Ltd, Telmar Communication Ltd, and BMRB (see other entries).
Address	Research Services House, Elmgrove Road, Harrow HA1 2QG
Telephone	0181 861 6000
Fax	0181 861 5515

126 BRITISH METALS FEDERATION

Title	**Annual Report**
Coverage	Commentary and statistics on trends in the industry with sections on production, scrap consumption, stocks, exports, imports, and prices. Based on a number of sources.
Frequency	Annual
Availability	General
Cost	On request
Comments	
Address	16 High Street, Brampton, Huntingdon, Cambridgeshire PE18 8TU
Telephone	01480 455249
Fax	01480 453680

127 BRITISH OFFICE SYSTEMS AND STATIONERY FEDERATION (BOSS)

Title	**Growth of Manufacturers' Turnover**
Coverage	The BOSS Federation survey of manufacturers' turnover gives quarterly data, and comparable data for previous quarters, for three sectors: furniture, machines, office products. The survey is based on returns from companies representing approximately one third of the total market.
Frequency	Quarterly
Availability	Detailed results only available to members. A summary of the results with sector statistics is issued as a press release to the trade press.
Cost	Free
Comments	
Address	6 Wimpole Street, London W1M 8AS
Telephone	0171 637 7692
Fax	0171 436 3137

128 BRITISH PHONOGRAPHIC INDUSTRY (BPI)

Title	**Market Information Sheets**
Coverage	Pamphlets with summary data and commentary on trends in the audio software market. Produced at regular intervals throughout the year.
Frequency	Regular
Availability	General
Cost	£20
Comments	
Address	25 Saville Row, London W1X 1AA
Telephone	0171 287 4422
Fax	0171 287 2252

129 BRITISH PHONOGRAPHIC INDUSTRY LTD (BPI)

Title	**BPI Yearbook**
Coverage	Includes statistics on the production of CDs, tapes and records plus imports and exports, deliveries, sales, prices, advertising expenditure, hardware ownership, video trends, piracy, and leisure market trends.
Frequency	Annual
Availability	General
Cost	£10 to non-members
Comments	
Address	25 Saville Row, London W1X 1AA
Telephone	0171 287 4422
Fax	0171 287 2252

130 BRITISH PLASTICS FEDERATION

Title	**BPF Business Trends Survey**
Coverage	A survey of companies in three areas: materials supplies, processing, and machinery manufacturers. Data on sales, orders, stocks, exports, investment, profits, prices, and capacity utilisation. Includes an opinion survey outlining likely future trends and a commentary supports the text.
Frequency	Twice per annum
Availability	General
Cost	Free to contributing members but priced for others
Comments	
Address	6 Bath Place, Rivington Street, London EC2A 3JE
Telephone	0171 457 5000
Fax	0171 235 8045

131 BRITISH PLASTICS FEDERATION

Title	**BPF Statistics Handbook**
Coverage	Statistics on the UK consumption of plastic materials, material consumption by major end-use, imports, exports, and plastics in packaging, building, and the automotive sectors. Based on BPF and other data with some supporting text.
Frequency	Annual
Availability	General
Cost	On request
Comments	
Address	6 Bath Place, Rivington Street, London EC2A 3JE
Telephone	0171 457 5000
Fax	0171 235 8045

132 BRITISH PRINTING INDUSTRIES FEDERATION

Title	**Manpower Survey**
Coverage	Details of the distribution of employees by region and occupation and detailed earnings data. Based on a survey by the federation.
Frequency	Annual
Availability	General
Cost	£1,900
Comments	
Address	11 Bedford Row, London WC1R 4DX
Telephone	0171 242 6904
Fax	0171 405 7784

133 BRITISH PRINTING INDUSTRIES FEDERATION

Title	**Profitability and Productivity Survey**
Coverage	Statistics include sales, value added, profits per employee by product group. Based on a survey by the federation.
Frequency	Annual
Availability	General
Cost	£1,900
Comments	
Address	11 Bedford Row, London WC1R 4DX
Telephone	0171 242 6904
Fax	0171 405 7784

134 BRITISH PRINTING INDUSTRIES FEDERATION

Title	**Salary Survey**
Coverage	Statistics on the distribution of salaries within the sector by occupation. Based on the federation's own survey.
Frequency	Annual
Availability	General
Cost	£1,900
Comments	
Address	11 Bedford Row, London WC1R 4DX
Telephone	0171 242 6904
Fax	0171 405 7784

135 BRITISH PRINTING INDUSTRIES FEDERATION

Title	**Facts and Figures about the Printing Industry**
Coverage	Basic data on sales, overseas trade, costs, prices, profits, redundancies etc. Based on a mixture of official and non-official sources.
Frequency	Every few years
Availability	General
Cost	Free
Comments	
Address	11 Bedford Row, London WC1R 4DX
Telephone	0171 242 6904
Fax	0171 405 7784

136

BRITISH RADIO AND ELECTRONIC EQUIPMENT
MANUFACTURERS' ASSOCIATION (BREEMA)

Title **Deliveries of Selected Consumer Electronics Products**

Coverage Deliveries to the trade of televisions, videography, music centres, CD players. Based on a survey of members and supported by a commentary.

Frequency Quarterly

Availability General

Cost Free

Comments

Address Landseer House, 19 Charing Cross Road, London WC2H 0ES

Telephone 0171 930 3206

Fax 0171 839 4613

137

BRITISH RADIO AND ELECTRONIC EQUIPMENT
MANUFACTURERS' ASSOCIATION (BREEMA)

Title **Market for Consumer Audio Equipment**

Coverage Detailed analysis and statistics on the market for audio equipment covering total UK production, imports, exports, deliveries to the trade, consumer offtake and stocks. Published in 2 volumes with the second volume giving historical data.

Frequency Annual

Availability General

Cost £130

Comments

Address Landseer House, 19 Charing Cross Road, London WC2H 0ES

Telephone 0171 930 3206

Fax 0171 839 4613

138

BRITISH RADIO AND ELECTRONIC EQUIPMENT
MANUFACTURERS' ASSOCIATION (BREEMA)

Title **Market for Domestic Television Receivers**

Coverage Detailed analysis and statistics on the UK market for televisions with data on total production, imports, exports, trade deliveries, consumer offtake, and stocks. The publication now includes satellite TV equipment. Published in 2 volumes with the second volume giving historical data.

Frequency Annual

Availability General

Cost £130

Comments

Address Landseer House, 19 Charing Cross Road, London WC2H 0ES

Telephone 0171 930 3206

Fax 0171 839 4613

139 BRITISH RADIO AND ELECTRONIC EQUIPMENT MANUFACTURERS' ASSOCIATION (BREEMA)

Title	**Market for Videography**
Coverage	Detailed analysis and statistics on the UK market for video equipment with statistics on total UK production, imports, exports, trade deliveries, consumer offtake, stocks. Published in 2 volumes with the second volume giving historical data.
Frequency	Annual
Availability	General
Cost	£130
Comments	
Address	Landseer House, 19 Charing Cross Road, London WC2H 0ES
Telephone	0171 930 3206
Fax	0171 839 4613

140 BRITISH RADIO AND ELECTRONIC EQUIPMENT MANUFACTURERS' ASSOCIATION (BREEMA)

Title	**Annual Report**
Coverage	The annual report contains some statistics on deliveries of consumer electronic products and a report on the statistical activities of the association.
Frequency	Annual
Availability	General
Cost	Free
Comments	
Address	Landseer House, 19 Charing Cross Road, London WC2H 0ES
Telephone	0171 930 3206
Fax	0171 839 4613

141 BRITISH RETAIL CONSORTIUM

Title	**Retail Crime Costs Survey**
Coverage	Based on a survey of approximately 53,000 outlets, the report analyses retail crime and includes data on the total cost, crime by retailers, type of crime.
Frequency	Annual
Availability	General
Cost	£25
Comments	
Address	Bedford House, 69-79 Fulham High Street, London SW6 3JW
Telephone	0171 371 5185
Fax	0171 371 0529

142 BRITISH RETAIL CONSORTIUM

Title	**Retail Sales Press Release**
Coverage	Volume and value of UK retail sales based mainly on government statistics supported by data from some non-official sources.
Frequency	Monthly
Availability	Usually only available to members and the press
Cost	Free
Comments	
Address	Bedford House, 69-79 Fulham High Street, London SW6 3JW
Telephone	0171 371 5185
Fax	0171 371 0529

143 BRITISH ROAD FEDERATION

Title	**Basic Road Statistics**
Coverage	Data on roads and road transport including data on traffic, energy, taxation, public expenditure, accidents, and some international comparisons. Mainly based on Central Government sources.
Frequency	Annual
Availability	General
Cost	£22
Comments	
Address	194-202 Old Kent Road, London SE1 5TY
Telephone	0171 703 9769
Fax	0171 701 0029

144 BRITISH ROBOT ASSOCIATION

Title	**Robot Facts**
Coverage	Statistics on robot use by industry sector with additional data on the country of origin of installed robots. Data usually given for a number of years and based on a survey by the association.
Frequency	Regular
Availability	General
Cost	£75
Comments	Also publishes a yearbook.
Address	Aston Science Park, Love Lane, Birmingham B7 4BJ
Telephone	0121 359 0981
Fax	0121 359 7520

145 BRITISH SCRAP FEDERATION

Title	**Annual Report**
Coverage	Includes statistics on scrap consumption, scrap stocks, exports, imports, and scrap prices. Based on a combination of the Federation's own data and official statistics.
Frequency	Annual
Availability	General
Cost	Free
Comments	
Address	16 High Street, Brampton, Huntingdon PE18 8TU
Telephone	01480 55249
Fax	01480 53680

146 BRITISH SECONDARY METALS ASSOCIATION

Title	**Member Survey**
Coverage	A survey of member companies by employment size, number of sites, investment, turnover.
Frequency	Regular
Availability	Primarily members but requests from non-members considered
Cost	Free
Comments	
Address	25 Park Road, Runcorn WA7 4SS
Telephone	09285 72400
Fax	09285 580493

147 BRITISH SECURITY INDUSTRY ASSOCIATION (BSIA)

Title	**CCTV Market Survey**
Coverage	An analysis of the UK closed-circuit television security market based on turnover figures from relevant BSIA member companies and some independent market research.
Frequency	Annual
Availability	Usually only members but some data may be made available to others on request
Cost	Free
Comments	Also publishes surveys of the manned guarding market.
Address	Security House, Barbourne Road, Worcester WR1 1RS
Telephone	01905 21464
Fax	01905 613625

148   BRITISH SECURITY INDUSTRY ASSOCIATION (BSIA)

Title	**Wage Survey**
Coverage	A wage survey covering security guards, alarm installations, and central station connections. Based on a survey by the association.
Frequency	Twice per annum
Availability	Usually members only but some data may be made available to others on request
Cost	Free
Comments	
Address	Security House, Barbourne Road, Worcester WR1 1RS
Telephone	01905 21464
Fax	01905 613625

149   BRITISH SOFT DRINKS ASSOCIATION LTD

Title	**Factsheets**
Coverage	Information sheets containing statistics on various aspects of the industry, eg sales, consumption, packaging etc. Each factsheet contains a large amount of text supported by statistics mainly collected by the association.
Frequency	Regular
Availability	General
Cost	Free
Comments	
Address	20-22 Stukely Street, London WC2B 5LR
Telephone	0171 430 0356
Fax	0171 831 6014

150   BRITISH TOURIST AUTHORITY

Title	**British on Holiday**
Coverage	A summary of the BTA annual survey of British residents' holiday-taking.
Frequency	Annual
Availability	General
Cost	£22.50
Comments	Published as a special report in Tourism Intelligence Quarterly (see other entry) but also available separately. The regional tourist boards also publish statistics.
Address	Department D, Thames Tower, Black's Road, Hammersmith, London W6 9EL
Telephone	0181 846 9000
Fax	0181 563 0302

151

BRITISH TOURIST AUTHORITY

Title	**Visits to Tourist Attractions**
Coverage	Gives details of attendances at tourist attractions in the UK, seasonal opening, ownership, and information on free admission. Attractions include: historic houses, gardens, museums and art galleries, wildlife attractions, country parks, steam railways, and workplaces.
Frequency	Annual
Availability	General
Cost	£16.50
Comments	The regional tourist boards also publish statistics.
Address	Department D, Thames Tower, Black's Road, Hammersmith, London W6 9EL
Telephone	0181 846 9000
Fax	0181 563 0302

152

BRITISH TOURIST AUTHORITY

Title	**Overseas Visitor Survey**
Coverage	A survey of overseas visitors to the UK based on the BTA's Overseas Visitor Survey. Some survey questions are asked each year while special topics are also covered in some years.
Frequency	Annual
Availability	General
Cost	£65
Comments	The regional tourist boards also publish statistics.
Address	Department D, Thames Tower, Black's Road, Hammersmith, London W6 9EL
Telephone	0181 846 9000
Fax	0181 563 0302

153

BRITISH TOURIST AUTHORITY

Title	**Sightseeing in the UK**
Coverage	Statistics and trends for the UK's tourist attractions. Data on visits and revenues, overseas visitors, child admissions, charges, new attractions, demand relative to capacity, capital expenditure, advertising expenditure, and employment. Also details of the above factors.
Frequency	Annual
Availability	General
Cost	£20
Comments	The regional tourist boards also publish statistics.
Address	Department D, Thames Tower, Black's Road, Hammersmith, London W6 9EL
Telephone	0181 846 9000
Fax	0181 563 0302

154

BRITISH TOURIST AUTHORITY

Title	**Facts of Tourism for England's Regions**
Coverage	Facts about tourism in each of the 11 tourist board regions. Information on the volume, value, characteristics of tourism by both UK residents and overseas visitors.
Frequency	Regular
Availability	General
Cost	£10 for each region, £90 for the complete set
Comments	The regional tourist boards also publish statistics.
Address	Department D, Thames Tower, Black's Road, Hammersmith, London W6 9EL
Telephone	0181 846 9000
Fax	0181 563 0302

155

BRITISH TOURIST AUTHORITY

Title	**The UK Tourist**
Coverage	An annual report based on the United Kingdom Tourism Survey (UKTS). Data includes the volume of UK residents' tourism, characteristics of their trips, and the people taking them. Subjects covered include purpose of trip, destinations, types of transport, accommodation used, categories of tourist spending. Also includes historical data.
Frequency	Annual
Availability	General
Cost	£60
Comments	The regional tourist boards also publish statistics.
Address	Department D, Thames Tower, Black's Road, Hammersmith, London W6 9EL
Telephone	0181 846 9000
Fax	0181 563 0302

156

BRITISH TOURIST AUTHORITY

Title	**English Heritage Monitor**
Coverage	Includes details of the numbers of historic buildings and conservation areas, admission charges, and visitor trends.
Frequency	Annual
Availability	General
Cost	£16
Comments	The regional tourist boards also publish statistics.
Address	Department D, Thames Tower, Black's Road, Hammersmith, London W6 9EL
Telephone	0181 846 9000
Fax	0181 563 0302

157 BRITISH TOURIST AUTHORITY

Title	**BTA Annual Report**
Coverage	Includes summary statistics on tourism in the UK with a general review of the short term outlook for tourism.
Frequency	Annual
Availability	General
Cost	£15
Comments	The regional tourist boards also publish statistics.
Address	Department D, Thames Tower, Black's Road, Hammersmith, London W6 9EL
Telephone	0181 846 9000
Fax	0181 563 0302

158 BRITISH TOURIST AUTHORITY

Title	**Digest of Tourist Statistics**
Coverage	Includes extracts and summaries from various travel and tourism surveys including the International Passenger Survey, the UK tourism survey of the residents of Britain, the British National Travel Survey, and many other BTA/ETB and other tourist boards' research results.
Frequency	Annual
Availability	General
Cost	£50
Comments	The regional tourist boards also publish statistics.
Address	Department D, Thames Tower, Black's Road, Hammersmith, London W6 9EL
Telephone	0181 846 9000
Fax	0181 563 0302

159 BRITISH TOY AND HOBBY ASSOCIATION

Title	**BTHA Handbook**
Coverage	Includes a section with statistics on the sales and imports and exports of specific types of toys and hobbies. Based on a combination of industry supplied data and Central Government statistics.
Frequency	Annual
Availability	General
Cost	£9
Comments	
Address	80 Camberwell Road, London SE5 0EG
Telephone	0171 701 7271
Fax	0171 708 2437

160 BRITISH VEHICLE RENTAL AND LEASING ASSOCIATION

Title	**BVRLA Annual Statistical Survey**
Coverage	Data on the size of the chauffer drive/private hire, rental, and leasing fleets operated by members of the BVRLA. Usually published around 6 months after the completion of the survey. A large amount of commentary supports the text.
Frequency	Annual
Availability	General
Cost	Free to members but priced for others
Comments	
Address	13 St John's Street, Chichester, West Sussex PO19 1UU
Telephone	01243 786782
Fax	01243 786930

161 BRITISH VEHICLE RENTAL AND LEASING ASSOCIATION

Title	**Residual Value Survey**
Coverage	Trends in the residual value of fleets operated by members and based on a survey of members.
Frequency	Quarterly
Availability	Members
Cost	Free
Comments	
Address	13 St John's Street, Chichester, West Sussex PO19 1UU
Telephone	01243 786782
Fax	01243 786930

162 BRITISH VENTURE CAPITAL ASSOCIATION

Title	**Report on Investment Activity**
Coverage	Investment trends and activities of member companies over the previous year. Commentary and statistics based on the association's own survey.
Frequency	Annual
Availability	General
Cost	£30
Comments	
Address	3 St Catherine Place, London SW1E 6DX
Telephone	0171 233 5212
Fax	0171 931 0563

163   BRITISH VIDEO ASSOCIATION

Title	**British Video Association Yearbook**
Coverage	Commentary, statistical tables and charts covering sales and rental of video tapes. The sales section includes data on distribution channels, sales by video type, sales by month, region, price group, retailer shares, number of tapes bought, best sellers, and a demographic breakdown. The rental section has data on the market value, seasonality, rentals by video type, source of rentals, frequency of rentals, viewing, and a demographic breakdown. A final section gives statistics on hardware, cinema admissions, employment. and lists BVA members. Many tables give historical data.
Frequency	Annual
Availability	General
Cost	£20
Comments	First published in 1994.
Address	22 Poland Street, London W1V 3DD
Telephone	0171 437 5722
Fax	0171 437 0477

164   BRITISH WOODPULP ASSOCIATION

Title	**Digest of Woodpulp Import Statistics**
Coverage	Tonnage imports of wood pulp for paper making and other purposes based on data supplied by HM Customs and Excise.
Frequency	Monthly
Availability	Members and some others on request
Cost	Free to members, annual subscription to others
Comments	
Address	9 Glenair Avenue, Lower Parkstone, Poole BH14 5AD
Telephone	01202 738732
Fax	01202 738747

165   BRITISH WOODPULP ASSOCIATION

Title	**Annual Report**
Coverage	Includes a statistical section with data on imports of pulp by grade and country of origin, production and consumption of paper and board.
Frequency	Annual
Availability	Members and some others on request
Cost	Free to members, a small charge to others
Comments	
Address	9 Glenair Avenue, Lower Parkstone, Poole BH14 5AD
Telephone	01202 738732
Fax	01202 738747

166 BRITISH WOOL MARKETING BOARD

Title	**Annual Statistics**
Coverage	Data on wool production, average clip size, weight of wool taken up, and the number of registered producers by UK region. Based on the Board's own survey and some text supports the tables.
Frequency	Annual
Availability	Primarily members and wool producers but other requests considered
Cost	Free
Comments	
Address	Oak Mills, Station Road, Bradford BD14 6JD
Telephone	01274 882091
Fax	01274 818277

167 BRITISH WOOL MARKETING BOARD

Title	**Annual Report and Accounts**
Coverage	Mainly details of the Board and its finances, but also contains statistics on wool production by type of wool produced. Based on the Board's own figures.
Frequency	Annual
Availability	Primarily members and wool producers but other requests considered
Cost	Free
Comments	
Address	Oak Mills, Station Road, Bradford BD14 6JD
Telephone	01274 882091
Fax	01274 818277

168 BRITISH WOOL MARKETING BOARD

Title	**Basic Data**
Coverage	Summary information on the sheep population, wool production, prices, registered producers, and the production of mutton and lamb. Based on a board survey.
Frequency	Annual
Availability	Primarily members and wool producers but other requests considered
Cost	Free
Comments	
Address	Oak Mills, Station Road, Bradford BD14 6JD
Telephone	01274 882091
Fax	01274 818277

169   BRITVIC SOFT DRINKS LTD

Title	**Britvic Soft Drinks Report**
Coverage	Graphs, tables, and commentary on trends in the soft drinks market with data on market values, brands, and consumer behaviour. Based on commissioned research.
Frequency	Annual
Availability	General
Cost	On request
Comments	
Address	Britvic House, Broomfield Road, Chelmsford, Essex CM1 1TU
Telephone	01245 261871
Fax	01245 267147

170   BUILDER GROUP

Title	**Building Economist**
Coverage	A regular newsletter with a Data File section containing statistics on housebuilding, new orders, contracting, prices, and features on specific market sectors. Based on a combination of official and non- official data.
Frequency	Monthly
Availability	General
Cost	£150
Comments	
Address	Builder House, 1 Millharbour, London E14 9RA
Telephone	0171 537 6073
Fax	0171 537 6004

171   BUILDERS MERCHANTS' FEDERATION

Title	**BMF Sales Index Survey**
Coverage	Indexed comparison of turnovers of builders merchants by region and commodity classification. Both adjusted and unadjusted figures are produced. Based on BMF's survey.
Frequency	Monthly
Availability	General
Cost	£100
Comments	
Address	15 Soho Square, London W1V 5FB
Telephone	0171 439 1753
Fax	0171 734 2766

172 BUILDING

Title	**Cost Update**
Coverage	Details of unit rates, material prices, and labour costs.
Frequency	Quarterly in a weekly journal
Availability	General
Cost	£2 per issue
Comments	Based on data compiled by quantity surveyors, Davis Langdon & Everest.
Address	1 Millharbour, London E14 9RA
Telephone	0171 537 6073
Fax	0171 537 6004

173 BUILDING

Title	**Employment Survey**
Coverage	A survey caried out by Gallup examining trends in temporary and permanent employment broken down into two sectors, consultants and contractors.
Frequency	Regular in a weekly journal
Availability	General
Cost	£2 per issue
Comments	The first survey was published in Building on 27th October 1995 and further surveys are planned.
Address	1 Millharbour, London E14 9RA
Telephone	0171 537 6073
Fax	0171 537 6004

174 BUILDING

Title	**Procurement Lead Times**
Coverage	Average procurement lead times for specific types of work and for specialist contractors.
Frequency	Six times per annum in a weekly journal
Availability	General
Cost	£2 per issue
Comments	The statistics are compiled by quantity surveyor, Gardiner & Theobold.
Address	1 Millharbour, London E14 9RA
Telephone	0171 537 6073
Fax	0171 537 6004

175	BUILDING
Title	**Indicators**
Coverage	Graphs and commentary on general trends in the building industry, based largely on Central Government data.
Frequency	Monthly in a weekly journal
Availability	General
Cost	£2 per issue
Comments	
Address	1 Millharbour, London E14 9RA
Telephone	0171 537 6073
Fax	0171 537 6004

176	BUILDING
Title	**Share Watch**
Coverage	General changes in share prices for the building sector plus specific details of the week's main gainers and losers.
Frequency	Weekly in a weekly journal
Availability	General
Cost	£2 per issue
Comments	
Address	1 Millharbour, London E14 9RA
Telephone	0171 537 6073
Fax	0171 537 6004

177	BUILDING
Title	**Construction Monitor**
Coverage	Includes statistics on building output, employment, and construction materials costs with different series published in different months. Also has news items and new legislation relating to the industry.
Frequency	Monthly in a weekly journal
Availability	General
Cost	£2 per issue
Comments	Published by Building for the Department of the Environment.
Address	1 Millharbour, London E14 9RA
Telephone	0171 537 6073
Fax	0171 537 6004

178   BUILDING

Title	**Tender Cost Forecast**
Coverage	Tender prices for various types of work, and broken down by region. Tender prices are compared with general price trends and forecasts are given for the coming year.
Frequency	Quarterly
Availability	General
Cost	£2 per issue
Comments	The figures are compiled by the quantity surveyor, Davis Langdon & Everest.
Address	1 Millharbour, London E14 9RA
Telephone	0171 537 6073
Fax	0171 537 6004

179   BUILDING EMPLOYERS' CONFEDERATION

Title	**BEC State of Trade Enquiry Report**
Coverage	Prospects for the building workload, capacity of operations. tender prices and the availability of labour and materials. Based on survey of members with the confederation stating that members account for 75% of all building work. Some commentary supports the survey results.
Frequency	Quarterly
Availability	General
Cost	£50, or £15 per issue
Comments	Subscriptions are handled by CIP Ltd, Federation House, 2309 Coventry Road, Birmingham B26 3PL, telephone 0121 742 0824.
Address	82 New Cavendish Street, London W1M 8AD
Telephone	0171 580 5588
Fax	0171 631 3872

180   BUILDING SERVICES RESEARCH AND INFORMATION ASSOCIATION (BSRIA)

Title	**BSRIA Statistics Bulletin**
Coverage	A bulletin with brief market reviews of the key building services and construction sectors. Also includes special features and forecasts of construction trends. Based on a mixture of Central Government sources, BSRIA's research, and other sources.
Frequency	Quarterly
Availability	General
Cost	£155
Comments	Also publishes various market reports and operates an inquiry service.
Address	Old Bracknell Lane West, Bracknell RG12 4AH
Telephone	01344 426511
Fax	01344 487575

181 BUILDING SOCIETIES ASSOCIATION

Title	**Building Society Yearbook**
Coverage	Key statistics on housing finance and building societies with data on loans, assets, mortgages, commitments etc. Based largely on data collected by the association.
Frequency	Annual
Availability	General
Cost	£60
Comments	Also publishes some titles jointly with the Council of Mortgage Lenders based at the same address (see separate entry).
Address	3 Savile Row, London W1X 1AF
Telephone	0171 437 0655
Fax	0171 734 6416

182 BUSINESS AND TRADE STATISTICS

Title	**UK Imports and Exports**
Coverage	Detailed statistics, from 1979 onwards, on product imports and exports, analysed by trading partners, port of entry and exit. Business and Trade Statistics is an official agent of HM Customs and Excise.
Frequency	Monthly
Availability	General
Cost	Depends on the amount and type of data required
Comments	Available in various machine readable formats.
Address	Lancaster House, More Lane, Esher, Surrey KT10 8AP
Telephone	01372 63121
Fax	01372 69847

183 BUSINESS AND TRADE STATISTICS LTD

Title	**UK Market Size Guide**
Coverage	Output data for approximately 5,000 product headings in the manufacturing sector. Based on Central Government data.
Frequency	Annual
Availability	General
Cost	£145
Comments	Also available in various machine-readable formats.
Address	Lancaster House, More Lane, Esher KT10 8AP
Telephone	01372 63121
Fax	01372 69847

184

BUSINESS AND TRADE STATISTICS LTD

Title	**Industrial and Economic Indicators**
Coverage	Data on output, investment, stocks, prices, and employment for 310 sectors. Data for the last 10 years and some forecasts. Based on Central Government data.
Frequency	Monthly
Availability	General
Cost	Varies according to the data required, number of sectors, time periods
Comments	Available in various machine-readable formats.
Address	Lancaster House, More Lane, Esher KT10 8AP
Telephone	01372 63121
Fax	01372 69847

185

BUSINESS AND TRADE STATISTICS LTD

Title	**Betting and Gaming Bulletin**
Coverage	Monthly revenue statistics from betting and gambling duties categorised by type of betting and gaming. Based on Central Government data.
Frequency	Monthly
Availability	General
Cost	£18
Comments	Also available in electronic format.
Address	Lancaster House, More Lane, Esher KT10 8AP
Telephone	01372 63121
Fax	01372 69847

186

BUSINESS GEOGRAPHICS LTD

Title	**Censys 95**
Coverage	A geodemographic service offering geodemographic profiles, lifestyle profiles, area profiles and geographical information systems. Based on an analysis of 1991 census data plus electoral roll data and market research sources including Target Group Index, BARB, NRS, and RAJAR.
Frequency	Continuous
Availability	General
Cost	On request
Comments	
Address	Garden Studios, 11-15 Betterton Street, London WC2H 9BP
Telephone	0171 379 0344
Fax	0171 379 0801

187 — BYRANT & MAY

Title	**Byrant & May Report**
Coverage	A report covering the UK market for lights (ie, matches and lighters), plus tobacco and smokers' sundries. Commentary supported by market size based on research commissioned by the company.
Frequency	Annual
Availability	General
Cost	Free
Comments	Previously titled the 'Lights Report' but name changed to reflect changing market.
Address	Sword House, Totteridge Road, High Wycombe, Buckinghamshire HP13 6EJ
Telephone	01494 556174
Fax	

188 — C CZARNIKOW SUGAR LTD

Title	**The UK Sugar Market**
Coverage	A brief review of the UK sugar market with commentary and statistics covering production, imports, consumption, and companies.
Frequency	Regular
Availability	General
Cost	Free
Comments	
Address	24 Chiswell Street, London EC1Y 4SG
Telephone	0171 972 6600
Fax	0171 972 6699

189 — CABLE TELEVISION ASSOCIATION

Title	**Statistics**
Coverage	The association produces regular statistics on cable penetration, ownership, and TV sets in the UK plus data on the major operators.
Frequency	Regular
Availability	General
Cost	On request
Comments	
Address	5th Floor, Artillery House, Artillery Row, London SW1P 1RT
Telephone	0171 222 2900
Fax	0171 799 1471

190 CACI INFORMATION SERVICES

Title	**Acorn Profiles/Areadata/Insite**
Coverage	Various demographic and area profiles based on an analysis of 1991 census data plus postcode address files and electoral roll data. Also uses Target Group Index and Financial Research Survey (FRS) data as well as some other market research sources.
Frequency	Continuous
Availability	General
Cost	On application, and depending on range and nature of information required
Comments	
Address	CACI House, Kensington Village, Avonmore Road, London W14 8TS
Telephone	0171 602 6000
Fax	0171 603 5862

191 CADBURY SCHWEPPES PLC

Title	**Confectionery Market Review**
Coverage	Figures for recent years on the confectionery market with data on specific sectors, eg chocolate, sugar, seasonal sales etc. Data on key brands, trade sector performance, advertising, retailing, the consumer. Includes a supporting commentary.
Frequency	Annual
Availability	General
Cost	On request
Comments	
Address	25 Berkeley Square, London W1X 6HT
Telephone	0171 262 1212
Fax	

192 CAMBRIDGE ECONOMETRICS

Title	**Industry and the British Economy**
Coverage	A detailed forecast of the British economy and industry with forecasts up to ten years ahead. Detailed analysis of over 40 industrial sectors and 19 service sectors.
Frequency	Regular
Availability	General
Cost	£1,750
Comments	
Address	Covent Garden, Cambridge CB1 2HS
Telephone	01223 460760
Fax	01223 464378

193 CAMBRIDGE ECONOMETRICS

Title	**Regional Economic Prospects**
Coverage	Detailed analysis and forecasts on economic trends in the UK regions. Long-term forecasts and commentary.
Frequency	Annual
Availability	General
Cost	£1,750
Comments	
Address	Covent Garden, Cambridge CB1 2HS
Telephone	01223 460760
Fax	01223 464378

194 CAMBRIDGE ECONOMETRICS

Title	**Construction Prospects**
Coverage	Detailed forecasts and analysis of the prospects for the construction industry over the medium- and long-term.
Frequency	Annual
Availability	General
Cost	£95
Comments	
Address	Covent Garden, Cambridge CB1 2HS
Telephone	01223 460760
Fax	01223 464378

195 CAN MAKERS INFORMATION SERVICE

Title	**Can Makers Report**
Coverage	Details of the beverage can industry and market, broken down by soft drinks and beer. The 1995 report includes a consumer attitudes survey and a profitability analysis. Market data covers the latest five years and there is also some data on European trends. Based mainly on a mixture of non-official sources including trade association, market research and Gallup data. Detailed commentary supports the tables.
Frequency	Annual
Availability	General
Cost	Free
Comments	Also publishes regular press releases and bulletins with statistics.
Address	1 Chelsea Manor Gardens, London SW3 5PN
Telephone	0171 351 2400
Fax	0171 352 6244

196

CAPEL, JAMES AND CO

Title **UK Economic Signals**

Coverage Data for the latest month, where available, and for the previous 12 months. Topics covered include inflation, PSBR, trade, earnings, banking etc.

Frequency Monthly

Availability Researchers and clients

Cost Free

Comments

Address Thames Exchange, 10 Queen Street Place, London EC4R 1BL

Telephone 0171 621 0011

Fax 0171 621 0496

197

CAPEL, JAMES AND CO

Title **Keynotes**

Coverage Weekly economic indicators presented in tabular and garphic form with supporting commentary.

Frequency Weekly

Availability Researchers and clients

Cost Free

Comments

Address Thames Exchange, 10 Queen Street Place, London EC4R 1BL

Telephone 0171 621 0011

Fax 0171 621 0496

198

CAPEL, JAMES AND CO

Title **UK Economics**

Coverage Statistics and commentary on UK economic trends and prospects.

Frequency Quarterly

Availability Researchers and clients

Cost Free

Comments

Address Thames Exchange, 10 Queen Street Place, London EC4R 1BL

Telephone 0171 621 0011

Fax 0171 621 0496

199 CAPSCAN LTD

Title	**Cenario**
Coverage	A CD-ROM providing access to the 1991 Census Small Area Statistics. The Cenario software provides a range of analytical functions including mapping, graphics, customer profiles, postcode sector ranking etc.
Frequency	Continuous
Availability	General
Cost	Minimum entry level – £3,000
Comments	
Address	Tranley House, Tranley Mews, Fleet Road, London NW3 2QW
Telephone	0171 267 7055
Fax	0171 267 2745

200 CARPET AND FLOORCOVERINGS REVIEW

Title	**Business Trends**
Coverage	A quarterly survey of trends in the carpet industry based on returns from carpet suppliers and retailers. Includes data on sales by carpet type.
Frequency	Quarterly
Availability	General
Cost	£61
Comments	Also publishes regular surveys on wholesaling, retailing, and specific carpet and floorcoverings markets.
Address	Miller Freeman Publications Ltd, Sovereign Way, Tonbridge TN9 1RW
Telephone	01732 364422
Fax	01732 361534

201 CARRICK JAMES MARKET RESEARCH

Title	**Youth Omnibus**
Coverage	Based on a sample of 1,200 young people aged between 11 and 24. Questions cover behaviour, spending, product and advertising awareness etc.
Frequency	Six times per annum
Availability	General
Cost	Varies according to the range of questions/information required
Comments	
Address	6 Homer Street, London W1H 1HN
Telephone	0171 724 3836
Fax	0171 224 8257

202

Title

Coverage

Frequency

Availability

Cost

Comments

Address

Telephone

Fax

CARRICK JAMES MARKET RESEARCH

Parent Omnibus

Based on a survey of 1,000 parents of children aged between 0 and 14. Parents of 5 to 14 year olds are surveyed every two months while parents of 0 to 14 year olds are surveyed quarterly.

Six times per annum

General

Varies according to the range of questions/information required

6 Homer Street, London W1H 1HN

0171 724 3836

0171 224 8257

203

Title

Coverage

Frequency

Availability

Cost

Comments

Address

Telephone

Fax

CARRICK JAMES MARKET RESEARCH

All Ages Omnibus

Based on a sample size of 3,000, this regular survey asks questions to adults and children from the age of seven upwards.

Monthly

General

Varies according to the range of questions/information required

6 Homer Street, London W1H 1HN

0171 724 3836

0171 224 8257

204

Title

Coverage

Frequency

Availability

Cost

Comments

Address

Telephone

Fax

CARRICK JAMES MARKET RESEARCH

Child and Teenage Omnibus

Continuous survey of children from the age of five upwards and teenagers up to the age of 19. Various questions relating to spending, behaviour, opinions, awareness etc.

Monthly

General

Varies according to the range of questions/information required

Also carries out a regular 'European Child Omnibus'.

6 Homer Street, London W1H 1HN

0171 724 3836

0171 224 8257

205

CATERER & HOTELKEEPER

Title	**Market Prices**
Coverage	Based on a survey of 18 specialist catering suppliers, prices are given for various fresh foods. Food categories covered are meat, poultry, game, fresh fish, fruit, vegetables, and salad.
Frequency	Weekly in a weekly journal
Availability	General
Cost	£68.25, £1.50 single issue
Comments	The journal also has occasional features on catering and hotel sectors.
Address	Reed Business Publishing Ltd, Quadrant House, The Quadrant, Sutton, Surrey SM2 5AS
Telephone	0181 652 3500
Fax	0181 652 8973

206

CATERER & HOTELKEEPER

Title	**Industry Trends**
Coverage	Various statistics on the catering and hotel trades including hotel occupancy rates, turnover figures for various catering sectors, share prices. The data available varies from week to week depending on the sources used.
Frequency	Weekly in a weekly journal
Availability	General
Cost	£68.25, £1.50 single issue
Comments	The journal also has occasional features on hotel and catering sectors.
Address	Reed Business Publishing Ltd, Quadrant House, The Quadrant, Sutton, Surrey SM2 5AS
Telephone	0181 652 3500
Fax	0181 652 8973

207

CCN BUSINESS INFORMATION

Title	**CCN Corporate Health Check**
Coverage	A review of corporate trends in the UK and the financial well-being of UK industry. Based on data collected by CCN from the financial statements of the UK's top 1,000 companies.
Frequency	Regular
Availability	General
Cost	£175
Comments	
Address	Talbot House, Talbot Street, Nottingham NG1 5HF
Telephone	01159 344944
Fax	01159 344903

208   CCN SYSTEMS LTD

Title	**Mosaic/Chorus**
Coverage	Geodemographic services based on various sources including census and lifestyle data, electoral roll data, postcode address files, Target Group Index (TGI) and Financial Research Survey (FRS).
Frequency	Continuous
Availability	General
Cost	On application, depending on the range and nature of the information required
Comments	
Address	Talbot House, Talbot Street, Nottingham NG1 5HF
Telephone	01159 344944
Fax	01159 344903

209   CDMS MARKETING SERVICES

Title	**Super Profiles**
Coverage	A geodemographic service based on a range of sources including the 1991 census, postcode address files, the electoral roll, Target Group Index (TGI), and specialist files from the Littlewoods organisation.
Frequency	Continuous
Availability	General
Cost	On application, depending on the range and nature of the information required
Comments	
Address	Kershaw Avenue, Crosby, Liverpool L23 0XA
Telephone	0151 949 1900
Fax	0151 920 1288

210   CEMENT ADMIXTURES ASSOCIATION

Title	**Statistical Return**
Coverage	Sales by weight and value for a variety of admixtures based on a survey of members.
Frequency	Regular
Availability	Members
Cost	Free
Comments	
Address	Harcourt, The Common, Kings Langley, Hertfordshire WD4 8BL
Telephone	01923 264314
Fax	01923 270778

211

CENTRE FOR THE STUDY OF REGULATED INDUSTRIES

Title **The UK Electricity Industry: Electricity Services and Costs**

Coverage The first edition of this publication appeared in 1994 following the privatisation of the electricity industry. Details of services and costs based on returns from companies and CIPFA research.

Frequency Annual

Availability General

Cost £12 to members, £15 to others

Comments CRI is a research centre of the Chartered Institute of Public Finance and Accountancy (see other entry).

Address 3 Robert Street, London WC2N 6BH

Telephone 0171 895 8623

Fax 0171 895 8825

212

CENTRE FOR THE STUDY OF REGULATED INDUSTRIES

Title **The UK Regulated Industries: Financial Figures**

Coverage The first edition of this publication appeared in 1994 and gives financial data on the newly privatised utilities. Based mainly on financial data supplied by the companies themselves.

Frequency Annual

Availability General

Cost £12 to members, £15 to others

Comments CRI is a research centre of the Chartered Institute of Public Finance and Accountancy (see other entry).

Address 3 Robert Street, London WC2N 6BH

Telephone 0171 895 8823

Fax 0171 895 8825

213

CENTRE FOR THE STUDY OF REGULATED INDUSTRIES

Title **The UK Water Industry: Charges for Water Services**

Coverage The first edition of this publication appeared in 1994 and gives details of water charges. Based on data supplied by the companies and some CIPFA analysis.

Frequency Annual

Availability General

Cost £8 to members, £10 to others

Comments CRI is a research centre of the Chartered Institute of Public Finance and Accountancy (see other entry).

Address 3 Robert Street, London WC2N 6BH

Telephone 0171 895 8623

Fax 0171 895 8825

214

	CENTRE FOR THE STUDY OF REGULATED INDUSTRIES
Title	**The UK Water Industry: Water Services and Costs**
Coverage	The first edition of this publication appeared in 1995 and gives details of water services and charges. Based on returns by the companies and some CIPFA research.
Frequency	Annual
Availability	General
Cost	£20 to members, £25 to others
Comments	CRI is a research centre of the Chartered Institute of Public Finance and Accountancy (see other entry).
Address	3 Robert Street, London WC2N 6BH
Telephone	0171 895 8623
Fax	0171 895 8825

215

	CENTRE FOR THE STUDY OF REGULATED INDUSTRIES
Title	**UK Airports Industry – Airport Statistics**
Coverage	Operating and financial statistics on UK airports with aggregate data and statistics on specific airports. Based on data collected by CIPFA and the Centre.
Frequency	Annual
Availability	General
Cost	£25
Comments	First published in 1996 to replace Airport – Statistics previously published by the Chartered Institute of Public Finance and Accountancy (CIPFA). CRI is a research centre of the Chartered Institute of Public Finance and Accountancy (see other entry).
Address	3 Robert Street, London WC2N 6BH
Telephone	0171 895 8623
Fax	0171 895 8825

216

	CENTRE FOR THE STUDY OF REGULATED INDUSTRIES
Title	**The UK Electricity Industry: Charges for Electricity Services**
Coverage	The first edition of this publication appeared in 1995 following the privatisation of the electricity industry. Based on returns from the companies and CRI research.
Frequency	Annual
Availability	General
Cost	£12 to CRI members, £15 to others
Comments	CRI is a research centre of the Chartered Institute of Public Finance and Accountancy (see other entry).
Address	3 Robert Street, London WC2N 6BH
Telephone	0171 895 8623
Fax	0171 895 8825

217	CHALVINGTON PRESS
Title	**The Business Book of the Electrical Retail Market in Great Britain**
Coverage	A general overview of the consumer electrical market is followed by specific sections on consumer electronics by product type, domestic appliances, and small appliances. Each section has details of market size, segments, brands, manufacturers, and distribution trends. Each market has statistics for the last five years. Based on various sources including research by the compiler.
Frequency	Annual
Availability	General
Cost	£80
Comments	First published in 1990.
Address	Plestor House, Farnham Road, West Liss, Hampshire GU33 6JQ
Telephone	01730 894059
Fax	01730 895298

218	CHAMBER OF SHIPPING
Title	**Statistical Brief**
Coverage	Statistics on the UK and world fleets, seaborne trade, freight and other market trends. Also analyses the balance of payments contribution from shipowning. Some data from the Chamber but the majority comes from other non-official sources and some official sources.
Frequency	Quarterly
Availability	General
Cost	On application
Comments	
Address	30-32 St Mary Axe, London EC3A 8ET
Telephone	0171 417 8400
Fax	0171 626 8135

219	CHAMBERS AND PARTNERS
Title	**Salary Survey of Lawyers in Industry**
Coverage	A survey of average salaries for various job categories broken down by sex, age, and industrial sector. Based on a survey by the company.
Frequency	Annual
Availability	General
Cost	Free
Comments	
Address	74 Long Lane, London EC1A 9ET
Telephone	0171 606 9371
Fax	0171 600 1793

220	CHARITIES AID FOUNDATION
Title	**Charity Trends**
Coverage	Commentary and statistics on the 'givers' and 'receivers' with tables giving historical figures. Based largely on the Foundation's own data with a detailed supporting text.
Frequency	Annual
Availability	General
Cost	£20
Comments	
Address	48 Pembury Road, Tonbridge TN9 2JD
Telephone	01732 771333
Fax	01732 350570

221	CHARITY RECRUITMENT
Title	**Annual Voluntary Sector Salary Survey**
Coverage	Salaries for various job categories and grades in large and small charities. Based on a survey by the company.
Frequency	Annual
Availability	General
Cost	£170 plus VAT, £120 plus VAT for charities with less than 30 staff
Comments	
Address	40 Rosebery Avenue, London EC1R 4RN
Telephone	0171 833 0770
Fax	0171 833 0188

222	CHART ANALYSIS LTD
Title	**UK Point and Figure Library**
Coverage	Comprehensive coverage of the UK Stock Market by market sector. Over 500 charts and tables cover industry group performance, share indices, British funds, money rates, and general indicators. Based on various sources and analysis by the company.
Frequency	Weekly and monthly
Availability	General
Cost	£1,315 weekly, £575 monthly
Comments	
Address	7 Swallow Street, London W1R 7HD
Telephone	0171 439 4961
Fax	0171 439 4966

223	CHART ANALYSIS LTD
Title	**Commodities**
Coverage	Trends and prices in UK and USA futures markets. Covers over 30 different commodities in the food, grain, livestock/meat, industrial, metals, and finance sectors. Based on the company's data.
Frequency	Weekly and monthly
Availability	General
Cost	£835 weekly, £250 monthly, £33 per issue
Comments	
Address	7 Swallow Street, London W1R 7HD
Telephone	0171 439 4961
Fax	0171 439 4966

224	CHARTERED INSTITUTE OF MARKETING
Title	**State of the Market Report**
Coverage	A review of economic and business trends and the effect of these trends on the marketing sector.
Frequency	Quarterly
Availability	Primarily members
Cost	Free
Comments	
Address	Moor Hall, Cookham SL6 9QH
Telephone	01628 524922
Fax	01628 531382

225	CHARTERED INSTITUTE OF MARKETING
Title	**Marketing Trends Survey**
Coverage	A quarterly survey of trends and prospects in the marketing sector, including the CIM Confidence Index. Based on a survey of members.
Frequency	Quarterly
Availability	Primarily members
Cost	Free
Comments	
Address	Moor Hall, Cookham SL6 9QH
Telephone	01628 524922
Fax	01628 531382

226

CHARTERED INSTITUTE OF PUBLIC FINANCE AND ACCOUNTANCY (CIPFA)

Title	**Probation – Combined Actuals and Estimates**
Coverage	Expenditure and income in the probation service per thousand population aged 15-29 and manpower for the service in England and Wales. Based on data collected by CIPFA.
Frequency	Annual
Availability	General
Cost	£55
Comments	
Address	3 Robert Street, London WC2N 6BH
Telephone	0171 895 8823
Fax	0171 895 8825

227

CHARTERED INSTITUTE OF PUBLIC FINANCE AND ACCOUNTANCY (CIPFA)

Title	**Housing Revenue Account – Combined Actuals and Estimates**
Coverage	Figures for Housing Revenue Account income in total and for each housing authority in England and Wales. Based on a combination of Central Government statistics and CIPFA data.
Frequency	Annual
Availability	General
Cost	£80
Comments	
Address	3 Robert Street, London WC2N 6BH
Telephone	0171 895 8823
Fax	0171 895 8825

228

CHARTERED INSTITUTE OF PUBLIC FINANCE AND ACCOUNTANCY (CIPFA)

Title	**Leisure and Recreation – Estimates**
Coverage	Estimated expenditure and income on sports and recreation, cultural and other related facilities by local authory area. Based on data collected by CIPFA from local authorities.
Frequency	Annual
Availability	General
Cost	£80
Comments	
Address	3 Robert Street, London WC2N 6BH
Telephone	0171 895 8823
Fax	0171 895 8825

229

CHARTERED INSTITUTE OF PUBLIC FINANCE AND ACCOUNTANCY (CIPFA)

Title	**Leisure Charges – Actuals**
Coverage	Sample survey of charges for leisure centre facilities, swimming pools and outdoor sports. Based on a sample of 150 local authorities.
Frequency	Annual
Availability	General
Cost	£55
Comments	
Address	3 Robert Street, London WC2N 6BH
Telephone	0171 895 8823
Fax	0171 895 8825

230

CHARTERED INSTITUTE OF PUBLIC FINANCE AND ACCOUNTANCY (CIPFA)

Title	**Local Authority Superannuation Fund Investment Statistics**
Coverage	A ten-year historical record of superannuation statistics with the first issue, published in 1995, covering the years 1985 to 1995. Based on data supplied by local authorities.
Frequency	Annual
Availability	General
Cost	£180
Comments	
Address	3 Robert Street, London WC2N 6BH
Telephone	0171 895 8823
Fax	0171 895 8825

231

CHARTERED INSTITUTE OF PUBLIC FINANCE AND ACCOUNTANCY (CIPFA)

Title	**Local Government Comparative Statistics**
Coverage	Summary statistical indicators covering the range of local authority services. Based on a combination of data collected by CIPFA and other non-official sources.
Frequency	Annual
Availability	General
Cost	£105
Comments	
Address	3 Robert Street, London WC2N 6BH
Telephone	0171 895 8823
Fax	0171 895 8825

232 CHARTERED INSTITUTE OF PUBLIC FINANCE AND ACCOUNTANCY (CIPFA)

Title	**Personal Social Services – Actuals**
Coverage	An analysis of residential, day, and community care provision giving gross and net expenditure and the number of clients by local authority area. Based on data collected by CIPFA.
Frequency	Annual
Availability	General
Cost	£80
Comments	
Address	3 Robert Street, London WC2N 6BH
Telephone	0171 895 8823
Fax	0171 895 8825

233 CHARTERED INSTITUTE OF PUBLIC FINANCE AND ACCOUNTANCY (CIPFA)

Title	**Waste Disposal – Actuals**
Coverage	Data on revenue income and expenditure, capital expenditure and financing, treatment methods, waste arising and reclaimed waste by tonnage, vehicle disposals, manpower, and unit costs. Summary data and by local authority area. Based on data collected by CIPFA.
Frequency	Annual
Availability	General
Cost	£80
Comments	
Address	3 Robert Street, London WC2N 6BH
Telephone	0171 895 8823
Fax	0171 895 8825

234 CHARTERED INSTITUTE OF PUBLIC FINANCE AND ACCOUNTANCY (CIPFA)

Title	**Planning and Development – Combined Actuals and Estimates**
Coverage	Capital and revenue expenditure on the planning and development functions in summary and by individual local authority. Based on data collected by CIPFA.
Frequency	Annual
Availability	General
Cost	£80
Comments	
Address	3 Robert Street, London WC2N 6BH
Telephone	0171 895 8823
Fax	0171 895 8825

235

CHARTERED INSTITUTE OF PUBLIC FINANCE AND ACCOUNTANCY (CIPFA)

Title **Police – Combined Actuals and Estimates**

Coverage Figures are given for income, expenditure, and manpower in total and by individual police force and regional crime squad. Based on data collected by CIPFA.

Frequency Annual

Availability General

Cost £105

Comments

Address 3 Robert Street, London WC2N 6BH

Telephone 0171 895 8823

Fax 0171 895 8825

236

CHARTERED INSTITUTE OF PUBLIC FINANCE AND ACCOUNTANCY (CIPFA)

Title **Public Libraries – Actuals**

Coverage Final outturn figures for income and expenditure, manpower, agency services, books, and other stocks and service points are given in total and for each library service in Great Britain and Northern Ireland.

Frequency Annual

Availability General

Cost £80

Comments

Address 3 Robert Street, London WC2N 6BH

Telephone 0171 895 8823

Fax 0171 895 8825

237

CHARTERED INSTITUTE OF PUBLIC FINANCE AND ACCOUNTANCY (CIPFA)

Title **Revenue Collection – Actuals**

Coverage Revenue collection statistics broken down by local authority area and based on returns to CIPFA from local authorities.

Frequency Annual

Availability General

Cost £80

Comments

Address 3 Robert Street, London WC2N 6BH

Telephone 0171 895 8823

Fax 0171 895 8825

238

CHARTERED INSTITUTE OF PUBLIC FINANCE AND ACCOUNTANCY (CIPFA)

Title **Trading Standards – Actuals**

Coverage Financial and non-financial data on trading standards departments with data for individual local authorities. Based on data collected by CIPFA.

Frequency Annual

Availability General

Cost £55

Comments

Address 3 Robert Street, London WC2N 6BH

Telephone 0171 895 8823

Fax 0171 895 8825

239

CHARTERED INSTITUTE OF PUBLIC FINANCE AND ACCOUNTANCY (CIPFA)

Title **Waste Collection – Actuals**

Coverage Data on waste collection including income and expenditure, staff numbers, charges, quantities collected, and methods and frequency of collection. Aggregate data and data by local authority area. Based on data collected by CIPFA.

Frequency Annual

Availability General

Cost £80

Comments

Address 3 Robert Street, London WC2N 6BH

Telephone 0171 895 8823

Fax 0171 895 8825

240

CHARTERED INSTITUTE OF PUBLIC FINANCE AND ACCOUNTANCY (CIPFA)

Title **Housing Rents – Actuals**

Coverage An analysis of the housing stock by age and type, average weekly rents and rebates, and allowances. Data for individual local authorities and summary tables for individual planning regions. Based on returns to CIPFA from local authorities.

Frequency Annual

Availability General

Cost £80

Comments

Address 3 Robert Street, London WC2N 6BH

Telephone 0171 895 8823

Fax 0171 895 8825

241   CHARTERED INSTITUTE OF PUBLIC FINANCE AND ACCOUNTANCY (CIPFA)

Title	**County Farms – Actuals**
Coverage	Financial and other data on county farms by local authority area. Based on data collected by CIPFA.
Frequency	Annual
Availability	General
Cost	£55
Comments	
Address	3 Robert Street, London WC2N 6BH
Telephone	0171 895 8823
Fax	0171 895 8825

242   CHARTERED INSTITUTE OF PUBLIC FINANCE AND ACCOUNTANCY (CIPFA)

Title	**Capital Payments**
Coverage	An analysis of capital payments and debt statistics for individual local authorities in England, Wales, Scotland, and Northern Ireland. Based on data collected by CIPFA.
Frequency	Annual
Availability	General
Cost	£105
Comments	
Address	3 Robert Street, London WC2N 6BH
Telephone	0171 895 8823
Fax	0171 895 8825

243   CHARTERED INSTITUTE OF PUBLIC FINANCE AND ACCOUNTANCY (CIPFA)

Title	**Administration of Justice – Combined Actuals and Estimates**
Coverage	Expenditure and income figures for both magistrates' and coroners' courts per thousand population. Based on returns received by CIPFA.
Frequency	Annual
Availability	General
Cost	£55
Comments	
Address	3 Robert Street, London WC2N 6BH
Telephone	0171 895 8823
Fax	0171 895 8825

244	CHARTERED INSTITUTE OF PUBLIC FINANCE AND ACCOUNTANCY (CIPFA)
Title	**Direct Service Organisations – Actuals**
Coverage	Financial, organizational, and related data on direct service organisations in local authorities. Based on returns to CIPFA from local authorities.
Frequency	Annual
Availability	General
Cost	£105
Comments	
Address	3 Robert Street, London WC2N 6BH
Telephone	0171 895 8823
Fax	

245	CHARTERED INSTITUTE OF PUBLIC FINANCE AND ACCOUNTANCY (CIPFA)
Title	**Archives – Estimates**
Coverage	Statistics on the organisation and financing of archives based on returns from local authorities collected by CIPFA.
Frequency	Annual
Availability	General
Cost	£55
Comments	
Address	3 Robert Street, London WC2N 6BH
Telephone	0171 895 8823
Fax	0171 895 8825

246	CHARTERED INSTITUTE OF PUBLIC FINANCE AND ACCOUNTANCY (CIPFA)
Title	**Housing Rent Arrears and Benefits – Actuals**
Coverage	An analysis of rent arrears and benefits by local authority area. Based on returns to CIPFA from local authorities.
Frequency	Annual
Availability	General
Cost	£80
Comments	
Address	3 Robert Street, London WC2N 6BH
Telephone	0171 895 8823
Fax	0171 895 8825

247

CHARTERED INSTITUTE OF PUBLIC FINANCE AND ACCOUNTANCY (CIPFA)

Title	**Cemetries – Actuals**
Coverage	Expenditure, income, fees, and non-financial data on cemetries in local authority areas. Based on data collected by CIPFA.
Frequency	Annual
Availability	General
Cost	£55
Comments	
Address	3 Robert Street, London WC2N 6BH
Telephone	0171 895 8823
Fax	0171 895 8825

248

CHARTERED INSTITUTE OF PUBLIC FINANCE AND ACCOUNTANCY (CIPFA)

Title	**Council Tax Demands and Precepts – Estimates**
Coverage	Statistics on the level of demands and revenues from council tax based on returns from local authorities collected by CIPFA.
Frequency	Annual
Availability	General
Cost	£55
Comments	
Address	3 Robert Street, London WC2N 6BH
Telephone	0171 895 8823
Fax	0171 895 8825

249

CHARTERED INSTITUTE OF PUBLIC FINANCE AND ACCOUNTANCY (CIPFA)

Title	**Crematoria – Actuals**
Coverage	Expenditure, income, fees and non-financial data on crematoria by local authority area. Based on data collected by CIPFA.
Frequency	Annual
Availability	General
Cost	£55
Comments	
Address	3 Robert Street, London WC2N 6BH
Telephone	0171 895 8823
Fax	0171 895 8825

250	CHARTERED INSTITUTE OF PUBLIC FINANCE AND ACCOUNTANCY (CIPFA)
Title	**Environmental Health – Actuals**
Coverage	Financial and other data relating to environmental health in specific local authorities. Based on data collected by CIPFA.
Frequency	Annual
Availability	General
Cost	£80
Comments	
Address	3 Robert Street, London WC2N 6BH
Telephone	0171 895 8823
Fax	0171 895 8825

251	CHARTERED INSTITUTE OF PUBLIC FINANCE AND ACCOUNTANCY (CIPFA)
Title	**Finance and General – Estimates**
Coverage	Summary information on local authority income and expenditure with data for each local authority in England and Wales. Based on estimates collected by CIPFA with additional data on estimated income and expenditure per head of the population.
Frequency	Annual
Availability	General
Cost	£105
Comments	
Address	3 Robert Street, London WC2N 6BH
Telephone	0171 895 8823
Fax	0171 895 8825

252	CHARTERED INSTITUTE OF PUBLIC FINANCE AND ACCOUNTANCY (CIPFA)
Title	**Fire – Combined Actuals and Estimates**
Coverage	Summary data on fire service income and expenditure and similar figures for each local authority and per thousand population. Also statistics on fire stations, training, manpower, applications, return of calls, inspections. Based on returns from local authorities received by CIPFA.
Frequency	Annual
Availability	General
Cost	£80
Comments	
Address	3 Robert Street, London WC2N 6BH
Telephone	0171 895 8823
Fax	0171 895 8825

253	CHARTERED INSTITUTE OF PUBLIC FINANCE AND ACCOUNTANCY (CIPFA)
Title	**Health Database**
Coverage	An annual survey of health service income and expenditure available in book and disc formats. The database consists of four volumes. Volume 1 is a financial overview available in hard copy format. Volumes 2, 3a, and 3b are discs covering the purchaser database, provider database on activity costs, and a provider database with accounts analysis respectively.
Frequency	
Availability	General
Cost	£360 – Volume 1, £390 – Volume 2, £450 – Volume 3a, £390 – Volume 3b. VAT must be added to the disc prices, discounts available for complete purchases of all volumes and for contributing organisations
Comments	
Address	3 Robert Street, London WC2N 6BH
Telephone	0171 895 8823
Fax	0171 895 8825

254	CHARTERED INSTITUTE OF PUBLIC FINANCE AND ACCOUNTANCY (CIPFA)
Title	**Highways and Transportation – Combined Actuals and Estimates**
Coverage	Data on highways and transportation expenditure by county councils in England and Wales. Based on returns received by CIPFA.
Frequency	Annual
Availability	General
Cost	£80
Comments	
Address	3 Robert Street, London WC2N 6BH
Telephone	0171 895 8823
Fax	0171 895 8825

255	CHARTERED INSTITUTE OF PUBLIC FINANCE AND ACCOUNTANCY (CIPFA)
Title	**Homelessness – Actuals**
Coverage	A financial survey of the operations of the Housing (Homeless Persons) Act with data for individual local authorities. Based on data collected by CIPFA.
Frequency	Annual
Availability	General
Cost	£55
Comments	
Address	3 Robert Street, London WC2N 6BH
Telephone	0171 895 8823
Fax	0171 895 8825

256	CHARTERED INSTITUTE OF PUBLIC FINANCE AND ACCOUNTANCY (CIPFA)
Title	**Education (Including Unit Costs) – Actuals**
Coverage	Non-financial data on pupil, school, and teacher numbers and financial data split by types of school and local authority area. The publication now also includes education unit costs, previously published in a separate volume. These costs cover institutional costs, pupil and student support costs, capital costs, salary costs, recurrent expenditure, and university costs. Based largely on Central Government data.
Frequency	Annual
Availability	General
Cost	£80
Comments	
Address	3 Robert Street, London WC2N 6BH
Telephone	0171 895 8823
Fax	0171 895 8825

257 CHARTERED INSTITUTE OF PUBLIC FINANCE AND ACCOUNTANCY (CIPFA)

Title **Airports – Actuals**

Coverage An analysis of the revenue accounts and balance sheets of local authority airports plus a range of non-financial information. Based on data supplied to CIPFA by local authorities.

Frequency Annual

Availability General

Cost £55

Comments The last issue was published in 1995 and replaced by UK Airports Industry – Airport Statistics published by the Centre for the Study of Regulated Industries (see other entry).

Address 3 Robert Street, London WC2N 6BH

Telephone 0171 895 8823

Fax 0171 895 8825

258 CHARTERHOUSE PLC

Title **UK Economica**

Coverage A review of UK economic trends with short-term forecasts. Forecasts produced by the company with existing data from Central Government sources.

Frequency Quarterly

Availability General

Cost On request

Comments

Address 1 Paternoster Row, London EC4M 7DH

Telephone 0171 248 4000

Fax 0171 246 2033

259 CHEMICAL INDUSTRIES ASSOCIATION

Title **UK Chemical Industry Facts**

Coverage Leaflet with basic statistics on the UK chemical industry with historical data over a ten-year period.

Frequency Annual

Availability General

Cost Free (single copy)

Comments Published in July each year. Also available on 35mm slides and overhead transparencies. The association also publishes international statistics.

Address Kings Building, Smith Square, London SW1P 3JJ

Telephone 0171 834 3399

Fax 0171 834 4469

260   CHEMICAL INDUSTRIES ASSOCIATION

Title	**Investment Intentions Survey**
Coverage	A survey of CIA member company investment intentions covering actual capital expenditure in the previous year together with investment intentions for the coming three years. Total figures plus a breakdown by region, chemicals sector, and purpose of investment.
Frequency	Annual
Availability	General
Cost	£20 to members, £50 to others
Comments	The results are announced at an annually held Investment Intentions Conference. The association also publishes international statistics.
Address	Kings Building, Smith Square, London SW1P 3JJ
Telephone	0171 834 3399
Fax	0171 834 4469

261   CHEMICAL INDUSTRIES ASSOCIATION

Title	**Economics Bulletin**
Coverage	Monitors, analyses and forecasts the economic performance of the UK chemical industry. A main table of chemical industry basic economic indicators is also included. Based on official and non-official sources.
Frequency	Three issues per year
Availability	General
Cost	Free to members, £70 to non-members
Comments	
Address	Kings Building, Smith Square, London SW1P 3JJ
Telephone	0171 834 3399
Fax	0171 834 4469

262   CHEMIST AND DRUGGIST

Title	**Chemist and Druggist Price List**
Coverage	Trade and retail prices for various products sold by chemists. Based on the journal's own survey with prices usually one month old.
Frequency	Monthly supplement to a weekly journal
Availability	General
Cost	£100, £2.10 single issue
Comments	The journal also has regular features on specific markets and specific products sold via chemists.
Address	Benn Publications, Sovereign Way, Tonbridge TN9 1RW
Telephone	01732 364422
Fax	01732 361534

263	CHESTERTON RESEARCH
Title	**City Centre Office Markets**
Coverage	A review of rents, rates, vacancies, occupancies in the major cities based on data collected by the company.
Frequency	Regular
Availability	General
Cost	£55
Comments	
Address	54 Brook Street, London W1A 2BU
Telephone	0171 499 0404
Fax	0171 629 7804

264	CHILDRENS RESEARCH UNIT
Title	**Juvenile Perspectives**
Coverage	An annual survey of 7 to 15 year olds in the UK and other European countries. Based on a sample of around 8,000, the survey is conducted by the company.
Frequency	Annual
Availability	General
Cost	On request
Comments	
Address	Albany House, Portslade Road, London SW8 3DJ
Telephone	0171 622 0286
Fax	0171 720 0537

265	CINEMA ADVERTISING ASSOCIATION
Title	**Caviar – Cinema and Video Industry Audience Research**
Coverage	Provides audience data for cinema and pre-recorded videos from the age of 7 upwards by film, genre, certificate. Based on a survey of almost 3,000 people in various randomly selected sampling points around the country.
Frequency	Annual
Availability	General
Cost	£5,600
Comments	The data is also available online, and on disc.
Address	127 Wardour Street, London W1V 4NL
Telephone	0171 439 9531
Fax	0171 439 2395

266   CINEMA ADVERTISING ASSOCIATION

Title	**Caviar – Cinema and Video Industry Audience Research**
Coverage	A guide to the levels of coverage and frequency achieved by cinema advertising campaigns. Statistics are taken from the National Readership Survey (NRS).
Frequency	Annual
Availability	General
Cost	On application
Comments	The data is also available online and on disc.
Address	127 Wardour Street, London W1V 4NL
Telephone	0171 439 9531
Fax	0171 439 2395

267   CINEMA ADVERTISING ASSOCIATION

Title	**CAA UK Advertising Admissions Monitor**
Coverage	A monthly measure of the attendances at all UK cinemas accepting advertising. Based on the association's own research.
Frequency	Monthly
Availability	General
Cost	On application
Comments	The data is also available online and on disc.
Address	127 Wardour Street, London W1V 4NL
Telephone	0171 439 9531
Fax	0171 439 2395

268   CIVIL AVIATION AUTHORITY

Title	**UK Airlines**
Coverage	Operating and traffic statistics for UK airlines by domestic and international services, and by types of operation, based on the CAA's own data. Statistics usually cover the previous month.
Frequency	Monthly
Availability	General
Cost	£59
Comments	CAA statistics also available on magnetic discs in Word for Windows format or on Excel spreadsheets. Disc subscription – £118 per annum, £11.80 for individual discs.
Address	Greville House, 37 Gratton Road, Cheltenham GL50 2BN
Telephone	01242 35151
Fax	01242 584139

269	CIVIL AVIATION AUTHORITY
Title	**UK Airports**
Coverage	Monthly statements of movements, passengers, and cargo at UK airports, based on data collected by the CAA. Statistics usually cover the previous month.
Frequency	Monthly
Availability	General
Cost	£59
Comments	CAA statistics also available on magnetic disc in Word for Windows format or on Excel spreadsheeets. Disc subscription – £118 per annum, £11.80 for individual discs.
Address	Greville House, 37 Gratton Road, Cheltenham GL50 2BN
Telephone	01242 35151
Fax	01242 584139

270	CIVIL AVIATION AUTHORITY
Title	**Punctuality Statistics**
Coverage	Punctuality statistics are available by airline and destination, for four London airports plus Manchester and Birmingham. Comparisons are made with the month in the previous year.
Frequency	Monthly
Availability	General
Cost	£310 for the detailed reports, £64 for summary reports
Comments	
Address	Greville House, 37 Gratton Road, Cheltenham GL50 2BN
Telephone	01242 35151
Fax	01242 584139

271	CIVIL AVIATION AUTHORITY
Title	**Annual Punctuality Statistics**
Coverage	Punctuality statistics are available by airline and destination, for four London airports plus Manchester and Birmingham. Comparisons with the previous year are given.
Frequency	Annual
Availability	General
Cost	£42 for the detailed report, £10.50 for the summary report
Comments	
Address	Greville House, 37 Gratton Road, Cheltenham GL50 2BN
Telephone	01242 35151
Fax	01242 584139

272   COCA-COLA & SCHWEPPES BEVERAGES LTD

Title	**Bottled Water Market Profile**
Coverage	A review of the UK bottled water market with sales data for the total market and by type of water. Also includes data on brands, retailing, new products.
Frequency	Regular
Availability	General
Cost	On request
Comments	
Address	Charter Place, Uxbridge UB8 1EZ
Telephone	01895 231313
Fax	01895 239092

273   COLLOROLL

Title	**Colloroll Wallcoverings Market Report**
Coverage	A review of the retail wallcoverings market with data on consumption, retail sale shares, design trends, and future trends. Based on commissioned research.
Frequency	Regular
Availability	General
Cost	On request
Comments	Available from John Wilman Ltd at the address below.
Address	7 Floral Street, London WC2E 9DH
Telephone	0171 836 9843
Fax	0171 497 2753

274   COMPANY CAR

Title	**Databank**
Coverage	Prices of new cars and the standing, running, and operating costs of car fleets.
Frequency	Monthly in a monthly journal
Availability	General
Cost	£61
Comments	
Address	International Trade Publications Ltd, Queensway House, 2 Queensway, Redhill, Surrey RH1 1QS
Telephone	01737 768611
Fax	01737 760564

275

COMPUTER BUSINESS REVIEW

Title **Trends and Indicators**

Coverage Basic data on general economic trends and indicators relevant to the computer sector based on information compiled from various sources.

Frequency Monthly in a monthly journal

Availability General

Cost £55

Comments

Address 12 Sutton Row, London W1V 5FH

Telephone 0171 208 4245

Fax 0171 439 1105

276

COMPUTER ECONOMICS LTD

Title **Computer Staff Salary Survey**

Coverage A survey of 50 job descriptions analysed by location, age, experience, areas of responsibility, fringe benefits etc. Based on a survey by the company. A small commentary supports the text.

Frequency Bi-annual

Availability General

Cost On application

Comments

Address Survey House, 51 Portland Road, Kingston-upon-Thames KT1 2SH

Telephone 0181 549 8726

Fax 0181 541 5705

277

COMPUTING SERVICES AND SOFTWARE ASSOCIATION

Title **Annual Report**

Coverage Includes the association's annual survey based on voluntary responses from member companies. Data on business activities, total revenue, revenue by business sector, revenue per employee, employment trends, profits, and future prospects. A detailed commentary supports the text.

Frequency Annual

Availability General

Cost Free

Comments

Address Hanover House, 73-74 High Holborn, London WC1V 6LE

Telephone 0171 405 2171

Fax 0171 404 4119

278	CONFEDERATION OF BRITISH INDUSTRY (CBI)
Title	**CBI/BSL Regional Trends Survey**
Coverage	A survey of economic and business trends in the UK regions based on a survey of a sample of companies in these regions.
Frequency	Annual
Availability	General
Cost	£33
Comments	Produced in association with Business Strategies Ltd.
Address	103 New Oxford Street, London WC1A 1DU
Telephone	0171 379 7400
Fax	0171 240 1578

279	CONFEDERATION OF BRITISH INDUSTRY (CBI)
Title	**Economic Situation Report**
Coverage	An economic survey plus a forecast up to six months ahead. Also a general survey of industrial and regional trends and some comparative data for other European countries. Based on a combination of CBI data and official statistics.
Frequency	Monthly
Availability	General
Cost	£220
Comments	
Address	103 New Oxford Street, London WC1A 1DU
Telephone	0171 379 7400
Fax	0171 240 1578

280	CONFEDERATION OF BRITISH INDUSTRY (CBI)
Title	**CBI Survey of the Disributive Trades**
Coverage	A survey of trends in over 20 distributive sectors with data on sales volume, orders, stocks, employment, investment, prices business expenditure etc. Based on a CBI survey.
Frequency	Monthly
Availability	General
Cost	£396, £240 to members
Comments	
Address	103 New Oxford Street, London WC1A 1DU
Telephone	0171 379 7400
Fax	0171 379 1578

281	CONFEDERATION OF BRITISH INDUSTRY (CBI)
Title	**CBI/Coopers and Lybrand Financial Services Survey**
Coverage	A survey of trends in various financial services sectors with data on income, employment, short term expectations etc. Based on a CBI survey.
Frequency	Quarterly
Availability	General
Cost	£300, £168 to members
Comments	
Address	103 New Oxford Street, London WC1A 1DU
Telephone	0171 379 7400
Fax	0171 240 1578

282	CONFEDERATION OF BRITISH INDUSTRY (CBI)
Title	**Industrial Trends Survey**
Coverage	Trends for over 40 industry groups covering orders, stocks, output, capital expenditure, exports, costs, labour etc for the last 4 months and the next 4 months. Based on a CBI survey of around 1,700 companies.
Frequency	Quarterly
Availability	General
Cost	£360, £200 to members, joint subscription with Monthly Trends Enquiry (see below) £552, £336 to members
Comments	
Address	103 New Oxford Street, London WC1A 1DU
Telephone	0171 379 7400
Fax	0171 240 1578

283	CONFEDERATION OF BRITISH INDUSTRY (CBI)
Title	**Monthly Trends Enquiry**
Coverage	Essentially an abbreviated version of the quarterly 'Industrial Trends Survey' with summary statistics on orders, stocks, output, prices etc. A short commentary supports the statistics. Data is based on a survey of companies with responses varying from around 1,300 to over 1,500.
Frequency	Monthly
Availability	General
Cost	£552, £336 to members, a joint subscription with Industrial Trends Survey (see entry above)
Comments	
Address	103 New Oxford Street, London WC1A 1DU
Telephone	0171 379 7400
Fax	0171 240 1578

284 CONSENSUS RESEARCH INTERNATIONAL

Title	**Unit Trust Survey**
Coverage	A survey of the awareness of, and attitudes towards, unit trusts amongst unitholders and intermediaries. Based on a company survey and a commentary supports the data.
Frequency	Quarterly
Availability	General
Cost	On application
Comments	Also produces an annual Stockbroker Survey, based on the ratings of brokers' analysts by company executives.
Address	8 St John's Hall, London SW11 1SA
Telephone	0171 738 1222
Fax	0171 738 1271

285 CONSTRUCTION FORECASTING AND RESEARCH LTD

Title	**Construction Forecasts**
Coverage	Short-term construction forecasts, and current trends, covering housing, industrial, commercial, and infrastructure. Value and volume forecasts are included and a detailed analysis of the forecasts accompanies the tables.
Frequency	Bi-annual
Availability	General
Cost	£75
Comments	Published on behalf of the Joint Forecasting Committee for the Construction Industries. Statistics on European construction trends and corporate performance in the construction industry also produced.
Address	Princes House, 39 Kingsway, London WC2B 6TP
Telephone	0171 379 5339
Fax	0171 379 5426

286 CONSTRUCTION FORECASTING AND RESEARCH LTD

Title	**Process Industries Investment Forecast**
Coverage	Forecasts of capital expenditure and expenditure on process plant in the chemical, nuclear fuel reprocessing, oil and gas production, petroleum refining, electricity generation, gas, steel, water and sewerage, and food and drink industries.
Frequency	Annual
Availability	General
Cost	On request
Comments	Statistics on European construction trends and corporate performance in the construction industry also produced.
Address	Princes House, 39 Kingsway, London WC2B 6TP
Telephone	0171 379 5339
Fax	0171 379 5426

287

CONSTRUCTION FORECASTING AND RESEARCH LTD

Title	**Construction Industry Focus**
Coverage	Data on contractors' activity, order books, tender prices, and short-term prospects for employment and tender prices. Based on a combination of official and non-official data.
Frequency	Monthly
Availability	General
Cost	On request
Comments	Statistics on European construction trends and corporate performance in the construction industry also produced.
Address	Princes House, 39 Kingsway, London WC2B 6TP
Telephone	0171 379 5339
Fax	0171 379 5426

288

CONSTRUCTION FORECASTING AND RESEARCH LTD

Title	**Consulting Engineers' Focus**
Coverage	Presents the results of a quarterly survey on consulting engineers' workloads.
Frequency	Quarterly
Availability	General
Cost	On request
Comments	Statistics on European construction trends and corporate performance in the construction sector also produced.
Address	Princes House, 39 Kingsway, London WC2B 6TP
Telephone	0171 379 5339
Fax	0171 379 5426

289

CONSTRUCTION NEWS

Title	**Annual Contracts Review**
Coverage	An annual review of contracts awarded by type of construction, eg residential, commercial, industrial, and by region. Also statistics on work out to tender. Based on data supplied by the Glenigan Group, Bournemouth.
Frequency	Annual in a weekly journal
Availability	General
Cost	£72.50
Comments	FT-Actuaries Indices are also included in each issue. The Glenigan Group address is 41-47 Seabourne Road, Bournemouth BH5 2HU. Tel. 01202 432121.
Address	EMAP Business Communications, Tower House, Sovereign Park, Lathkill Street, Market Harborough, Leicestershire LE16 9EF
Telephone	01858 468888
Fax	01858 434958

CONSTRUCTION NEWS

Title **Workload Trends**

Coverage Statistics covering new contracts awarded by construction type updating the data in the annual survey noted in the previous entry. Based on information supplied by the Glenigan Group, Bournemouth.

Frequency Monthly in a weekly journal

Availability General

Cost £72.50

Comments FT-Actuaries Indices are also included in each issue.The Glenigan Group address is 41-47 Seabourne Road, Bournemouth BH5 2HU, Tel. 01202 432121.

Address EMAP Business Communications, Tower House, Sovereign Park, Lathkill Street, Market Harborough, Leicestershire LE16 9EF

Telephone 01858 468888

Fax 01858 434958

CONSTRUCTION PLANT HIRE ASSOCIATION

Title **CPA Driver Cost Studies**

Coverage Details of the costs attached to the employment of drivers under civil engineering or plant hire working rule agreements. Based on a survey by the association.

Frequency Annual

Availability General

Cost Free to members but there may be a small charge to others

Comments

Address 28 Eccleston Place, London SW1W 9PY

Telephone 0171 730 7117

Fax 0171 730 7110

CONSTRUCTION PLANT HIRE ASSOCIATION

Title **CPA Activity and Hire Rate Studies**

Coverage Activity percentages and average hire rates for typical machines. Based on a survey of members.

Frequency Quarterly

Availability Only available to participating members.

Cost Free

Comments

Address 28 Eccleston Place, London SW1W 9PY

Telephone 0171 730 7117

Fax 0171 730 7110

293   CONSTRUCTION PLANT HIRE ASSOCIATION

Title	**CPA Machine Cost Studies**
Coverage	Details of the costs to plant hire companies of running typical machines and cost movement indices. Based on data collected by the association.
Frequency	Twice per annum
Availability	General
Cost	Free to members but there may be a small charge to others
Comments	
Address	28 Eccleston Place, London SW1W 9PY
Telephone	0171 730 7117
Fax	0171 730 7110

294   CONSUMER CREDIT TRADE ASSOCIATION

Title	**Consumer Credit**
Coverage	Commentary and statistics on consumer credit trends with comparisons trends in the previous year.
Frequency	Six issues per year
Availability	General
Cost	On request
Comments	
Address	1st Floor, Tennyson House, 159-163 Great Portland Street, London W1N 5FD
Telephone	0171 636 7564
Fax	0171 323 0796

295   CONSUMER PROFILE RESEARCH LTD

Title	**Decisions**
Coverage	A regular omnibus survey aimed at researching issues relating to advertising, packaging, new product development etc.
Frequency	Regular
Availability	General
Cost	On application
Comments	
Address	18 High Street, Thame, Oxford OX4 2BZ
Telephone	01844 215672
Fax	01844 261324

296

	CONTEXT
Title	**Hardware Sales Report**
Coverage	An analysis of distribution channels and sales trends for computer hardware based on a dealer survey by the company.
Frequency	Monthly
Availability	General
Cost	£5,450
Comments	Other regular reports on European computer markets.
Address	96 Kensington High Street, London W8 4SG
Telephone	0171 937 3595
Fax	0171 937 1159

297

	CONTEXT
Title	**Printer Sales Report**
Coverage	An analysis of distribution channels and sales trends for computer printers based on a dealer survey by the company.
Frequency	Monthly
Availability	General
Cost	£4,950
Comments	Other regular reports on European computer markets.
Address	96 High Street Kensington, London W8 4SG
Telephone	0171 937 3595
Fax	0171 937 1159

298

	CONTEXT
Title	**Software Sales Report**
Coverage	An analysis of distribution channels and sales trends for computer software based on a dealer survey by the company.
Frequency	Monthly
Availability	General
Cost	£5,450
Comments	Other regular reports on European computer markets.
Address	96 Kensington High Street, London W8 4SG
Telephone	0171 937 3595
Fax	0171 937 1159

299

CONTINENTAL RESEARCH

Title	**Satellite Monitor Report**
Coverage	Monthly commentary and statistics on the number of satellite dishes, SMATV, and cable installations in the UK. Also figures on intentions to purchase and viewing levels. Based on original research by the company.
Frequency	Monthly
Availability	General
Cost	£2,200
Comments	Also carries out other surveys of financial and media sectors, including the Fintrak omnibus survey.
Address	37-42 Compton Street, London EC1V 0AP
Telephone	0171 490 5944
Fax	0171 490 1174

300

CONTINENTAL RESEARCH

Title	**Satellite Television Audience Report**
Coverage	A monthly review of audience figures for satellite television and satellite channels. Also includes audience share, reach figures, an analysis by demographic sector, forecasts up to five years ahead, and details of the top 50 programmes. Based on research by the company.
Frequency	Monthly
Availability	General
Cost	£1,200
Comments	Also carries out other surveys of financial and media sectors, including the Fintrak omnibus survey.
Address	37-42 Compton Street, London EC1V 0AP
Telephone	0171 490 5944
Fax	0171 490 1174

301

CONTROL RISKS GROUP

Title	**Business Security Outlook**
Coverage	Based on a survey of senior executives in the UK, and the USA, the report considers the main security issues for UK and US overseas investors.
Frequency	Annual
Availability	General
Cost	£140
Comments	
Address	83 Victoria Street, London SW1H 0HW
Telephone	0171 222 1552
Fax	0171 222 2296

302	**COOPERATIVE UNION LTD**
Title	**Cooperative Statistics**
Coverage	Retail distribution by individual cooperative societies and other information on cooperative wholesaling, banking, and insurance. Based almost entirely on the organisation's own research.
Frequency	Annual
Availability	General
Cost	On request
Comments	
Address	Holyoake House, Hanover Street, Manchester M60 0AS
Telephone	0161 832 4300
Fax	0161 831 7684

303	**CORPORATE INTELLIGENCE ON RETAILING**
Title	**Retail Research Report**
Coverage	Each report contains a number of surveys of specific retail sectors, with statistics, and most of these surveys are updated on a regular basis.
Frequency	10 issues per annum
Availability	General
Cost	£495
Comments	Also publishes various other reports on UK retailing sectors and European retailing.
Address	51 Doughty Street, London WC1N 2LS
Telephone	0171 696 9006
Fax	0171 696 9004

304	**CORPORATE INTELLIGENCE ON RETAILING**
Title	**UK Retail Rankings**
Coverage	Mainly financial and operating information on specific companies but it also has general statistics on retail sales, by sector, for the latest 2 years based on estimates produced by the company.
Frequency	Annual
Availability	General
Cost	
Comments	Also publishes various other reports on UK retailing sectors and European retailing.
Address	51 Doughty Street, London WC1N 2LS
Telephone	0171 696 9006
Fax	0171 696 9004

305 COSMETIC WORLD NEWS

Title	**London Market Report**
Coverage	Prices of specific cosmetics and raw materials including essential oils, aroma chemicals, raw materials etc. Based on data collected by the journal.
Frequency	Monthly in a monthly journal
Availability	General
Cost	£90, £14.50 for single issue
Comments	
Address	World News Publications, 130 Wigmore Street, London W1H 0AT
Telephone	0171 486 6757
Fax	0171 487 5436

306 COUNCIL OF MORTGAGE LENDERS

Title	**Housing Finance**
Coverage	Includes articles and a diary of events plus a statistical section covering trends in housing, building, mortgage lending, prices, transactions, and savings. Also data on specific building societies.
Frequency	Quarterly
Availability	General
Cost	£20 per issue
Comments	Based at the same address as the Building Societies Association and involved in some joint publications (see next entry).
Address	3 Savile Row, London W1X 1AF
Telephone	0171 437 0655
Fax	0171 734 6416

307 COUNCIL OF MORTGAGE LENDERS

Title	**Compendium of Housing Finance Statistics**
Coverage	Historical statistics covering housing tenure, stock, transactions, prices, mortgages, rates of interest, and building society information.
Frequency	Regular
Availability	General
Cost	On request
Comments	Published jointly with the Building Societies Association. The latest edition was published in 1995 following the previous edition in 1990.
Address	3 Savile Row, London W1X 1AF
Telephone	0171 437 0655
Fax	0171 734 6416

308 CREMATION SOCIETY OF GREAT BRITAIN

Title	**Directory of Crematoria**
Coverage	Progress of cremation over the last 100 years. Facts and figures section includes number of crematoria, cremations carried out, fees etc. Based on the Society's own survey.
Frequency	Regular
Availability	General
Cost	On request
Comments	
Address	16A Albion Place, Maidstone ME17 1XH
Telephone	01622 688292
Fax	01622 686698

309 CROOKES HEALTHCARE LTD

Title	**Farley's Market Report**
Coverage	A review of the baby food market with statistics and commentary on various product sectors. Based on commissioned research.
Frequency	Regular
Availability	General
Cost	On request
Comments	
Address	Central Park, Lenton Lane, Nottingham NG7 2LJ
Telephone	0115 953 9922
Fax	0115 968 8722

310 CSU (PUBLICATIONS) LTD

Title	**First Destination Statistics of Graduates and Diplomats from UK Higher Education Institutions**
Coverage	Supply of graduates and those entering employment by employer, type of work and field of study. Comparative figures for earlier years. Based on data supplied by various institutions and some supporting text.
Frequency	Annual
Availability	General
Cost	£9
Comments	
Address	Armstrong House, Oxford Road, Manchester M1 7ED
Telephone	0161 236 8677
Fax	0161 236 8541

311	CSU (PUBLICATIONS) LTD
Title	**Statistical Quarterly**
Coverage	An analysis of graduate vacancies and salaries arranged by work type, employer type, subject of study, and location. Based on data collected by CSU. A commentary is included with the data.
Frequency	Quarterly
Availability	General
Cost	£75
Comments	
Address	Armstrong House, Oxford Road, Manchester M17 1ED
Telephone	0161 236 8677
Fax	0161 236 8541

312	CSU (PUBLICATIONS) LTD
Title	**Supply of University Graduates: Trends and Predictions**
Coverage	Output of university first degree graduates over a six year period and the output of specific disciplines. Supply of university graduates available for employment. Based on a combination of CSU data and Central Government data with some supporting text.
Frequency	Annual
Availability	General
Cost	£25
Comments	
Address	Armstrong House, Oxford Road, Manchester M17 1ED
Telephone	0161 236 8677
Fax	0161 236 8541

313	DAIRY INDUSTRY FEDERATION
Title	**Dairy Industry**
Coverage	Statistics covering the prices, consumption, and general market for milk and other dairy products. Data from various sources with a significant amount of supporting text.
Frequency	Annual
Availability	General
Cost	Free
Comments	
Address	19 Cornwall Terrace, London NW1 4QP
Telephone	0171 486 7244
Fax	0171 487 4734

314		DAIWA BANK
Title		**Quarterly Fixed Income Strategy**
Coverage		A review of economic and financial trends in the UK with forecasts for the short- and medium-term.
Frequency		Quarterly
Availability		General
Cost		Free
Comments		
Address		5th Floor, 4 Broadgate, London EC2M 2QS
Telephone		0171 418 8800
Fax		0171 418 8850

315		DARTMOUTH PUBLISHING CO
Title		**British Social Attitudes**
Coverage		A survey of social values and attitudes in the UK in the 1980s and 1990s, based on interviews with approximately 3,000 people. Supported by detailed analysis.
Frequency		Annual
Availability		General
Cost		£15
Comments		
Address		Gower House, Croft Road, Aldershot GU11 3HR
Telephone		01252 331551
Fax		01252 343151

316		DATASTREAM INTERNATIONAL LTD
Title		**Economic Series Database**
Coverage		Datastream is primarily a provider of company information but it also has a database of economic statistics covering the UK and various other countries.
Frequency		Continuous
Availability		General
Cost		On request
Comments		
Address		Monmouth House, 58-64 City Road, London EC1Y 2AL
Telephone		0171 250 3000
Fax		0171 253 0171

DEFENCE MANUFACTURERS' ASSOCIATION OF GREAT BRITAIN

317

Title	**DMA Market Report**
Coverage	Text and statistics on the defence market, based on various sources.
Frequency	Quarterly
Availability	General
Cost	On request
Comments	
Address	Marlborough House, Headley Road, Grayshott, Hindhead GU26 6LG
Telephone	01428 607788
Fax	01428 604567

DEL MONTE FOODS INTERNATIONAL

318

Title	**Canned Fruit and Juices Report**
Coverage	Commentary and statistics on the canned fruit and juices market with data on market size, brands, consumer trends in specific product sectors. Based on commissioned research.
Frequency	Annual
Availability	General
Cost	On request
Comments	
Address	Del Monte House, London Road, Staines TW18 4JD
Telephone	01784 447400
Fax	01784 465301

DHL INTERNATIONAL (UK) LTD

319

Title	**Quarterly Export Indicator**
Coverage	This publication surveys the level of business confidence amongst the UK's manufacturing export industries and it is based on telephone interviews with approximately 500 directors and managers responsible for exports in British manufacturing. The survey results include export expectations over the next 3 and 12 months, trends in the main factors affecting exports, opinions on the role of the EU and the Single European Currency, trends in raw material costs.
Frequency	Quarterly
Availability	General
Cost	Free
Comments	The opinion survey is carried out by Gallup on behalf of DHL.
Address	Orbital Park, 178-188 Great South West Road, Hounslow, Middlesex TW4 6JS
Telephone	0181 818 8000
Fax	0181 818 8038

320

DIRECT MARKETING ASSOCIATION

Title **Direct Marketing Statistics**

Coverage A compilation of statistics on direct marketing from a variety of non-official sources.

Frequency Annual

Availability General

Cost Free

Comments The association changed its name from the British Direct Marketing Association in 1992.

Address 1 Oxenden Street, London SW1Y 4EE

Telephone 0171 321 2525

Fax 0171 321 0191

321

DIRECT MARKETING ASSOCIATION

Title **DMA Census of the UK Direct Marketing Industry**

Coverage A detailed survey of the industry covering structure, sales, postings etc based largely on original research.

Frequency Regular

Availability General

Cost £350

Comments Published by the Henley Centre (see other entry) in association with the DMA.

Address 1 Oxenden Street, London SW1Y 4EE

Telephone 0171 321 2525

Fax 0171 321 0191

322

DIRECT SELLING ASSOCIATION

Title **Direct Selling in the UK**

Coverage Annual review of direct selling with statistics on the value and range of products and services sold by direct selling. Based on a survey of members with some supporting text.

Frequency Annual

Availability General

Cost £18

Comments Other reports on the industry also produced.

Address 29 Floral Street, London WC2E 9DP

Telephone 0171 497 1234

Fax 0171 497 3144

323 DIY SUPERSTORE

Title	**Review of the Year and Statistical Analysis**
Coverage	Commentary and statistics on developments in the DIY superstore sector with data on the number of superstores, openings during the year, and market shares.
Frequency	Annual in a monthly journal
Availability	General
Cost	
Comments	Usually appears in the November/December issue of the journal.
Address	Colebrooke House, Ducklington Road, Witney, Oxfordshire OX8 7TT
Telephone	01993 706848
Fax	01933 706955

324 DIY WEEK

Title	**DIY Trak Market Monitor**
Coverage	Statistics on DIY retail sales by product sector and by retail channels based on continuous research carried out by GfK Marketing Services (see other entry).
Frequency	Quarterly in a weekly journal
Availability	General
Cost	£65, £3.80 single issue
Comments	The journal also has regular features and market reports on specific DIY product sectors and DIY retailers, wholesalers.
Address	Miller Freeman Publications, Sovereign Way, Tonbridge TN9 1RW
Telephone	01732 364422
Fax	01732 361534

325 DONOVAN DATA SYSTEMS

Title	**Donovan Database Services**
Coverage	Donovan has access to a number of media and consumer surveys held on computer, including the British Business Survey (see other entry), and other advertising and audience/readership surveys.
Frequency	Continuous
Availability	General
Cost	On request, depending on the nature and range of information required
Comments	
Address	7 Farm Street, London W1X 7RB
Telephone	0171 629 7654
Fax	0171 493 0239

326 DTZ DEBENHAM THORPE

Title	**Regional Annual Property Reviews**
Coverage	Regional trends in floorspace, rents, and availability. Based on surveys carried out by the company.
Frequency	Annual
Availability	General
Cost	Free
Comments	Publishes various other reports on key European cities and one-off reports on property issues, eg business parks, retailing, overseas investment in commercial property.
Address	44 Brook Street, London W1A 4AG
Telephone	0171 408 1161
Fax	0171 491 4593

327 DTZ DEBENHAM THORPE

Title	**Core – Central London Offices Research**
Coverage	Office floorspace and rent trends in the centre of London based on surveys by the company.
Frequency	Quarterly
Availability	General
Cost	On request
Comments	Publishes various other reports on key European cities and one-off reports on property issues, eg business parks, retailing, overseas investment in commercial property.
Address	DTZ Debenham Thorpe, 44 Brook Street, London W1A 4AG
Telephone	0171 408 1161
Fax	0171 491 4593

328 DUN AND BRADSTREET LTD

Title	**Key Business Ratios**
Coverage	20 key ratios arranged by SIC industry group with data for the latest three years available. Based on the company's own analysis of company financial data.
Frequency	Annual
Availability	General
Cost	
Comments	
Address	Holmers Farm Way, High Wycombe HP12 4UL
Telephone	01494 423689
Fax	01494 422332

329 DUN AND BRADSTREET LTD

Title	**Business Failure Statistics**
Coverage	Company liquidations and bankruptcies analysed by sector and region. A commentary supports the data which comes from records maintained by the company.
Frequency	Quarterly
Availability	General
Cost	Free
Comments	
Address	Holmers Farm Way, High Wycombe HP12 4UL
Telephone	01494 423689
Fax	01494 422332

330 ECONOMIC DEVELOPMENT BRIEFING

Title	**London Office Location Survey**
Coverage	Statistics and analysis of trends in the London office market based on research by the company.
Frequency	Annual
Availability	General
Cost	£120
Comments	
Address	PO Box 625, London NW3 2TZ
Telephone	0181 209 1722
Fax	

331 ECONOMIC DEVELOPMENT BRIEFING

Title	**Property Manpower and Media Study**
Coverage	Statistics and trends covering the UK property professions and the British property media. Based on the company's own survey with some supporting text.
Frequency	Annual
Availability	General
Cost	£100
Comments	
Address	PO Box 625, London NW3 2TZ
Telephone	0181 209 1722
Fax	

332

ECONOMIST PUBLICATIONS LTD

Title	**Retail Business – Retail Trade Review**
Coverage	A monthly journal with articles on specific retailing sectors which also includes a quarterly update of retailing trends and an annual survey of prospects for consumer spending.
Frequency	Monthly
Availability	General
Cost	£225
Comments	Various other one-off and regular reports published on UK and international markets.
Address	15 Regent Street, London SW1Y 4LR
Telephone	0171 830 1000
Fax	0171 499 9767

333

ECONOMIST PUBLICATIONS LTD

Title	**United Kingdom Quarterly Economic Review**
Coverage	Commentary and statistics on general economic trends and business conditions in the UK. Based mainly on official sources.
Frequency	Quarterly
Availability	General
Cost	On request
Comments	Various other one-off and regular reports published on UK and international markets.
Address	15 Regent Street, London SW1Y 4LR
Telephone	0171 830 1000
Fax	0171 499 9767

334

ELECTRIC VEHICLE ASSOCIATION OF GREAT BRITAIN

Title	**Yardstick Costs for Battery Electrics**
Coverage	Basic costs for electric vehicles used in warehouses and airports. Based on data collected by the association.
Frequency	Regular
Availability	General
Cost	On request
Comments	Also produces the EVA Manual.
Address	Alexandra House, Harrowden Road, Wellingborough NN8 5BD
Telephone	01933 276618
Fax	01933 276618

335		**ELLIS, RICHARD**
	Title	**Monthly Index**
	Coverage	General commentary and statistics on property values and yields with a monthly index covering the latest 12 months. Based on data collected by the company.
	Frequency	Monthly
	Availability	General
	Cost	Free
	Comments	Occasional reports on property trends and issues.
	Address	Berkeley Square House, London W1X 6AN
	Telephone	0171 629 6290
	Fax	0171 493 3734

336		**ELLIS, RICHARD**
	Title	**London Market Bulletin**
	Coverage	Rents, values and property availability in various areas of London, eg Docklands, West End, City, Mid-Town etc. Based on data collected by the company.
	Frequency	Quarterly
	Availability	General
	Cost	Free
	Comments	Occasional reports on property trends and issues.
	Address	Berkeley Square House, London W1X 6AN
	Telephone	0171 629 6290
	Fax	0171 493 3734

337		**EMAP MEDIA LTD**
	Title	**British Rate and Data (BRAD)**
	Coverage	Details of all UK media advertising rates, subscription rates, cover prices, circulation trends etc. Also general data on advertising expenditure, number of cinemas.
	Frequency	Monthly
	Availability	General
	Cost	£130 per issue
	Comments	
	Address	33-39 Bowling Green Lane, London EC1R 0DA
	Telephone	0171 505 8275
	Fax	0171 505 8293

338

ENGINEERING EMPLOYERS' FEDERATION

Title	**Business Trends Survey**
Coverage	National and regional statistics on industry and sector trends based on surveys carried out by the regional associations of the federation. Commentary supports the data.
Frequency	Quarterly
Availability	General
Cost	£35
Comments	Produced in association with Alex Lawrie.
Address	Broadway House, Tothill Street, London SW1H 9NQ
Telephone	0171 222 7777
Fax	0171 222 2782

339

ENGINEERING EMPLOYERS' FEDERATION

Title	**Engineering Economic Trends**
Coverage	Graphs, tables, and commentary on engineering output and sales and imports and exports. Some forecasts are included usually up to one year ahead and a commentary accompanies the data. Based on a combination of official and non-official sources.
Frequency	Bi-annual
Availability	General
Cost	£25
Comments	
Address	Broadway House, Tothill Street, London SW1H 9NQ
Telephone	0171 222 7777
Fax	0171 222 2782

340

ENVIRONMENTAL TRANSPORT ASSOCIATION

Title	**Factsheets**
Coverage	Various factsheets relating to transport and the environment and based on various sources.
Frequency	Regular
Availability	General
Cost	Free
Comments	The association is relatively new having been established in 1990.
Address	The Old Post, Heath Road, Weybridge KT13 8RJ
Telephone	01932 828882
Fax	01932 829015

341 EQUIFAX EUROPE

Title	**Define/Portrait**
Coverage	Define is a census-based geodemographic system including 1991 census data, financial data from the Equifax database, unemployment statistics, and electoral roll variables. Portrait is a geolifestyle system based on results from 11 million questionnaires.
Frequency	Continuous
Availability	General
Cost	On application, depending on the range and nature of the information required
Comments	
Address	Sentinel House, 16 Harcourt Street, London W1H 2AE
Telephone	0171 724 6116
Fax	0181 686 7777

342 ERDMAN LEWIS

Title	**Midsummer Retail Report**
Coverage	Analysis and statistics covering trends in the retailing sector and the retail property market. Based on data collected by the company.
Frequency	Annual
Availability	General
Cost	On request
Comments	Various other property reports and town reports produced.
Address	6 Grosvenor Street, London W1X 0AD
Telephone	0171 629 8121
Fax	0171 409 3124

343 ERNST AND YOUNG ITEM CLUB

Title	**UK Economic Prospects**
Coverage	A detailed review of economic trends and prospects with data on all the main economic indicators.
Frequency	Quarterly
Availability	Item Club participants.
Cost	£3,900
Comments	
Address	Becket House, 1 Lambeth Palace Road, London SE1 7EU
Telephone	0171 931 4226
Fax	0171 928 1345

ESA MARKET RESEARCH LTD

Title	**ESA Monthly Shopping Basket Report**
Coverage	A regular report analysing price differences between retailers during the current month and price differences over time. Based on a survey of 132 product categories at 85 outlets covering different retailing formats.
Frequency	Monthly
Availability	General
Cost	£195 per month
Comments	
Address	4 Woodland Court, Soothouse Spring, St Albans AL3 6NR
Telephone	01727 847572
Fax	01727 837337

ESRC DATA ARCHIVE

Title	**ESRC Data Archive**
Coverage	The archive holds surveys from various official and non-official sources including all the major CSO continuous surveys such as the Family Expenditure Survey, General Household Survey, National Food Survey plus many non-official surveys from organisations such as NOP, Gallup, Research Services etc.
Frequency	Continuous
Availability	General
Cost	On request
Comments	Data can be supplied in various formats including diskette, magnetic tape, and CD-ROM.
Address	Wivenhoe Park, University of Essex, Colchester CO4 3SO
Telephone	01206 872001
Fax	01206 872003

ESTATES GAZETTE

Title	**Figures and Figures**
Coverage	General data relating to the property market including house prices, farm prices, rent index, housing starts and completions, land prices, property yields, interest rates. Based mainly on various non-official sources supported by some official statistics.
Frequency	Monthly in a weekly journal
Availability	General
Cost	£108, £1.85 for single issue
Comments	
Address	Estates Gazette Ltd, 151 Wardour Street, London W1V 4BN
Telephone	0171 437 0141
Fax	0171 437 0295

347

	EURODIRECT DATABASE MARKETING
Title	**Demograf/Neighbours and PROSPECTS**
Coverage	Demograf is a Windows-based GIS marketing system incorporating demographic data. Neighbours and PROSPECTS is a demographic classification system based on 1991 Census data with additional information from the electoral roll.
Frequency	Continuous
Availability	General
Cost	On application, and depending on the range and nature of the information required
Comments	
Address	Onward House, 2 Baptist Place, Bradford BD1 2PS
Telephone	01274 737144
Fax	01274 741126

348

	EUROMONITOR
Title	**Euromonitor Market and Media Guide**
Coverage	A compilation of statistics covering economic trends, regional data, consumer trends, advertising, labour market data, transport, key markets etc. Based on Euromonitor data and statistics from other sources.
Frequency	Monthly
Availability	General
Cost	£450 (annual subscription to Market Research Great Britain)
Comments	Included as part of Market Research Great Britain. Various consumer reports on international markets also produced.
Address	60-61 Britton Street, London EC1M 5NA
Telephone	0171 251 8024
Fax	0171 608 3149

349 EUROPEAN COSMETIC MARKETS

Title	**Market Reviews**
Coverage	Market reports are scheduled throughout the year and each report has a review of UK trends, alongside reviews of the other major European markets. The 1995 schedule is bathroom products (January), skin care (February), men's lines (March), sun care (April), women's fragrances (May), body care (June), deodorants (August), hair care (September), hair styling (October), colour cosmetics (November), oral hygiene (December). Mainly based on original consumer research.
Frequency	Monthly in a monthly journal
Availability	General
Cost	£550
Comments	
Address	Nicholas Hall & Co, 35 Alexandra Street, Southend on Sea, Essex SS1 1BW
Telephone	01702 430804
Fax	01702 430787

350 EUROPEAN PLASTICS NEWS

Title	**UK Plastics Annual Review**
Coverage	A commentary on the market performance of plastics raw materials in the UK with tables on the consumption of major plastics. A general outlook for the coming year is given.
Frequency	Annual in a monthly journal
Availability	General
Cost	£99
Comments	
Address	EMAP Business Publications, Maclaren House, 19 Scarbrook Road, Croydon CR9 1QH
Telephone	0181 688 7788
Fax	0181 688 8375

351 EXHIBITION SURVEYS

Title	**Networks Exhibition Audience Profile**
Coverage	A profile of international visitors to the Networks exhibitions, based on a postal survey by the company. Data on networking products and services, audience analysis, purchasing influences, and future buying patterns.
Frequency	Annual
Availability	General
Cost	£260
Comments	
Address	PO Box 7, Melton Mowbray, Leicestershire LE13 0BR
Telephone	01664 67666
Fax	01664 67528

352

EXHIBITION SURVEYS

Title	**Audience Profile Reports**
Coverage	Regular reports profiling the audiences at major exhibitions based on postal surveys by the company. Data includes audience analysis, product interests, purchasing influences, and future buying patterns.
Frequency	Every one to three years
Availability	Exhibiting companies and other interested parties.
Cost	Varies according to the exhibitions covered
Comments	Frequency of surveys depends on the frequency of the exhibitions.
Address	PO Box 7, Melton Mowbray, Leicestershire LE13 0BR
Telephone	01664 67666
Fax	01664 67528

353

FACTS INTERNATIONAL LTD

Title	**Telefacts**
Coverage	An omnibus survey of 1,000 adults each month. It is a telephone survey covering the whole of the UK.
Frequency	Monthly
Availability	General
Cost	Varies according to questions and analysis
Comments	Results available on disc.
Address	Facts Centre, Kennington Road, Ashford, Kent TN24 0TD
Telephone	01233 643551
Fax	01233 626950

354

FARMERS' WEEKLY

Title	**Farmland Market**
Coverage	Land value prices analysed over the previous 6 months. Includes a county-by-county analysis and the report is based on various sources.
Frequency	Twice per annum
Availability	General
Cost	£90, £50 to chartered surveyors
Comments	The publication is produced jointly by Farmers Weekly and the Royal Institution of Chartered Surveyors.
Address	Quadrant House, The Quadrant, Sutton, Surrey SM2 5AS
Telephone	0181 652 4920
Fax	0181 652 8920

355

FAST FACTS LTD

Title **Food Trends**

Coverage Household consumption trends over the last ten years for over 200 product categories. Also includes projections for the next two years.

Frequency Quarterly

Availability General

Cost £250

Comments Factfinder is a disc version of the above report.

Address Hannington Road, Walgrave, Northamptonshire NN6 9QF

Telephone 01604 781 392

Fax 01604 781 392

356

FAST FACTS LTD

Title **Fast Food Figures**

Coverage Regular reports on various food sectors including meat, bakery products, savoury products, chocolate and sugar confectionery. Food sectors can be added when specified by the client.

Frequency Monthly

Availability General

Cost £1,500 (total subscription to all Fast Facts services)

Comments

Address Hannington Road, Walgrave, Northamptonshire NN6 9QF

Telephone 01604 781 392

Fax 01604 781 392

357

FAST FACTS LTD

Title **Fast fax**

Coverage Fast fax is a daily service, available via the fax or post, providing updated information on food markets and based on data arriving at Fast Facts offices.

Frequency Continuous

Availability General

Cost Varies depending on the data required

Comments

Address Hannington Road, Walgrave, Northamptonshire NN6 9QF

Telephone 01604 781 392

Fax 01604 781 392

358 FEDERATION OF BAKERS

Title	**Annual Report**
Coverage	Includes a section with statistics on production trends in the UK bakery industry.
Frequency	Annual
Availability	General
Cost	Free
Comments	
Address	20 Bedford Square, London WC1B 3HF
Telephone	0171 580 4252
Fax	0171 255 1389

359 FEDERATION OF BRITISH CREMATION AUTHORITIES

Title	**Annual Report**
Coverage	Includes cremation statistics for individual crematoria over a five year period. Based on the Federation's own survey. A large amount of supporting text accompanies the data.
Frequency	Annual
Availability	General
Cost	Free
Comments	
Address	41 Salisbury Road, Carshalton, Surrey SM5 3HA
Telephone	0181 669 4521
Fax	

360 FEDERATION OF MASTER BUILDERS

Title	**FMB State of Trade Survey**
Coverage	Results of a survey of member firms in England and Wales with data on workload for the previous quarter and predictions for the coming quarter. Various topical questions are also included in each survey. Text supports the data.
Frequency	Quarterly
Availability	General
Cost	On application
Comments	Also produces irregular factsheets.
Address	14-15 Great James Street, London WC1N 3DP
Telephone	0171 242 7583
Fax	0171 404 0296

361 FEDERATION OF OPTHALMIC & DISPENSING OPTICIANS

Title	**Optics at a Glance**
Coverage	General statistics on optics including the number of opticians, average spectacle prices. Based on a combination of the Federation's own survey and Central Government data. Some supporting commentary.
Frequency	Annual
Availability	General
Cost	Free
Comments	Produced as a double-sided A4 page.
Address	113 Eastbourne Mews, London W2 6LQ
Telephone	0171 258 0240
Fax	0171 724 1175

362 FEDERATION OF THE ELECTRONICS INDUSTRY (FEI)

Title	**The FEI Review**
Coverage	Mainly text describing the activities of the Federation but the 'Focus on the Industry' section includes graphs and tables on sector value, and data on the components and business equipment sectors. Based on data collected by the federation.
Frequency	Annual
Availability	General
Cost	Free
Comments	The federation was only established in 1993.
Address	Russell Square House, 10-12 Russell Square, London WC1B 5EE
Telephone	0171 331 2000
Fax	0171 331 2040

363 FEDERATION OF THE ELECTRONICS INDUSTRY (FEI)

Title	**Interface**
Coverage	Contains regular statistics on the electronics industry and markets in the UK based on the Federation's own survey plus government data.
Frequency	Six issues per year
Availability	Usually only available to members.
Cost	Free
Comments	The federation was only established in 1993.
Address	Russell Square House, 10-12 Russell Square, London WC1B 5EE
Telephone	0171 331 2000
Fax	0171 331 2040

364 FERTILISER MANUFACTURERS' ASSOCIATION

Title	**Fertiliser Review**
Coverage	Covers area of crops, consumption of inorganic fertilisers, straight fertilisers, and compound fertilisers. Also concentration, application rates, and usage of compound fertilisers. Based mainly on the association's own research with additional data from Central Government. Most of the review is made up of text.
Frequency	Annual
Availability	General
Cost	£5
Comments	
Address	Greenhill House, Thorpe Wood, Peterborough PE3 6GT
Telephone	01733 331303
Fax	01733 333617

365 FINANCE AND LEASING ASSOCIATION

Title	**Annual Report**
Coverage	Contains commentary and statistics on trends in the credit and leasing market with most tables giving figures for the last two years. Based on transactions by FLA members.
Frequency	Annual
Availability	General
Cost	Free
Comments	
Address	18 Upper Grosvenor Street, London W1X 9PB
Telephone	0171 491 2783
Fax	0171 629 0396

366 FINANCIAL TIMES INFORMATION

Title	**FT-Actuaries Share Indices Service**
Coverage	A loose/leaf folder, updated monthly, with statistics on shares, prices, equities, gilts etc.
Frequency	Monthly
Availability	General
Cost	On request
Comments	
Address	Fitzroy House, 13-17 Epworth Street, London EC2A 4DL
Telephone	0171 825 8000
Fax	0171 825 7999

367

	FINANCIAL TIMES INFORMATION
Title	**FT-SE 100 Monthly Review**
Coverage	Includes daily index values, market activity information, total returns, performance data, plus information on individual company shares.
Frequency	Monthly
Availability	General
Cost	£95
Comments	Also available are similar reports on the FT-SE Mid 250, FT-SE Mid 250 Ex Investment Trusts, FT-SE Actuaries 350.
Address	Fitzroy House, 13-17 Epworth Street, London EC2A 4DL
Telephone	0171 825 8000
Fax	0171 825 7999

368

	FINANCIAL TIMES INFORMATION
Title	**Finstat**
Coverage	The FT's online service providing daily updates of share prices, equities, gilts etc.
Frequency	Continuous
Availability	General
Cost	On request
Comments	
Address	Fitzroy House, 13-17 Epworth Street, London EC2A 4DL
Telephone	0171 825 8000
Fax	0171 825 7999

369

	FISH TRADER
Title	**Imports and Exports**
Coverage	Imports and exports of fish by volume and value broken down by type of fish. A short commentary accompanies the data which is based on official statistics.
Frequency	Quarterly in a monthly journal
Availability	General
Cost	£74.85, £6.60 per issue
Comments	
Address	Queensway House, 2 Queensway, Redhill RH1 1QS
Telephone	01737 768611
Fax	01737 761685

370 FLOUR ADVISORY BUREAU

Title	**Bread at work – Market Report**
Coverage	Analysis and statistics on the bread market with data on consumption patterns, consumer attitudes to bread, the role of bread in diets, new and speciality breads, and bread sales to the catering sector. A section of summary statistics is included at the end. Based on commissioned research and some official sources.
Frequency	Annual
Availability	General
Cost	Free
Comments	-
Address	21 Arlington Street, London SW1A 1RN
Telephone	0171 493 2521
Fax	0171 493 6785

371 FLOWER TRADES JOURNAL

Title	**Annual Statistics**
Coverage	Cultivation and production data on non-edible horticultural products. Based on trade association data.
Frequency	Annual in a monthly journal
Availability	General
Cost	£41, or £2.50 per issue
Comments	
Address	Yewtree Publishing Ltd, 17 Wickham Road, Beckenham BR3 2JS
Telephone	0181 658 8688
Fax	0181 658 2250

372 FLYMO LTD

Title	**Power Lawnmower Statistics**
Coverage	Tables and graphs on the power lawnmower market with data on total market size, by type of lawnmower, brand shares, price trends, and lawn numbers. Based on data from market research sources.
Frequency	Annual
Availability	General
Cost	Free
Comments	
Address	Aycliffe Industrial Estate, Preston Road, Newton Aycliffe DL5 6UP
Telephone	01325 300303
Fax	01325 310339

373 FOOD FROM BRITAIN

Title	**Annual Report**
Coverage	Includes statistics on food exports and the key export markets for UK food companies plus general details of trends in the industry. Based primarily on official statistics.
Frequency	Annual
Availability	General
Cost	Free
Comments	
Address	123 Buckingham Palace Road, London SW1W 9SA
Telephone	0171 233 5111
Fax	0171 233 9515

374 FOOTBALL TRUST

Title	**Digest of Football Statistics**
Coverage	Details of attendances, match receipts, other financial data, miscellaneous data. Separate section on Scottish football and section also on the Football Trust. Many tables have historical series. Based mainly on non-official sources.
Frequency	Annual
Availability	General
Cost	On request
Comments	
Address	Centre for Football Research, University of Leicester, University Road, Leicester LE1 7RH
Telephone	01533 522741
Fax	

375 FORUM FOR PRIVATE BUSINESS

Title	**Banks' Attitudes to Borrowing**
Coverage	A regular survey of UK banks' attitudes to borrowings with a review of general attitudes torwards specific sectors. Data for the latest quarter and earlier quarters.
Frequency	Quarterly
Availability	General
Cost	On request
Comments	
Address	Ruskin Chambers, Drury Lane, Knutsford WA16 6HA
Telephone	01565 634467
Fax	01565 650059

376	FORVUS
Title	**UK Imports and Exports**
Coverage	Detailed statistics on UK product imports and exports, with data on total trade, trading partners, port of entry and exit. Appointed as an official agent of HM Customs and Excise.
Frequency	Monthly
Availability	General
Cost	Depends on the amount of information required
Comments	Available in various machine readable formats.
Address	Forvus House, 53 Clapham Common, South Side, London SW4 9BX
Telephone	0171 498 2602
Fax	0171 498 1939

377	FOUNDRY TRADE JOURNAL
Title	**Metal Prices**
Coverage	Prices of ferro-alloy and other metals and non-ferrous metals by type in the UK. Based on various non official sources.
Frequency	Twice a month in a twice-monthly journal
Availability	General
Cost	£128.60, or £15.60 for a single issue
Comments	
Address	FMJ International Publications Ltd, 2 Queensway, Redhill RH1 1QS
Telephone	01737 768611
Fax	01737 761685

378	FRASER OF ALLENDER INSTITUTE
Title	**Scottish Chambers' Business Survey**
Coverage	Trends in the Scottish economy and business sectors based on returns from a sample of members of Scottish chambers of commerce.
Frequency	Quarterly
Availability	General
Cost	On request
Comments	
Address	Strathclyde University, Cathedral Street, Glasgow G4 0LN
Telephone	0141 552 4400
Fax	

379 FRASER OF ALLENDER INSTITUTE

Title	**Quarterly Economic Bulletin**
Coverage	Trends and outlook for the Scottish economy with individual reviews of industrial performance, service sector, labour market, and the regions. Also some feature articles. Based mainly on Central Government data and a supporting commentary.
Frequency	Quarterly
Availability	General
Cost	£60
Comments	
Address	Strathclyde University, 100 Cathedral Street, Glasgow G4 0LN
Telephone	0141 552 4400
Fax	

380 FREIGHT TRANSPORT ASSOCIATION

Title	**Freight Transport Trends**
Coverage	A review of freight transport by air, road, sea, and rail with data on demand, markets, prices, costs, safety, accidents, and forecasts. Based on census returns from members, data from the Department of Transport, and other sources.
Frequency	Annual
Availability	General
Cost	£15
Comments	
Address	Hermes House, St John's Road, Tunbridge Wells, Kent TN4 9UZ
Telephone	01892 526171
Fax	01892 534989

381 FREIGHT TRANSPORT ASSOCIATION

Title	**Managers' Guide to Distribution Costs**
Coverage	Statistics on road transport costs including wages, vehicle operating costs, haulage rates. Actual costs and indices are included. Based on the association's own survey with supporting commentary.
Frequency	Quarterly
Availability	Members
Cost	£87.50
Comments	
Address	Hermes House, St John's Road, Tunbridge Wells, Kent TN4 9UZ
Telephone	01892 526171
Fax	01892 534989

382 FREIGHT TRANSPORT ASSOCIATION

Title	**Managers' Fuel Price Information Service**
Coverage	Prices of derv and fuel oil with a general analysis of market trends. Based on the association's own survey with some supporting text.
Frequency	Monthly
Availability	Members
Cost	£118
Comments	
Address	Hermes House, St John's Road, Tunbridge Wells, Kent TN4 9UZ
Telephone	01892 526171
Fax	01892 534989

383 FRESH FRUIT AND VEGETABLE INFORMATION BUREAU

Title	**UK Fresh Fruit and Vegetable Market Review**
Coverage	Commentary and statistics on the fresh produce market with sections on specific fruits and vegetables.
Frequency	Annual
Availability	General
Cost	On request
Comments	Latest issue produced in association with Checkout Fresh Magazine. Available from public relations consultants, Cameron Choat & Partners, at the address below.
Address	126-128 Cromwell Road, London SW7 4ET
Telephone	0171 373 4537
Fax	0171 373 3926

384 FURNITURE INDUSTRY RESEARCH ASSOCIATION

Title	**Furniture Industry in the UK – A Statistical Digest**
Coverage	Statistics include turnover, sales, deliveries, consumption, imports, exports, prices, and advertising. Mainly based on Central Government data, supplemented by association and non-official sources.
Frequency	Annual
Availability	General
Cost	£30, reduced price to members
Comments	Also produces statistics on the international market.
Address	Maxwell Road, Stevenage SG1 2EW
Telephone	01438 313433
Fax	01438 727607

385 FURNITURE INDUSTRY RESEARCH ASSOCIATION

Title	**FIRA Bulletin**
Coverage	Includes statistics updating the annual publication (see previous entry) including sales, imports, exports, prices etc. Mainly based on Central Government data.
Frequency	Quarterly
Availability	General
Cost	On request
Comments	Also produces statistics on the international furniture market.
Address	Maxwell Road, Stevenage SG1 2EW
Telephone	01438 313433
Fax	01438 727607

386 GALLUP

Title	**Gallup Omnibus**
Coverage	Sample surveys of around 1,000 adults form the basis of this omnibus survey. Based on face-to-face interviews with adults.
Frequency	2 or 3 times a week
Availability	General
Cost	On request
Comments	Results available in various machine-readable formats.
Address	307 Finchley Road, London NW3 6EH
Telephone	0171 794 0461
Fax	0171 435 5947

387 GALLUP

Title	**Gallup Political Index**
Coverage	Summary data on the various opinion polls carried out by Gallup on political, economic, and social issues.
Frequency	Monthly
Availability	General
Cost	On application
Comments	Gallup data also available in machine readable formats.
Address	307 Finchley Road, London NW3 6EH
Telephone	0171 794 0461
Fax	0171 435 5947

388

GEOPLAN (UK) LTD

Title **Geoplan**

Coverage A service supplying statistical and geographical data, and the provision of Geographical Information Systems. Based on census data and the postcode address file.

Frequency Continuous

Availability General

Cost On application, and depending on the range and nature of the information required

Comments

Address 14-15 Regent Parade, Harrogate HG1 5AW

Telephone 01423 569538

Fax 01423 525545

389

GfK MARKETING SERVICES

Title **Computers in the Home**

Coverage A quarterly survey of ownership levels for computers in households around the country. Trends are monitored over time. Based on research by the company.

Frequency Quarterly

Availability General

Cost On request

Comments Also carries out an annual survey of the installed base of computers in the home.

Address Sheer House, Station Approach, West Byfleet, Surrey KT 14 6NL

Telephone 01932 354911

Fax 01932 354827

390

GfK MARKETING SERVICES

Title **Photopanel**

Coverage A continuous audit of the photographic market in the UK. Research by the company.

Frequency Continuous

Availability Participants

Cost On request

Comments

Address Sheer House, Station Approach, West Byfleet, Surrey KT14 6NL

Telephone 01932 354911

Fax 01932 354827

391

GfK MARKETING SERVICES

Title

IT-Trak

Coverage

A retail audit covering office technology products and telecommunications equipment. Research by the company.

Frequency

Continuous

Availability

Participants

Cost

On request

Comments

Address

Sheer House, Station Approach, West Byfleet, Surrey KT14 6NL

Telephone

01932 354911

Fax

01932 354827

392

GfK MARKETING SERVICES

Title

LEK-Trak

Coverage

A retail audit covering electrical products and domestic electronic appliances. Research carried out by the company.

Frequency

Continuous

Availability

Participants

Cost

On request

Comments

Address

Sheer House, Station Approach, West Byfleet, Surrey KT14 6NL

Telephone

01932 354911

Fax

01932 354827

393

GfK MARKETING SERVICES

Title

DIY-Trak

Coverage

A retail audit covering products sold in DIY outlets in the UK, mainly DIY and gardening products. Research carried out by the company.

Frequency

Continuous

Availability

Participants

Cost

On request

Comments

Address

Sheer House, Station Approach, West Byfleet, Surrey KT14 6NL

Telephone

01932 354911

Fax

01932 354827

394 GfK MARKETING SERVICES

Title **Home Audit**

Coverage A quarterly survey of around 35,000 households examining ownership and purchasing of consumer durables. Based on research by the company.

Frequency Quarterly

Availability General

Cost On request

Comments

Address Sheer House, Station Approach, West Byfleet, Surrey KT14 6NL

Telephone 01932 354911

Fax 01932 354827

---

395 GfK MARKETING SERVICES

Title **Home Trak**

Coverage A monthly survey of around 6,000 households based on a diary kept by the households. Data on purchasing and household spending.

Frequency Monthly

Availability General

Cost On request

Comments

Address Sheer House, Station Approach, West Byfleet, Surrey KT14 6NL

Telephone 01932 354911

Fax 01392 354827

---

396 GIN AND VODKA ASSOCIATION OF GREAT BRITAIN

Title **Returns for the Four Half Years Ended 31st December**

Coverage Gives production of gin, home trade sales and export sales to EU countries and non-EU countries for the last four six-month periods. Based on returns from members.

Frequency Annual

Availability General

Cost Free

Comments

Address Strangford, Amport, Andover SP11 8AX

Telephone 01264 773085

Fax

397	GLOBUS OFFICE WORLD
Title	**Office World Quarterly Small Business Survey**
Coverage	A survey of investment and financial arrangements and trends for small businesses in the UK. Based on a survey commissioned by the company.
Frequency	Quarterly
Availability	General
Cost	On request
Comments	
Address	WSM Wordsworth, 37-39 London End, Beaconsfield, Buckinghamshire HP9 2HW
Telephone	01494 674101
Fax	01494 674202

398	GMAP LTD
Title	**GMAP**
Coverage	A geodemographic service based primarily on the 1991 census population data.
Frequency	Continuous
Availability	General
Cost	On application, and depending on the range and nature of the information required
Comments	
Address	Cromer Terrace, Leeds LS2 9JU
Telephone	0113 2446164
Fax	0113 2433173

399	GROCER
Title	**Grocer Price List**
Coverage	A supplement usually produced on the first Saturday of each month giving detailed prices for various foods and grocery products.
Frequency	Monthly supplement to a weekly journal
Availability	General
Cost	£45 (subscription to The Grocer)
Comments	The Grocer also has regular market surveys of the main food and non-food markets.
Address	William Reed Publishing Ltd, Broadfield Park, Crawley, West Sussex RH11 9RT
Telephone	01293 613400
Fax	01293 613156

400 GROCER

Title	**Market Figures**
Coverage	Prices of various foods including vegetables, meat, salad, cheese, egg, butter, lard etc. Based on various non-official sources with some supporting text.
Frequency	Weekly in a weekly journal
Availability	General
Cost	£45
Comments	The Grocer also has regular market surveys of the main food and non-food markets.
Address	William Reed Publishing Ltd, Broadfield Park, Crawley, West Sussex RH11 9RT
Telephone	01293 613400
Fax	01293 613156

401 HALIFAX

Title	**Halifax House Price Index**
Coverage	Commentary plus indices and average values for different types of houses. Also includes a regional analysis and additional data for first time buyers, mortgage demand etc. Based on Halifax records.
Frequency	Quarterly
Availability	General
Cost	Free
Comments	The separate regional price index publication is now included in this publication.
Address	Trinity Road, Halifax HX1 2RG
Telephone	01422 333333
Fax	01422 332043

402 HARDWARE TODAY

Title	**Today's Trading Trends**
Coverage	Performance trends in various hardware sectors based on a summary of the results of a survey of members of the British Hardware Federation.
Frequency	Quarterly in a monthly journal
Availability	General
Cost	On request
Comments	
Address	225 Bristol Road, Edgbaston, Birmingham B5 7SB
Telephone	0121 446 6688
Fax	0121 446 5215

	403	HARRIS RESEARCH
Title		**Harris Response**
Coverage		A weekly omnibus survey involving face-to-face interviews with 1,000 adults. Demographic breakdowns and detailed information on purchasing, consumer attitudes etc.
Frequency		Weekly
Availability		General
Cost		On application
Comments		
Address		34-38 Hill Rise, Richmond, Surrey TW10 6UA
Telephone		0181 332 9898
Fax		0181 948 6335

404 HARRIS RESEARCH

Title **55+ Omnibus**

Coverage A quarterly face-to-face survey based on a sample of 1,500 adults aged 55 and over. A specialist service for those whose products and services are targeted at the 'grey' market.

Frequency Quarterly

Availability General

Cost On application

Comments

Address 34-38 Hill Rise, Richmond, Surrey TW10 6UA

Telephone 0181 332 9898

Fax 0181 948 6335

405 HARRIS RESEARCH

Title **Young Persons' Omnibus**

Coverage A quarterly omnibus survey of 1,500 young people aged between 12 and 24. Face-to-face interviews collect information on the purchasing trends, attitudes, and preferences of this consumer group.

Frequency Quarterly

Availability General

Cost On application

Comments

Address 34-38 Hill Rise, Richmond, Surrey TW10 6UA

Telephone 0181 332 9898

Fax 0181 948 6335

406

HAY MANAGEMENT CONSULTANTS LTD

Title   **Hay Compensation Report**

Coverage   Statistics and analysis on the salaries and main benefits of executive, managerial, and supervisory positions. Analysis by major industrial and service sector, location, and function. Based on a quarterly updated database of over 500 companies and thousands of jobs.

Frequency   Quarterly

Availability   Participants

Cost   £1,000, or £375 per quarterly report

Comments

Address   52 Grosvenor Gardens, London SW1W 0AU

Telephone   0171 873 9123

Fax   0171 873 9152

407

HAY MANAGEMENT CONSULTANTS LTD

Title   **Information Technology Remuneration**

Coverage   A survey of salaries and benefits for IT staff in over 400 organisations. Based on a survey by the company.

Frequency   Annual

Availability   Participants

Cost   £720

Comments

Address   52 Grosvenor Gardens, London SW1W 0AU

Telephone   0171 873 9123

Fax   0171 873 9152

408

HAY MANAGEMENT CONSULTANTS LTD

Title   **Human Resources and Personnel Remuneration**

Coverage   A survey of salaries and benefits for personnel and human resources managers and related jobs. Based on a survey of over 600 organisations.

Frequency   Annual

Availability   Participants

Cost   £720

Comments

Address   52 Grosvenor Gardens, London SW1W 0AU

Telephone   0171 873 9123

Fax   0171 873 9152

409	HAY MANAGEMENT CONSULTANTS LTD
Title	**Solicitors and Legal Executives' Remuneration**
Coverage	A survey of salaries and benefits of solicitors and related professionals based on data collected by the company.
Frequency	Annual
Availability	Participants
Cost	£720
Comments	
Address	52 Grosvenor Gardens, London SW1W 0AU
Telephone	0171 873 9123
Fax	0171 873 9152

410	HAY MANAGEMENT CONSULTANTS LTD
Title	**Investment Fund Remuneration**
Coverage	Covers the pay and benefits of investment fund managers and related jobs down to the level of investment analysts. Analyses available by sector, and geographical location. Based on data collected by the company.
Frequency	Annual
Availability	Participants
Cost	£675
Comments	
Address	52 Grosvenor Gardens, London SW1W 0AU
Telephone	0171 873 9123
Fax	0171 873 9152

411	HAY MANAGEMENT CONSULTANTS LTD
Title	**HAY/PA Publishers' Survey**
Coverage	A survey of salaries and benefits in the book and magazine publishing sectors. Based on data collected by the company and the Publishers Association.
Frequency	Annual
Availability	Participants
Cost	£860
Comments	
Address	52 Grosvenor Gardens, London SW1W 0AU
Telephone	0171 873 9123
Fax	0171 873 9152

412

HAY MANAGEMENT CONSULTANTS LTD

Title — **Engineers' Remuneration**

Coverage — A survey of salaries and benefits for engineers based on 22 job levels. Based on a survey by the company of over 300 organisations.

Frequency — Annual

Availability — Participants

Cost — £675

Comments —

Address — 52 Grosvenor Gardens, London SW1W 0AU

Telephone — 0171 873 9123

Fax — 0171 873 9152

413

HAY MANAGEMENT CONSULTANTS LTD

Title — **Accountants and Taxation Professionals**

Coverage — A salary and benefits survey of accountants and related professionals based around 19 job levels and sampling over 500 organisations. Based on a survey by the company.

Frequency — Annual

Availability — Participants

Cost — £720

Comments —

Address — 52 Grosvenor Gardens, London SW1W 0AU

Telephone — 0171 873 9123

Fax — 0171 873 9152

414

HAY MANAGEMENT CONSULTANTS LTD

Title — **Boardroom Guide – A Survey of Directors' Remuneration**

Coverage — A survey focusing on the remuneration of top management and directors with data on over 4,000 top jobs from over 400 companies. Based on salary data collected by the company with additional data on share options, cars, pensions and other benefits.

Frequency — Annual

Availability — Participants

Cost — £1,400

Comments —

Address — 52 Grosvenor Gardens, London SW1W 0AU

Telephone — 0171 873 9123

Fax — 0171 873 9152

415

HAY MANAGEMENT CONSULTANTS LTD

Title **Retail Survey**

Coverage A survey of salaries and benefits for various jobs in the retailing sector. Based on a survey of almost 100 organisations.

Frequency Annual

Availability Participants

Cost £720

Comments

Address 52 Grosvenor Gardens, London SW1W 0AU

Telephone 0171 873 9123

Fax 0171 873 9152

416

HAY MANAGEMENT CONSULTANTS LTD

Title **Consumer Sector Salesforce Survey**

Coverage A survey of salaries and benefits in fast-moving consumer goods (FMCG) companies. Based on a range of jobs in over 60 organisations.

Frequency Annual

Availability Participants

Cost £700

Comments

Address 52 Grosvenor Gardens, London SW1W 0AU

Telephone 0171 873 9123

Fax 0171 873 9152

417

HAY MANAGEMENT CONSULTANTS LTD

Title **Local Authority Survey**

Coverage A survey of salaries and benefits for various levels of local authority staff based on a survey of around 70 local authorities.

Frequency Annual

Availability Participants

Cost £675

Comments

Address 52 Grosvenor Gardens, London SW1W 0AU

Telephone 0171 873 9123

Fax 0171 873 9152

418	HAY MANAGEMENT CONSULTANTS LTD
Title	**Health Service Survey**
Coverage	A survey of salaries and benefits for 17 job levels in the health service. Based on a survey of around 70 hospitals.
Frequency	Annual
Availability	Participants
Cost	£365
Comments	
Address	52 Grosvenor Gardens, London SW1W 0AU
Telephone	0171 873 9123
Fax	0171 873 9152

419	HCIS
Title	**Fitzhugh Directory of Independent Healthcare and Long Term Care**
Coverage	A directory of the independent healthcare sector which includes statistical data on market size and trends, plus details of the number of mergers and acquisitions.
Frequency	Annual
Availability	General
Cost	£240
Comments	
Address	12 Riverview Grove, London W4 3QJ
Telephone	0181 995 1752
Fax	0181 742 2418

420	HEALEY AND BAKER
Title	**Prime**
Coverage	Commentary and statistics on the trends in property rents with data for industrial, office, and retail property. Figures for the standard regions and a table of summary data covering a ten year period. Based on the company's own research with supporting text.
Frequency	Bi-annual
Availability	General
Cost	Free
Comments	
Address	29 George Street, Hanover Square, London W1A 3BG
Telephone	0171 629 9292
Fax	0171 355 4299

421	
	HEALEY AND BAKER
Title	**Quarterly Market Report**
Coverage	Data on investment trends in the retail, office, and industrial property sectors. Commentary supported by various tables.
Frequency	Quarterly
Availability	General
Cost	Free
Comments	
Address	29 George Street, Hanover Square, London W1A 3BG
Telephone	0171 629 9292
Fax	0171 355 4299

422	
	HEALEY AND BAKER
Title	**Shop Expansion Plans Survey**
Coverage	A survey of expansion intentions based on information from approximately 118 organisations covering 30,000 outlets.
Frequency	Annual
Availability	General
Cost	£25
Comments	
Address	29 George Street, Hanover Square, London W1A 3BG
Telephone	0171 629 9292
Fax	0171 355 4299

423	
	HENLEY CENTRE
Title	**Directors' Guide**
Coverage	A digest providing a regular review of economic and social trends and forecasts up to 2 years ahead. A commentary analyses the implications of changes in the business environment.
Frequency	Monthly
Availability	General
Cost	£225
Comments	Various other one-off reports and regular services available.
Address	9 Bridewell Place, London EC4Y 6AY
Telephone	0171 353 9961
Fax	0171 353 2899

424

Title

Coverage

Frequency

Availability

Cost

Comments

Address

Telephone

Fax

HENLEY CENTRE

UK Economic Forecasts

Statistics and forecasts of the UK economy. Forecasts up to 5 years ahead for economic trends, business trends, consumer spending, costs and prices, and the stock market. Based on existing Central Government data and Henley forecasts with some supporting text.

Monthly

General

£1,225

Various other one-off reports and regular services available.

9 Bridewell Place, London EC4Y 6AY

0171 353 9961

0171 353 2899

425

Title

Coverage

Frequency

Availability

Cost

Comments

Address

Telephone

Fax

HENLEY CENTRE

Leisure Futures

Statistics and forecasts up to 5 years ahead for leisure spending in total and for specific leisure sectors. Data on leisure time use, activities and spending patterns.

Quarterly

General

£1,225

Various other one-off reports and regular services available.

9 Bridewell Place, London EC4Y 6AY

0171 353 9961

0171 353 2899

426

Title

Coverage

Frequency

Availability

Cost

Comments

Address

Telephone

Fax

HENLEY CENTRE

Planning Consumer Markets

Statistics and forecasts of consumers' income and expenditure and social trends with a regional analysis. Forecasts by quarter up to 18 months ahead and annually for the next 5 years.

Quarterly

General

£1,225

Various other one-off reports and regular services available.

9 Bridewell Place, London EC4Y 6AY

0171 353 9961

0171 353 2899

427	HEWITT ASSOCIATES
Title	**Salary Increase Survey Report - UK**
Coverage	A survey of salary increases for various categories of jobs based on a sample of around 250 companies.
Frequency	Annual
Availability	General
Cost	Free
Comments	The company carries out various specialist salary surveys, eg consumer electronics, consumer finance, and also maintains a salaries database. These services are available to clients only.
Address	Romeland House, Romeland Hill, St Albans AL3 4EZ
Telephone	01727 866233
Fax	01727 830122

428	HILLIER PARKER
Title	**Retail Warehouse Parks in the Pipeline**
Coverage	Details of specific warehouse parks and aggregate data on numbers and floorspace. Based on the company's own data.
Frequency	Regular
Availability	General
Cost	£8
Comments	
Address	77 Grosvenor Street, London W1A 2BT
Telephone	0171 629 7666
Fax	0171 409 3016

429	HILLIER PARKER
Title	**Specialised Property**
Coverage	Statistics on trends in office parks, retail warehouses, supermarkets. Based on data collected by the company.
Frequency	Annual
Availability	General
Cost	£8
Comments	
Address	77 Grosvenor Street, London W1A 2BT
Telephone	0171 629 7666
Fax	0171 409 3016

430

HILLIER PARKER

Title	**Shopping Centre Vacancies**
Coverage	Details of vacancy levels in shopping centres. Based on data collected by the company.
Frequency	Annual
Availability	General
Cost	£8
Comments	
Address	77 Grosvenor Street, London W1A 2BT
Telephone	0171 629 7666
Fax	0171 409 3016

431

HILLIER PARKER

Title	**Shopping Centres Investment Activity**
Coverage	Investment trends in the shop property sector. Based on a survey by the company.
Frequency	Regular
Availability	General
Cost	£8
Comments	
Address	77 Grosvenor Street, London W1A 2BT
Telephone	0171 629 7666
Fax	0171 409 3016

432

HILLIER PARKER

Title	**Residual Land Values**
Coverage	A survey of the theoretical values of residual land calculated by reference to the potential development of the land and the likely cost of this development.
Frequency	Twice per annum
Availability	General
Cost	£15
Comments	
Address	77 Grosvenor Street, London W1A 2BT
Telephone	0171 629 7666
Fax	0171 409 3016

433

	HILLIER PARKER
Title	**Average Yields**
Coverage	Average property yields for shops, offices, and industrial property with comparative data for gilt and equity yields. Includes a regional breakdown. Based on the company's own survey.
Frequency	Quarterly
Availability	General
Cost	£8
Comments	
Address	77 Grosvenor Street, London W1A 2BT
Telephone	0171 629 7666
Fax	0171 409 3016

434

	HILLIER PARKER
Title	**Secondary Property**
Coverage	Indices by property type and region. Based on data colected by the company.
Frequency	Annual
Availability	General
Cost	£8
Comments	
Address	77 Grosvenor Street, London W1A 2BT
Telephone	0171 629 7666
Fax	0171 409 3016

435

	HILLIER PARKER
Title	**Property Market Values**
Coverage	An index of capital market values and rates of return for types of property by UK region. Based on the company's own survey.
Frequency	Regular
Availability	General
Cost	£8
Comments	
Address	77 Grosvenor Street, London W1A 2BT
Telephone	0171 629 7666
Fax	0171 409 3016

436	HILLIER PARKER
Title	**HP Rent Index**
Coverage	Statistics on the general rents for shops, offices, and industrial premises with data over a 5 year period, and a regional breakdown. Based on the company's own survey.
Frequency	Quarterly
Availability	General
Cost	£8
Comments	
Address	77 Grosvenor Street, London W1A 2BT
Telephone	0171 629 7666
Fax	0171 409 3016

437	HILLIER PARKER
Title	**Shopping Centres in the Pipeline**
Coverage	Details of specific shopping centres, aggregate data and projected floorspace. Based on the company's own survey.
Frequency	Regular
Availability	General
Cost	£8
Comments	
Address	77 Grosvenor Street, London W1A 2BT
Telephone	0171 629 7666
Fax	0171 409 3016

438	HOLBORN RESEARCH SERVICES (HRS)
Title	**HRS Databases**
Coverage	HRS has access to a range of media and consumer databases including the British Business Survey from the British Media Research Committee.
Frequency	Continuous
Availability	General
Cost	On request
Comments	
Address	Grosvenor House, Grosvenor Gardens, London SW1W 0BS
Telephone	0171 630 5033
Fax	0171 828 3642

439

HOME GROWN CEREALS AUTHORITY

Title	**Weekly Bulletin**
Coverage	Statistics on prices, imports, exports, and the futures market for cereals. International data is also included.
Frequency	Weekly
Availability	General
Cost	£45, combined subscription with the Weekly Digest
Comments	
Address	Hamlyn House, Highgate Hill, London N19 5PR
Telephone	0171 263 3391
Fax	0171 561 6218

440

HOME GROWN CEREALS AUTHORITY

Title	**Weekly Digest**
Coverage	Statistics on cereal output, prices, grain fed to livestock and compound feed production. Based on a combination of Central Government statistics, data from the Authority, and other non-official sources.
Frequency	Weekly
Availability	General
Cost	£45, combined subscription with Weekly Bulletin
Comments	
Address	Hamlyn House, Highgate Hill, London N19 5PR
Telephone	0171 263 3391
Fax	0171 561 6218

441

HOME GROWN CEREALS AUTHORITY

Title	**Cereal Statistics**
Coverage	Production and supplies of specific types of cereals plus data on prices and imports and exports. Some international comparisons are included and there is a section of historical statistics. Based mainly on Central Government data with additional material from the Authority and other non-official sources.
Frequency	Annual
Availability	General
Cost	£25
Comments	
Address	Hamlyn House, Highgate Hill, London N19 5PR
Telephone	0171 263 3391
Fax	0171 561 6218

442 HOME GROWN CEREALS AUTHORITY

Title	**Annual Report**
Coverage	Mainly a general commentary on the cereals sector but includes some general statistics on production, supplies etc.
Frequency	Annual
Availability	General
Cost	Free
Comments	
Address	Hamlyn House, Highgate Hill, London N19 5PR
Telephone	0171 263 3391
Fax	0171 561 6218

443 HONG KONG AND SHANGHAI BANKING CORPORATION (HSBC)

Title	**UK Economic Prospects**
Coverage	A review of economic trends and short- and medium-term forecasts for the UK economy.
Frequency	Monthly
Availability	General
Cost	On request
Comments	
Address	3rd Floor, 10 Lower Thames Street, London EC3R 6HH
Telephone	0171 638 2366
Fax	0171 260 0119

444 HORWATH CONSULTING LTD

Title	**UK Hotel Industry**
Coverage	Part of a worldwide survey of hotels comparing London, provincial England, and Scotland. Covers room occupancy, analysis of guests, revenue, expenses, and costs. Includes comparisons with the previous year.
Frequency	Annual
Availability	General
Cost	£100
Comments	Various other international surveys produced plus detailed occupancy surveys in the UK.
Address	8 Baker Street, London W1M 1DA
Telephone	0171 486 5191
Fax	0171 487 3686

445	HOTEL CATERING AND INSTITUTIONAL MANAGEMENT ASSOCIATION
Title	**Hospitality Yearbook**
Coverage	Includes an Annual Review section with commentary and statistics on developments over the previous 12 months.
Frequency	Annual
Availability	General
Cost	On request
Comments	
Address	William Reed Publishing Ltd, Broadfield Park, Crawley, West Sussex RH11 9RT
Telephone	01293 610301
Fax	01293 613304

446	HOUSEBUILDERS' FEDERATION AND HOUSEBUILDER PUBLICATIONS
Title	**Housing Market Report**
Coverage	Includes a survey of housebuilding and a survey of confidence and affordability in the market. Also data on housing market activity, building, labour market trends, mortgages. News items on the housing market are also included and historical data is included in many tables.
Frequency	Quarterly
Availability	General
Cost	On request
Comments	
Address	82 New Cavendish Street, London W1M 8AD
Telephone	0171 580 5588
Fax	0171 323 1697

447	HOUSEWARES BUSINESS CENTRE (HBC)
Title	**Housewares Datapack**
Coverage	Market information on 85 product sectors classified as non-electrical housewares used in the kitchen. Over 900 pages of analysis and data based on research by the company.
Frequency	Annual
Availability	General
Cost	£2,750
Comments	Also undertakes commissioned research on the housewares sector. Summary data from the Housewares Datapack included in DIY Week.
Address	45 Parkfield Road, Coleshill, Birmingham B46 3LD
Telephone	01675 464216
Fax	

448

Title

Coverage

Frequency

Availability

Cost

Comments

Address

Telephone

Fax

HP FOODS LTD

HP Retail Sauce Report

Commentary and statistics on market trends, brands, product developments etc based on commissioned research.

Annual

General

On request

45 Northampton Road, Market Harborough, Leicestershire LE16 9BQ

01858 410144

01858 410053

449

Title

Coverage

Frequency

Availability

Cost

Comments

Address

Telephone

Fax

ICD MARKETING SERVICES

The National Lifestyle Report

ICD is a geodemographic service and the National Lifestyle Report is a customer profile analysis allocating every record on ICD's database into one of 100 cells, based on 280 lifestyle variables.

Continuous

General

On application, and depending on the range and nature of the information required

Boundary House, 91-93 Charterhouse Street, London EC1M 6HR

0171 251 2883

0171 250 0298

450

Title

Coverage

Frequency

Availability

Cost

Comments

Address

Telephone

Fax

ICM RESEARCH

Consumer Omnibus

An omnibus survey of 1,500 adults aged 15 and over at 103 sampling points around the country.

Fortnightly

General

On application

90-92 Great Portland Street, London W1N 5PB

0171 436 3114

0171 436 3179

451	IMPERIAL CHEMICAL INDUSTRIES PLC
Title	**Dulux Paints Review**
Coverage	A review of the UK paints market with data on sales, distribution, and key brands. Based largely on market research sources.
Frequency	Regular
Availability	General
Cost	On request
Comments	
Address	9 Millbank, London SW1P 3JF
Telephone	0171 834 4444
Fax	0171 834 2042

452	IMS (UK) LTD
Title	**IMS Databases**
Coverage	IMS has access to a range of media and consumer databases including the British Business Survey produced by the Business Media Research Committee.
Frequency	Continuous
Availability	General
Cost	On request
Comments	
Address	Grosvenor House, Grosvenor Gardens, London SW1W 0BS
Telephone	0171 630 5033
Fax	0171 828 3642

453	INCOMES DATA SERVICES
Title	**IDS Management Pay Review Executive Pay Report**
Coverage	A survey of salary movements for management staff in FTSE 250 companies. Additional information on bonuses, share options, benefits, and contracts. Based on a survey by the company.
Frequency	Annual
Availability	General
Cost	On request
Comments	
Address	193 St John Street, London EC1V 4LS
Telephone	0171 250 3434
Fax	0171 608 0949

INCOMES DATA SERVICES

Title	**Pay Settlement Analysis**
Coverage	Data on trends in pay settlements with figures for changes in the level of settlements over a twelve month period. Based on data collected by IDS.
Frequency	Quarterly in a twice-monthly journal
Availability	General
Cost	On request
Comments	The survey is included as a quarterly feature in the journal, IDS Report. IDS publishes a range of reports on the UK and European labour market and conditions.
Address	193 St John Street, London EC1V 4LS
Telephone	0171 250 3434
Fax	0171 608 0949

INCOMES DATA SERVICES

Title	**Datable**
Coverage	General statistics on retail prices and average earnings, in index form, with historical data for previous months. Based on Central Government data.
Frequency	Twice monthly in a twice monthly journal
Availability	General
Cost	On request
Comments	Published in the IDS journal, IDS Report. IDS publishes a range of reports on the UK and European labour market and conditions.
Address	193 St John Street, London EC1V 4LS
Telephone	0171 250 3434
Fax	0171 608 0949

INCOMES DATA SERVICES

Title	**IDS Report Fax Service**
Coverage	A call-back fax service offering a range of statistics to callers, often out of office hours. Data includes the latest retail price indices, average earnings indices, pay settlements, and summary economic forecasts.
Frequency	Continuous
Availability	General
Cost	On request
Comments	The service is available on 0336 424575. IDS publishes a range of reports on the UK and European labour market and conditions.
Address	193 St John Street, London EC1V 4LS
Telephone	0171 250 3434
Fax	0171 608 0949

457

INCOMES DATA SERVICES

Title **Public Sector Labour Market Survey**

Coverage An IDS survey of the public sector labour market based on a survey of employers' perceptions of the market and their recent recruitment and training experiences.

Frequency Annual

Availability General

Cost On request

Comments The survey is included as a special feature in the twice-monthly IDS Report. IDS publishes a range of reports on the UK and European labour market and conditions.

Address 193 St John Street, London EC1V 4LS

Telephone 0171 250 3434

Fax 0171 608 0949

458

INCOMES DATA SERVICES

Title **Pay and Bargaining Prospects**

Coverage Commentary and statistics on the outlook for pay and bargaining in the next twelve months. Based on an analysis of current and likely economic and pay trends by IDS.

Frequency Annual

Availability General

Cost On request

Comments The survey is included as a special feature in the twice-monthly IDS Report, usually in a September issue.

Address 193 St John Street, London EC1V 4LS

Telephone 0171 250 3434

Fax 0171 608 0949

459

INCOMES DATA SERVICES

Title **IDS Management Pay Review Pay and Progression for Graduates**

Coverage A survey of salary and related trends in the graduate labour market based on a sample survey of over 100 organisations.

Frequency Annual

Availability General

Cost £202

Comments

Address 193 St John Street, London EC1V 4LS

Telephone 0171 250 3434

Fax 0171 608 0949

460

INCORPORATED SOCIETY OF BRITISH
ADVERTISERS LTD

Title **Exhibition Expenditure Review**

Coverage Expenditure by UK exhibitors on trade and consumer exhibitions by venue and by media. Based on a survey of around 2,000 exhibitors at various types of exhibitions. A small amount of supporting text.

Frequency Annual

Availability General

Cost On request

Comments

Address 44 Hertford Street, London W1Y 8AE

Telephone 0171 499 7502

Fax 0171 629 5355

461

INDEPENDENT HEALTHCARE ASSOCIATION

Title **Survey of Acute Hospitals in the Independent Sector**

Coverage Details of the size of, and growth trends for, the private hospital market in the UK. Regional data is also included. Based on information collected by the association.

Frequency Annual

Availability General

Cost £25

Comments

Address 22 Little Russell Street, London WC1A 2HT

Telephone 0171 430 0537

Fax 0171 242 2681

462

INDEPENDENT SCHOOLS INFORMATION SERVICE (ISIS)

Title **ISIS Annual Census**

Coverage General statistical information about the number of pupils in ISIS schools, spending, current trends in independent education etc. Based on a regular ISIS survey.

Frequency Annual

Availability General

Cost Free

Comments

Address 56 Buckingham Gate, London SW1E 6AG

Telephone 0171 630 8793

Fax 0171 630 5013

463

	INDEPENDENT TELEVISION COMMISSION (ITC)
Title	**Television: the Public's View**
Coverage	Annual survey, from 1970 onwards, of consumer opinions of television plus ownership levels. Includes data on the number of TV sets, subscriptions to cable and satellite television, programme selection, motives for choosing specific programmes, opinions on standards and quality, comments on specific types of programmes.
Frequency	Annual
Availability	General
Cost	£7.50
Comments	Also produces an annual report with a general review of viewing trends.
Address	33 Foley Street, London W1P 7LB
Telephone	0171 255 3000
Fax	0171 306 7800

464

	INDICES PUBLICATIONS LTD
Title	**The New Grey List**
Coverage	Market prices for over 30,000 hardware and DIY products based on a survey by Indices Publications of prices throughout the country.
Frequency	Monthly
Availability	General
Cost	£119, £99 to British Hardware Federation members
Comments	
Address	14-16 Church Street, Rickmansworth WD3 1WD
Telephone	01923 711434
Fax	01923 896063

465

	INDUSTRIAL COMMON OWNERSHIP MOVEMENT LTD
Title	**Cooperative Statistics**
Coverage	Regular statistics on the number of cooperative businesses in the UK based on data collected by the movement.
Frequency	Regular
Availability	General
Cost	On request
Comments	
Address	20 Central Road, Leeds LS1 6DE
Telephone	0113 2461737
Fax	0113 2440002

INDUSTRIAL RELATIONS SERVICES (IRS)

Title	**IRS Employment Review**
Coverage	The Employment Review comprises five journals which have been brought together under one cover. These include Pay and Benefits Bulletin, with data on earnings, settlements, prices etc. and IRS Employment Trends.
Frequency	Twice a month
Availability	General
Cost	On request
Comments	
Address	18-20 Highbury Place, London N5 1QP
Telephone	0171 354 5858
Fax	0171 359 4000

INFORMATION RESEARCH NETWORK (IRN)

Title	**Travelstat**
Coverage	Detailed statistics covering inbound and outbound tourist profiles, tourist flows by origin and destination, tourist flows by purpose of visit, expenditure breakdowns, traffic by mode of transport, market shares etc. Based primarily on Central Government's International Passenger Survey plus IRN's own database of travel and tourism data.
Frequency	Continuous
Availability	General
Cost	Varies according to the nature and range of data required
Comments	Available in hard copy or disc formats.
Address	Davis House, 129 Wilton Road, London SW1V 1LD
Telephone	0171 416 8107
Fax	0171 828 2030

INFORMATION RESEARCH NETWORK (IRN)

Title	**Townstat**
Coverage	Economic and social profiles of over 700 UK towns and 150 towns in Continental Europe, plus data on counties, regions, and other specified local areas. Based on official statistics, geodemographic sources, and chartered surveyors.
Frequency	Continuous
Availability	General
Cost	£38 per town profile, reduced rates for multiple orders, negotiated fees for tailormade reports on specific areas
Comments	Produced in association with Property Intelligence PLC (see other entry).
Address	Davis House, 129 Wilton Road, London SW1V 1LD
Telephone	0171 416 8107
Fax	0171 828 2030

469 INGLEBY TRICE

Title	**City Floorspace Survey**
Coverage	Details of floorspace in the centre of London with a geographical breakdown into 3 areas: city, central city, city fringe. Based on data held by the company.
Frequency	Monthly
Availability	General
Cost	Free
Comments	Ingleby Trice was previously Richard Saunders & Partners.
Address	11 Old Jewry, London EC2R 8DU
Telephone	0171 606 7461
Fax	0171 726 2578

470 INSTITUTE FOR EMPLOYMENT STUDIES

Title	**IES Graduate Review**
Coverage	Statistics on graduates and the graduate recruitment market, plus characteristics of the student population. Also examines major issues relevant to graduate recruitment. Based on data collected and analysed by the Institute.
Frequency	Annual
Availability	General
Cost	£30
Comments	Various other reports on the labour market produced and a publications catalogue is available.
Address	Mantell Building, University of Sussex, Falmer, Brighton
Telephone	01273 686751
Fax	01273 690430

471 INSTITUTE OF GROCERY DISTRIBUTION

Title	**Food Industry Statistics Digest**
Coverage	Food retailing trends by sector, company, region and the number and size of outlets. Also includes data on costs, profits, employment , stocks, capital, wholesaling, cash and carry, along with consumption and expenditure patterns plus key economic indicators. Details of the leading operators are also included. A compilation from various sources.
Frequency	Monthly
Availability	General
Cost	£120, £90 to members
Comments	Produced in a loose/leaf format each month with a binder provided. Various other occasional and one-off reports are produced on the grocery sector.
Address	Letchmore Heath, Watford, Hertfordshire WD2 8DQ
Telephone	01923 857141
Fax	01923 852531

472

INSTITUTE OF GROCERY DISTRIBUTION

Title **Grocery Market Bulletin**

Coverage News items, features and statistics covering trends in the UK grocery market. Based on various sources.

Frequency Monthly

Availability General

Cost £75, for both members and non-members

Comments Various other occasional and one-off reports are produced on the grocery sector.

Address Letchmore Heath, Watford, Hertfordshire WD2 8DQ

Telephone 01923 857141

Fax 01923 852531

473

INSTITUTE OF GROCERY DISTRIBUTION

Title **Grocery Retailing**

Coverage A regularly updated report on grocery retailing in the UK with details of sales and sectors, companies, consumer trends, and new developments. Based on various sources.

Frequency Regular

Availability General

Cost £260, £190 for members

Comments Various other occasional and one-off reports are produced on the grocery sector.

Address Letchmore Heath, Watford, Hertfordshire WD2 8DQ

Telephone 01923 857141

Fax 01923 852531

474

INSTITUTE OF GROCERY DISTRIBUTION

Title **Grocery Wholesaling**

Coverage A regularly updated report on grocery wholesaling with commentary and statistics covering sales, wholesaling sectors, companies, employment, and new developments. Based on various sources.

Frequency Regular

Availability General

Cost £230, £175 for members

Comments Various other occasional and one-off reports are produced on the grocery sector.

Address Letchmore Heath, Watford, Hertfordshire WD2 8DQ

Telephone 01923 857141

Fax 01923 852531

475	INSTITUTE OF INFORMATION SCIENTISTS (IIS)
Title	**IIS Remuneration Survey**
Coverage	Salary statistics for Institute members in full time employment. Analysis by grade of membership, age, and sectors of employment. A commentary accompanies the data.
Frequency	Every two years
Availability	General
Cost	£12, free to members
Comments	
Address	44 Museum Street, London WC1A 1LY
Telephone	0171 831 8003
Fax	0171 430 1270

476	INSTITUTE OF PERSONNEL AND DEVELOPMENT (IPD)
Title	**IPD Labour Turnover Survey**
Coverage	A survey of employee turnover and job tenure with analysis by type of job, sectors, and manual/non-manual workers. Based on a survey by IPD.
Frequency	Annual
Availability	General
Cost	On request
Comments	The survey was carried out for the first time in 1995 but the aim is to continue it as an annual survey.
Address	IPD House, Camp Road, Wimbledon, London SW19 4UX
Telephone	0181 971 9000
Fax	

477	INSTITUTE OF PETROLEUM
Title	**IP Statistics Folder**
Coverage	A folder with data sheets providing summary information on the main indicators relating to the UK petroleum sector. Based largely on the Institute's own data.
Frequency	Regular
Availability	General
Cost	On request
Comments	Also produces the monthly Petroleum Review which contains some statistics.
Address	61 New Cavendish Street, London W1M 8AR
Telephone	0171 636 1004
Fax	0171 255 1472

478

INSTITUTE OF PETROLEUM

Title **Ten-year Cumulation Booklet**

Coverage Historical statistics covering the key indicators in the UK petroleum sector.

Frequency Regular

Availability General

Cost On request

Comments Also publishes the monthly Petroleum Review which contains some statistics.

Address 61 New Cavendish Street, London W1M 8AR

Telephone 0171 636 1004

Fax 0171 255 1472

479

INSTITUTE OF PETROLEUM

Title **UK Petroleum Industry Statistics: Consumption and Refinery Production**

Coverage Deliveries, end-use, and production of petroleum products with data for the latest 2 years. Based on the Institute's data with a small amount of supporting text.

Frequency Annual

Availability General

Cost Free

Comments Also produces the monthly Petroleum Review which contains some statistics.

Address 61 New Cavendish Street, London W1M 8AR

Telephone 0171 636 1004

Fax 0171 255 1472

480

INSTITUTE OF PETROLEUM

Title **UK Retail Marketing Survey**

Coverage Statistics and commentary on the retail market for petrol with data on sites, sales, company performance, and new developments and sites. Also data on forecourt retailing.

Frequency Regular

Availability General

Cost £50

Comments Also publishes the monthly Petroleum Review which contains some statistics.

Address 61 New Cavendish Street, London W1M 8AR

Telephone 0171 636 1004

Fax 0171 255 1472

481	INSTITUTE OF PHYSICS
Title	**Remuneration Survey**
Coverage	Analysis of salaries of members by class of membership, age, sex, type of work etc. Based on a survey of members and supported by a brief commentary.
Frequency	Annual
Availability	General
Cost	Free
Comments	Available in the house journal Physics World.
Address	47 Belgrave Square, London SW1X 8QX
Telephone	0171 470 4800
Fax	0171 470 4848

482	INSTITUTE OF PRACTITIONERS IN ADVERTISING
Title	**IPA Agency Census**
Coverage	Estimated number of people employed in IPA member advertising agencies categorised by location, staff category, size of agency. Based on the IPA's own survey with some supporting text. Usually published early in the year following a survey in autumn of the previous year.
Frequency	Annual
Availability	General
Cost	£15
Comments	Also produces surveys of agency costs usually only available to members.
Address	44 Belgrave Square, London SW1X 8QS
Telephone	0171 235 7020
Fax	0171 245 9904

483	INSTITUTION OF CHEMICAL ENGINEERS
Title	**Remuneration Survey**
Coverage	Remuneration and employment trends for members of the Institution based on the organization's own survey.
Frequency	Every two years
Availability	General
Cost	£75, free to members
Comments	
Address	Davis Building, 165-171 Railway Terrace, Rugby CV21 3HQ
Telephone	01788 578214
Fax	01788 560833

484 INSTITUTION OF CIVIL ENGINEERS

Title	**ICE Salary Survey**
Coverage	An analysis by employer, age, type of work, overtime payments, location, firm size, qualifications etc. Based on a survey of members.
Frequency	Annual
Availability	General
Cost	£130
Comments	
Address	Thomas Telford Ltd, 1 Heron Quay, London E14 4JD
Telephone	0171 987 6999
Fax	0171 538 4101

485 INSTITUTION OF ELECTRICAL ENGINEERS (IEE)

Title	**IEE Salary Survey**
Coverage	A random sample of members, analysed by age, position, class, type of work, levels of responsibility, size of work, qualifications, location of employment, fringe benefits etc. A small amount of supporting text.
Frequency	Annual
Availability	General
Cost	£50, £30 to members
Comments	
Address	Michael Faraday House, Six Hills Way, Stevenage SG1 2SD
Telephone	01438 313311
Fax	01438 313465

486 INSTITUTION OF ELECTRONICS AND ELECTRICAL INCORPORATED ENGINEERS (IEEIE)

Title	**199– Survey of Members**
Coverage	A survey of salaries by various job grades broken down by class of employment, levels of responsibility, age, geographical location, number at the workplace etc.
Frequency	Annual
Availability	General
Cost	£25, free to members
Comments	
Address	Savoy Hill House, Savoy Hill, London WC2R 0BS
Telephone	0171 836 3357
Fax	0171 497 9006

487 INSTITUTION OF MECHANICAL ENGINEERS

Title **Salary Survey**

Coverage Salary survey of the members of the Institution with data by type of work, sector, type of member, and geographical location. Also includes data on fringe benefits and overtime.

Frequency Every two years

Availability General

Cost £95

Comments Latest survey – April 1994.

Address 1 Birdcage Walk, London SW1H 9JJ

Telephone 0171 973 1298

Fax 0171 222 4557

488 INSTITUTIONAL FUND MANAGERS' ASSOCIATION

Title **Fund Management Survey**

Coverage A survey of IFMA members with data on fund ownership, funds under management, client analysis, overseas earnings, and staff.

Frequency Regular

Availability General

Cost On request

Comments First published in 1992.

Address Garrard House, 31-45 Gresham Street, London EC2V 7DN

Telephone 0171 600 3914

Fax

489 INTERNATIONAL STOCK EXCHANGE OF THE UNITED KINGDOM

Title **Stock Exchange Fact Book**

Coverage Commentary, graphs, and tables providing summary information on the workings of the Stock Exchange. Based on statistics maintained by the Stock Exchange.

Frequency Annual

Availability General

Cost £119 as part of the Stock Exchange Fact Service

Comments

Address Stock Exchange, London EC2N 1HP

Telephone 0171 588 2355

Fax 0171 588 2355

490

INTERNATIONAL STOCK EXCHANGE OF THE
UNITED KINGDOM

Title	**AIM Market Statistics**
Coverage	Statistics covering trends in the recently established AIM market based on information maintained by the Stock Exchange.
Frequency	Monthly
Availability	General
Cost	On request
Comments	
Address	Stock Exchange, London EC2N 1HP
Telephone	0171 588 2355
Fax	0171 588 2355

491

INTERNATIONAL STOCK EXCHANGE OF THE
UNITED KINGDOM

Title	**Stock Exchange Quarterly**
Coverage	Articles and commentary followed by a statistical section covering funds, turnover, new work, sector analysis etc. Based on statistics maintained by the Stock Exchange.
Frequency	Quarterly
Availability	General
Cost	£71, or £119 as part of the Stock Exchange Fact Service
Comments	
Address	Stock Exchange, London EC2N 1HP
Telephone	0171 588 2355
Fax	0171 588 2355

492

INTERNATIONAL STOCK EXCHANGE OF THE
UNITED KINGDOM

Title	**Quality of Markets Monthly Fact Sheet**
Coverage	Statistics on the daily market trends for the month plus data on equities, gilts, renewable issues, traded options etc. Based on a general review of Stock Exchange activities.
Frequency	Monthly
Availability	General
Cost	£119, as part of the Stock Exchange Fact Service
Comments	
Address	Stock Exchange, London EC2N 1HP
Telephone	0171 588 2355
Fax	0171 588 2355

493	INVESTMENT PROPERTY DATABANK
Title	**IPD Annual Review**
Coverage	Presents and interprets statistics about current trends in the commercial property market. Utilises records of over 9,000 properties on the IPD and includes ten-year's worth of data on total returns, capital growth, income return, value growth, fund strategies etc. A large amount of text accompanies the data.
Frequency	Annual
Availability	General
Cost	On request
Comments	Also offers a telephone inquiry service.
Address	7-8 Greenland Place, London NW1 0AP
Telephone	0171 482 5149
Fax	0171 267 0208

494	INVESTMENT PROPERTY DATABANK
Title	**Monthly Index**
Coverage	A monthly index examining the trends in the value of commercial property analysed by region and sector. Based on data collected by IPD.
Frequency	Monthly
Availability	General
Cost	£250
Comments	
Address	7-8 Greenland Place, London NW1 0AP
Telephone	0171 482 5149
Fax	0171 267 0208

495	INVESTMENT PROPERTY DATABANK
Title	**Quarterly Review**
Coverage	A quarterly review of the trends in the value of commercial property with an analysis by region and sector. Based on data collected by IPD.
Frequency	Quarterly
Availability	General
Cost	£750
Comments	
Address	7-8 Greenland Place, London NW1 0AP
Telephone	0171 482 5149
Fax	0171 267 0208

496

Title	**IPD/Savills Agricultural Performance Analysis**
Coverage	Data on institutional investment in farmland including rental growth, capital growth, total returns, and the future. A number of tables and graphs give historical trends. Data by land grade and type of tenancy and some regional figures. Based on IPD's records of investments with some supporting text.
Frequency	Annual
Availability	General
Cost	On request
Comments	Published in association with Savills (see separate entry).
Address	7-8 Greenland Place, London NW1 0AP
Telephone	0171 482 5149
Fax	0171 267 0208

497

JONES LANG WOOTTON

Title	**JLW Property Index**
Coverage	Analysis of the returns to property by type and comparisons with other investments. Figures given over a ten-year period and portfolio statistics by region. Data calculated from various sources and some supporting text.
Frequency	Quarterly
Availability	General
Cost	On request
Comments	Publications also cover London City offices and West End offices.
Address	22 Hanover Square, London W1A 2BN
Telephone	0171 413 1347
Fax	0171 355 3732

498

JONES LANG WOOTTON

Title	**50 Centres: A Guide to Office and Industrial Rental Trends**
Coverage	Statistics on 50 main urban centres based on JLW's Centres database which records transactions at the top end of the prime property market. Some supporting text.
Frequency	Twice per annum
Availability	General
Cost	On request
Comments	Publications also cover London City offices and West End offices.
Address	22 Hanover Square, London W1A 2BN
Telephone	0171 413 1347
Fax	0171 355 3732

499	JONES, ALAN & ASSOCIATES
Title	**Charities Salary Survey**
Coverage	A survey by the company of salaries for various jobs in 30 charities.
Frequency	Annual
Availability	General
Cost	On request
Comments	
Address	Apex House, Wonastow Road, Monmouth, Gwent NP5 4YE
Telephone	01600 716916
Fax	

500	JOSEPH ROWNTREE FOUNDATION
Title	**Housing Finance Review**
Coverage	A compendium of data on the housing sector with 150 tables covering key housing issues. Based on data collected from various sources.
Frequency	Annual
Availability	General
Cost	£17.50
Comments	
Address	The Homestead, 40 Water End, York YO3 6LP
Telephone	01904 654328
Fax	01904 620072

501	KEY NOTE PUBLICATIONS
Title	**Key Note Reports**
Coverage	A range of over 200 reports on UK markets and sectors, with many of the reports updated every 12 to 18 months. Each report follows a standard format with sections on market definition, market size, industry background, competitor analysis, SWOT analysis, buying behaviour, outside suppliers, current issues, forecasts, and company profiles. Based on various sources including official statistics, trade association data, company reports, TGI data, and, occasionally, commissioned research.
Frequency	Regular
Availability	General
Cost	£185 each
Comments	Key Note reports are now available on a Key Note CD-ROM.
Address	Field House, 72 Oldfield Road, Hampton, Middlesex TW12 2HQ
Telephone	0181 783 0755
Fax	0181 783 0049

502

Title	**Key Note Market Reviews**
Coverage	These are reviews of general market sectors in the UK, such as food, drinks, catering, clothing, leisure and recreation, and travel and tourism. Within each report, the market sector is broken down into its main segments. There is also a section profiling the major companies in the sector and, normally, some original consumer data. Most market reviews are updated regularly and there are approximately 40 titles in the series.
Frequency	Regular
Availability	General
Cost	£375
Comments	Key Note reports are now also available on a Key Note CD-ROM.
Address	Field House, 72 Oldfield Road, Hampton, Middlesex TW12 2HQ
Telephone	0181 783 0755
Fax	0181 783 1940

503 KNIGHT FRANK & RUTLEY

Title	**Central London**
Coverage	Property development trends, including rents and floorspace, in Central London.
Frequency	Quarterly
Availability	General
Cost	Free
Comments	Various other reports produced on property issues in the UK and Europe.
Address	20 Hanover Square, London W1A 2BN
Telephone	0171 629 8171
Fax	0171 629 1610

504 KNIGHT RIDDER INFORMATION LTD

Title	**Tradstat**
Coverage	An online database of UK import and export statistics with data on specific products. Based on data supplied by HM Customs and Excise and part of an international database of foreign trade statistics.
Frequency	Regular
Availability	General
Cost	On request
Comments	
Address	Haymarket House, 1 Oxenden Street, London SW1Y 4EE
Telephone	0171 930 7646
Fax	0171 930 2581

505	KORN/FERRY CARRE/ORBAN INTERNATIONAL
Title	**Boards of Directors Study**
Coverage	A survey of salaries and benefits for around 830 executive and non-executive company directors based on a survey by the company. Also includes information on the composition of company boards, special committees, and the data is broken down by company type, sector, and number of employees.
Frequency	Annual
Availability	General
Cost	£99 plus VAT
Comments	
Address	252 Regent Street, London W1R 5DA
Telephone	0171 312 3100
Fax	0171 312 3130

506	KPMG CORPORATE FINANCE
Title	**New Issue Statistics**
Coverage	Commentary and statistics on UK flotations, new issues by quarter. Also contains details of specific new issues. Based on an analysis of Stock Exchange data.
Frequency	Quarterly
Availability	General
Cost	On request
Comments	
Address	8 Salisbury Square, London EC4Y 8BB
Telephone	0171 236 8805
Fax	0171 248 6552

507	KPMG CORPORATE FINANCE
Title	**Management Buyout Statistics**
Coverage	Commentary and statistics on the total value of buy-outs plus data by category, size of buy-out. The publication also includes historical data.
Frequency	Quarterly
Availability	General
Cost	On request
Comments	
Address	8 Salisbury Square, London EC4Y 8BB
Telephone	0171 236 8805
Fax	0171 248 6552

508

Title

Coverage

Frequency

Availability

Cost

Comments

Address

Telephone

Fax

KPMG CORPORATE FINANCE

Alternative Investment Market (AIM)

Commentary and statistics on trends in the alternative investment market including total size, companies etc.

Quarterly

General

On request

8 Salisbury Square, London EC4Y 8BB

0171 236 8805

0171 248 6552

509

Title

Coverage

Frequency

Availability

Cost

Comments

Address

Telephone

Fax

LABOUR RESEARCH

Labour Research Fact Service

A weekly pamphlet containing news and statistics relating to the labour market. Based on various sources.

Weekly

General

£46.95

Also publishes reports on directors' pay and bargaining plus a monthly journal, Labour Research.

78 Blackfriars Road, London SE1 8HF

0171 928 3649

0171 928 0621

510

Title

Coverage

Frequency

Availability

Cost

Comments

Address

Telephone

Fax

LAING & BUISSON PUBLICATIONS LTD

Laing's Review of Private Healthcare

Analysis and statistics covering the private healthcare market with information on three sectors: acute healthcare services, medical insurance, and long term care of the elderly. Based on research by the company.

Annual

General

£120

Lymehouse Studios, Block B, 38 Georgiana Street, London NW1 0EB

0171 284 1268

0171 267 8269

511	LAING & BUISSON PUBLICATIONS LTD
Title	**Private Medical Insurance Market**
Coverage	A regular review of the private medical insurance market based on returns from insurers representing virtually 100% of the private medical insurance business.
Frequency	Regular
Availability	General
Cost	On request
Comments	
Address	Lymehouse Studios, Block B, 38 Georgiana Street, London NW1 0EB
Telephone	0171 284 1268
Fax	0171 267 8269

512	LEATHER
Title	**Prices**
Coverage	Leather and hide prices in the UK based on data collected from leather markets.
Frequency	Monthly in a monthly journal
Availability	General
Cost	£66
Comments	The journal also has regular surveys of the UK leather industry and similar surveys of European and international markets.
Address	Miller Freeman Publications Ltd, Sovereign Way, Tonbridge TN9 1RW
Telephone	01732 364422
Fax	01732 361534

513	LEATHERHEAD FOOD RA
Title	**UK Food and Drinks Report**
Coverage	A two-volume report reviewing the UK food market, industry, and new product trends by sector. Based on a combination of original research and various published sources.
Frequency	Regular
Availability	General
Cost	On application
Comments	Also publishes various one-off reports on the UK and European food industry.
Address	Randalls Road, Leatherhead, Surrey KT22 7RY
Telephone	01372 376761
Fax	01372 386228

514   LEISURE CONSULTANTS

Title	**Leisure Forecasts**
Coverage	Published in 2 volumes with the first volume covering leisure away from the home and the second volume relating to leisure in the home. Forecasts are given for 5 years ahead for consumer spending, prices, and key market indicators. Based largely on the company's own research with some supporting commentary.
Frequency	Annual
Availability	General
Cost	£120 for each volume
Comments	
Address	Lint Growis, Foxearth, Sudbury CO10 7JX
Telephone	01787 375777
Fax	01787 375777

515   LEX SERVICE PLC

Title	**LEX Report on Motoring**
Coverage	A sample survey of approximately 1,500 drivers providing information on purchasing, ownership, attitudes etc. It also includes forecasts relating to the motoring sector.
Frequency	Annual
Availability	General
Cost	£295
Comments	
Address	Lex House, 17 Connaught Place, London W2 2EL
Telephone	0171 723 1212
Fax	0171 724 5234

516   LIBRARY AND INFORMATION STATISTICS UNIT (LISU)

Title	**Average Prices of British Academic Books**
Coverage	A survey of thousands of published titles with prices analysed by various subject categories, and academic and calender year indexing.
Frequency	Bi-annual
Availability	General
Cost	£9.50
Comments	The survey is published in February and August each year and there is a companion publication on academic book prices in the USA. LISU also publishes a range of occasional and one-off surveys of the library and publishing sectors.
Address	Loughborough University of Technology, Loughborough, Leicestershire LE11 3TU
Telephone	01509 223071
Fax	01509 223072

517

LIBRARY AND INFORMATION STATISTICS UNIT (LISU)

Title	**UK Public Library Materials Fund and Budget Survey**
Coverage	Originally concentrating on public library book funds, this survey now also covers audio and video material, service points, opening hours, and staffing levels. Comparisons are presented between individual Authorities responding to the survey, and the latest year's budgets are compared to the previous year.
Frequency	Annual
Availability	General
Cost	£22.50, £17.50 to contributing institutions
Comments	Published in July each year. LISU also publishes a range of occasional and one-off surveys of the library and publishing sectors.
Address	Loughborough University of Technology, Loughborough, Leicestershire LE11 3TU
Telephone	01509 223071
Fax	01509 223072

518

LIBRARY AND INFORMATION STATISTICS UNIT (LISU)

Title	**Survey of Public Library Services to Schools and Children in the UK**
Coverage	An analysis of services based on a questionnaire survey carried out with guidance from AMDECL, SOCCEL, and other groups of specialist librarians. It includes tables of detailed information by authority with explanatory comments, summaries, and per capita indicators. The delegation effect of Local Management of Schools on the Schools Library Service is monitored.
Frequency	Annual
Availability	General
Cost	£19.50, £16.50 to contributing institutions
Comments	LISU also publishes a range of occasional and one-off surveys of the library and publishing sectors.
Address	Loughborough University of Technology, Loughborough, Leicestershire LE11 3TU
Telephone	01509 223071
Fax	01509 223072

519

	LIBRARY AND INFORMATION STATISTICS UNIT (LISU)
Title	**LISU Annual Library Statistics**
Coverage	A compendium of statistics on UK libraries including public libraries, university libraries, the national libraries, and the book trade. Historical statistics are included for the last ten years and the data is based on returns to CIPFA, UFC, and SCONUL supplemented by some special surveys.
Frequency	Annual
Availability	General
Cost	£27.50
Comments	LISU also publishes a range of occasional and one-off surveys of the library and publishing sectors.
Address	Loughborough University of Technology, Loughborough, Leicestershire LE11 3TU
Telephone	01509 223071
Fax	01509 223072

520

	LIBRARY ASSOCIATION RECORD
Title	**Annual Periodical Prices**
Coverage	Brief commentary and statistics of periodical prices arranged by subject, with figures for the latest year and the previous year. Based on data collected by Blackwells from a broad selection of journals.
Frequency	Annual
Availability	General
Cost	£79.50
Comments	Usually published in May (from 1977 to 1995).
Address	7 Ridgmount Street, London WC1E 7AE
Telephone	0171 636 7543
Fax	0171 436 7218

521

	LIVERPOOL COTTON ASSOCIATION LTD
Title	**Raw Cotton Report**
Coverage	The Liverpool market for cotton, UK cotton supply and consumption, futures market, conference freight rates to Liverpool, and world raw cotton markets.
Frequency	26 issues per year
Availability	General
Cost	£30 members, £41 non-members
Comments	
Address	620 Cotton Exchange Building, Edmund Street, Liverpool L3 9LH
Telephone	0151 236 6041
Fax	0151 255 0174

522

LIVERPOOL MACROECONOMIC RESEARCH LTD

Title **Quarterly Economic Review**

Coverage Quarterly commentary on economic trends supported by statistics and forecasts of future trends.

Frequency Quarterly

Availability General

Cost £85

Comments

Address University of Liverpool, PO Box 147, Liverpool LS9 3DX

Telephone 0151 794 3032

Fax 0151 794 3028

523

LLOYDS OF LONDON

Title **Lloyds' Nautical Yearbook**

Coverage Includes a section on the 'Year in Shipping', plus casualty statistics, port statistics, and country information. Based on various sources.

Frequency Annual

Availability General

Cost On request

Comments Publishes various regular statistical reports on international shipping trends.

Address Lloyds of London Press Ltd, Sheepen Place, Colchester CO3 3LP

Telephone 01206 772277

Fax 01206 46273

524

LONDON BUSINESS SCHOOL

Title **Economic Outlook**

Coverage Three major forecasts and nine intermediate forecast releases per annum. A forecast summary is followed by the forecast in detail and topical articles. The main reports also have detailed forecast tables at the back of each issue with long-term forecasts.

Frequency Three issues per annum plus monthly updates

Availability General

Cost £190

Comments Published by Basil Blackwell Publishers Ltd at the address below. London Business School also produces a monthly Exchange Rate Outlook.

Address 108 Cowley Road, Oxford OX4 1JF

Telephone 01865 791100

Fax 01865 791347

525 LONDON CHAMBER OF COMMERCE

Title	**London Chamber Economic Report and Survey**
Coverage	A review of economic and business trends in London including statistics on domestic business, investment, profits, exports, labour. Based on a survey of around 250 companies in the capital with additional data from official sources.
Frequency	Quarterly
Availability	General
Cost	On request
Comments	
Address	69 Cannon Street, London EC4N 5AB
Telephone	0171 248 4444
Fax	0171 489 0391

526 LONDON CHAMBER OF COMMERCE

Title	**Annual Review of the London Economy**
Coverage	A review of economic trends in the capital based on data from the Chamber and other sources.
Frequency	Annual
Availability	General
Cost	On request
Comments	
Address	69 Cannon Street, London EC4N 5AB
Telephone	0171 248 4444
Fax	0171 489 0391

527 LONDON CLEARING HOUSE

Title	**London Clearing House Statistics**
Coverage	Statistics relating to cleared volumes with monthly figures for the latest year. Based on data collected by the clearing house.
Frequency	Monthly
Availability	General
Cost	On request
Comments	
Address	Roman Wall House, 1-2 Crutched Friars, London EC3N 2AN
Telephone	0171 265 2000
Fax	0171 265 2056

528	**LONDON CORN CIRCULAR**
Title	**Market Prices**
Coverage	Prices of cereals and various other crops with some forecasts of future prices.
Frequency	Weekly in a weekly journal
Availability	General
Cost	£75
Comments	
Address	Nene House, Town Bridge, London Road, Peterborough PE2 8AH
Telephone	01733 555079
Fax	01733 896046

529	**LONDON METAL EXCHANGE**
Title	**Statistics at a Glance**
Coverage	A regular market report including data on price movements, liquidity, and volume. Based on the Exchange's own data.
Frequency	Monthly
Availability	General
Cost	On request
Comments	
Address	56 Leadenhall Street, London EC3A 2BJ
Telephone	0171 264 5555
Fax	0171 680 0505

530	**LONDON RESEARCH CENTRE**
Title	**London 9–**
Coverage	A compilation of statistics on the London area with historical data in many tables. Data for London as a whole and for specific boroughs. Based on a combination of central and local government data.
Frequency	Annual
Availability	General
Cost	£29
Comments	Publishes various other statistics and surveys on the London area.
Address	81 Black Prince Road, London SE1 7SZ
Telephone	0171 735 4250
Fax	0171 627 9606

531 LONDON RESEARCH CENTRE

Title	**London Housing Statistics**
Coverage	Detailed statistics on housing in London ranging from housebuilding and the housing stock through to data on household composition, homelessness. Data is given for the individual London boroughs.
Frequency	Annual
Availability	General
Cost	£32
Comments	Also publishes various other statistics and surveys.
Address	81 Black Prince Road, London SE1 7SZ
Telephone	0171 735 4250
Fax	0171 627 9606

532 LONGMAN

Title	**Directory of Independent Hospitals and Health Services**
Coverage	Mainly details of organizations and services but it includes a statistical survey of acute healthcare hospitals with data for the last 15 years. Includes aggregate statistics plus ownership categories and a regional breakdown of the data.
Frequency	Annual
Availability	General
Cost	On request
Comments	
Address	Fourth Avenue, Harlow, Middlesex CM19 5AA
Telephone	01279 442601
Fax	01279 444501

533 LONGMAN

Title	**British Leisure Centre Directory**
Coverage	Details of leisure centres around the country but it also includes statistics on the number of centres, admission charges, admissions, and seating capacities.
Frequency	Annual
Availability	General
Cost	On request
Comments	
Address	Fourth Avenue, Harlow, Middlesex CM19 5AA
Telephone	01279 442601
Fax	01279 444501

534	LYONS WADDELL
Title	**Premier Beverages Hot Beverages Report**
Coverage	A review of the UK hot beverages market with commentary and statistics on market size, brands, products etc.
Frequency	Annual
Availability	General
Cost	On request
Comments	
Address	11-12 Bouverie Street, London EC4Y 8AH
Telephone	0171 583 2523
Fax	

535	M.A.C.E
Title	**Information Technology in UK Banks**
Coverage	A review of IT developments in UK banking with data on branches, IT budgets, IT trends, and the IT outlook. Based on research by the company.
Frequency	Annual
Availability	General
Cost	£195
Comments	
Address	Brenfield House, Bolney Road, Ansty, West Sussex RH17 5AW
Telephone	01444 459151
Fax	01444 454061

536	M.A.C.E.
Title	**Information Technology in UK Building Societies**
Coverage	A review of IT developments in UK building societies with data on branches, budgets, IT trends, and IT outlook. Based on research by the company.
Frequency	Annual
Availability	General
Cost	£195
Comments	
Address	Brenfield House, Bolney Road, Ansty, West Sussex RH17 5AW
Telephone	01444 459151
Fax	01444 454061

537	M.A.C.E.
Title	**Information Technology in Financial and Commodity Exchanges**
Coverage	A review of IT developments in financial and commodity exchanges with data on budgets, IT trends, and IT outlook. Based on research by the company.
Frequency	Annual
Availability	General
Cost	£195
Comments	
Address	Brenfield House, Bolney Road, Ansty, West Sussex RH17 5AW
Telephone	01444 459151
Fax	01444 454061

538	M.A.C.E.
Title	**Information Technology in the Insurance Industry**
Coverage	A review of IT developments in the insurance industry with data on budgets, IT trends, and IT outlook. Based on research by the company.
Frequency	Annual
Availability	General
Cost	£195
Comments	
Address	Brenfield House, Bolney Road, Ansty, West Sussex RH17 5AW
Telephone	01444 459151
Fax	01444 454061

539	M.A.C.E.
Title	**Information Technology in Other Financial Institutions**
Coverage	A review of IT developments in various financial institutions with data on budgets, IT trends, and IT outlook. Based on research by the company.
Frequency	Annual
Availability	General
Cost	£195
Comments	
Address	Brenfield House, Bolney Road, Ansty, West Sussex RH17 5AW
Telephone	01444 459151
Fax	01444 454061

540

MACHINE TOOL TECHNOLOGIES ASSOCIATION

Title   **UK CNC Machine Tool Survey**

Coverage   A survey of the purchasing patterns and purchasing intentions of manufacturing industry. Includes analysis by industry and by type of machine, plus a breakdown of sales by size of company. Based on original research by Benchmark Research with 879 sites participating in 1994.

Frequency   Annual

Availability   General

Cost   £250 for members, £750 to others

Comments   An executive summary of the report is available free to members and for £250 to others.

Address   62 Bayswater Road, London W2 3PS

Telephone   0171 402 6671

Fax   0171 724 7250

541

MACHINE TOOL TECHNOLOGIES ASSOCIATION

Title   **MTTA Statistical Report**

Coverage   Details of imports and exports by product type for the latest quarter, and compared to the corresponding quarter in the previous year. A brief commentary accompanies the data. Based on Central Government statistics.

Frequency   Quarterly

Availability   General

Cost   Free

Comments   Produced as a press release.

Address   62 Bayswater Road, London W2 3PS

Telephone   0171 402 6671

Fax   0171 724 7250

542

MACHINE TOOL TECHNOLOGIES ASSOCIATION

Title   **Machine Tool Statistics**

Coverage   Machine tool production, orders, imports, exports, population, prices, investment, and employment. Based mainly on Central Government sources plus some non-official data and data for a number of years is usually given. Some supporting text.

Frequency   Annual

Availability   General

Cost   £30

Comments

Address   62 Bayswater Road, London W2 3PS

Telephone   0171 402 6671

Fax   0171 724 7250

543

MACHINE TOOL TECHNOLOGIES ASSOCIATION

Title	**Basic Figures**
Coverage	Basic figures on production, sales, investment, imports, exports, and consumption over a ten-year period. Also information on the leading export markets and leading import sources plus the UK's share of total world production and exports. Based on a mixture of Central Government and non-official sources.
Frequency	Annual
Availability	General
Cost	Free
Comments	Produced in pocketbook format.
Address	62 Bayswater Road, London W2 3PS
Telephone	0171 402 6671
Fax	0171 724 7250

544

MAID

Title	**Maid Online**
Coverage	An online database service offering access to a wide range of market research reports, many of which have been included as separate entries in this directory. For example, reports from EIU, Datamonitor, Key Note, MAPS etc.
Frequency	Regular
Availability	General
Cost	£5,950
Comments	MAID also has databases covering company and news information.
Address	48 Leicester Square, London WC2H 7DB
Telephone	0171 930 6900
Fax	0171 930 6006

545

MANAGEMENT CONSULTANCIES ASSOCIATION

Title	**President's Statement and Annual Report**
Coverage	Includes five pages of statistical data with details of total turnover, numbers of clients, number of consultants employed, and a breakdown of turnover by service category. Based on a survey of members.
Frequency	Annual
Availability	General
Cost	Free
Comments	
Address	11 West Halkin Street, London SW1X 8JL
Telephone	0171 235 3897
Fax	0171 235 0825

546	MANAGEMENT CONSULTANCY
Title	**Surveys**
Coverage	Regular surveys of the management consultancy sector with surveys of particular types of consultants and specific work areas. Based on various sources and some research by the journal.
Frequency	Regular in a monthly journal
Availability	General
Cost	£45
Comments	
Address	VNU Business Publications, VNU House, 32-34 Broadwick Street, London W1A 2HG
Telephone	0171 316 9000
Fax	0171 316 9250

547	MANAGEMENT CONSULTANCY INFORMATION SERVICE
Title	**Management Consultancy Fee Rate Survey**
Coverage	The survey analyses fees charged by management consultants ranging in size from sole practitioners to major international practices. The results are analysed by seven different practice areas and by four sector groups, as well as geographical variations, analysis by size of consultancy, fees charged for different levels of consultant, recruitment charges, and terms of working. Based on original research.
Frequency	Annual
Availability	General
Cost	£25
Comments	A relatively new survey, first published in 1992.
Address	38 Blenheim Avenue, Gants Hill, Ilford, Essex IG2 6JQ
Telephone	0181 554 4695
Fax	0181 554 4695

548	MANPOWER PLC
Title	**Survey of Employment Prospects**
Coverage	Short-term forecasts of employment for specific sectors in manufacturing, services, and the public sector based on the stated intentions of over 2,000 companies and organisations. Data by region is included and a commentary accompanies the statistics.
Frequency	Quarterly
Availability	General
Cost	Free
Comments	
Address	International House, 66 Chiltern Street, London W1M 1PR
Telephone	0171 224 6688
Fax	0171 224 5267

MANUFACTURING CHEMIST

Title	**Aerosol Review**
Coverage	Listing of all aerosols filled in the UK and imported. Also lists all types of aerosols filled by company, brand name, type etc. Based on non-official sources.
Frequency	Annual and as a separate item from the journal
Availability	General
Cost	£24
Comments	
Address	Morgan Grampian Ltd, 30 Calderwood Street, London SE18 69H
Telephone	0171 855 7777
Fax	0171 316 3206

550

MAPS

Title	**Top Markets**
Coverage	A digest of statistics and commentary on the top 150 markets covered in the MAPS market research report series. Each market summary has data on value, trade, brands, advertising, and general trends.
Frequency	Annual
Availability	General
Cost	£350 (combined subscription with Market Forecasts - £550)
Comments	
Address	4 Crinan Street, London N1 9UE
Telephone	0171 278 2388
Fax	0171 833 2124

551

MAPS

Title	**Market Forecasts**
Coverage	Forecasts over a five-year period of trends in 150 markets covered in the MAPS market research report series.
Frequency	Annual
Availability	General
Cost	£350 (combined subscription with Top Markets - £550)
Comments	
Address	4 Crinan Street, London N1 9UE
Telephone	0171 278 2388
Fax	0171 833 2124

552 MAPS

Title	**Market Reports**
Coverage	Over 100 regular reports are published on UK consumer markets with data and analysis on market value, brands, market segments, consumers, advertising, companies, distribution, and forecasts. Based on various sources.
Frequency	Regular
Availability	General
Cost	On request
Comments	
Address	4 Crinan Street, London N1 9UE
Telephone	0171 278 2388
Fax	0171 833 2124

553 MARKET LOCATION LTD

Title	**Industry Analysis**
Coverage	Tables giving the distribution of industry by region and SIC classification. Based on Market Location's database of establishments.
Frequency	Regular
Availability	General
Cost	On request
Comments	
Address	1 Warwick Street, Leamington Spa CV32 5LW
Telephone	01926 450388
Fax	01926 450592

554 MARKET RESEARCH SCOTLAND

Title	**Scottish Consumer Omnibus**
Coverage	An omnibus survey based around a sample of 1,000 consumers in Scotland.
Frequency	Monthly
Availability	General
Cost	On application
Comments	
Address	9 Park Quadrant, Glasgow G3 6BS
Telephone	0141 332 5751
Fax	0141 332 3035

555	MARKETING STRATEGIES FOR INDUSTRY (UK) LTD
Title	**MSI Data Reports/MSI Data Briefs**
Coverage	MSI publishes over a 100 reports per year on UK consumer and industrial sectors and many of these are updated on a regular basis. Based primarily on research by the company supported by data from official non-official sources.
Frequency	Regular
Availability	General
Cost	£236 upwards, depending on type of report
Comments	
Address	Viscount House, Riverside Business Park, River Lane, Saltney, Chester CH4 8QY
Telephone	01244 681424
Fax	01244 681457

556	MARKETING WEEK
Title	**Salary Survey**
Coverage	Based on a survey of subscribers to Marketing Week, this annual salary survey examines pay and conditions for 11 marketing job titles.
Frequency	Annual
Availability	General
Cost	£80.85 + VAT
Comments	
Address	50 Poland Street, London W1V 4AX
Telephone	0171 439 9381
Fax	0171 439 9669

557	MARKETLINE
Title	**UK Marketline CD-ROM**
Coverage	Reports on over 700 industrial, business-to-business, and consumer sectors in the UK with data, analysis, and commentary. All reports are written to the same structure and include an analysis of published data as well as original research based on industry interviews. Many of the reports are regularly updated.
Frequency	Annual
Availability	General
Cost	£995
Comments	Individual reports are also available in hard copy format. USA Marketline and European Marketline are also available.
Address	16 Connaught Street, London W2 2AF
Telephone	0171 624 2200
Fax	0171 316 0655

558 MARKETPOWER LTD

Title	**Consumer Express**
Coverage	A quarterly omnibus survey of 750 consumers who frequently eat out from the age of 12 upwards. Issues covered include types of establishments visited, brands, frequency of eating out, amount spent, methods of payments, regional differences, attitudes to menu items etc.
Frequency	Quarterly
Availability	General
Cost	On request
Comments	Also publishes various one-off and occasional reports on the catering market.
Address	84 Uxbridge Road, London W13 8RA
Telephone	0181 840 5252
Fax	0181 840 6173

559 MARKETPOWER LTD

Title	**Quarterly Catering Barometer**
Coverage	A survey of meals served by caterers in each of nine sectors: hotels, restaurants, public houses, cafes, take-aways, leisure, staff catering, health care, education. Also includes a Balance of Confidence indicator and a special feature in each issue.
Frequency	Quarterly
Availability	General
Cost	£300 + VAT
Comments	Also publishes various one-off and occasional reports on the catering market.
Address	84 Uxbridge Road, London W13 8RA
Telephone	0181 840 5252
Fax	0181 840 6173

560	MARKETPOWER LTD
Title	**Catering Industry Population File**
Coverage	A study of the structure of the catering industry giving number of outlets, value of caterers' food purchases, outlet sizes, number of meals served, sector buying concentration, and a regional analysis. Eleven catering sectors are covered in detail with historical trends over a ten-year period. Based on Marketpower research, non-official sources, and some official statistics.
Frequency	Annual
Availability	General
Cost	£950
Comments	A disc containing key data can also be supplied with the report for an additional £25. Various other one-off and occasional reports on the catering market are also published.
Address	84 Uxbridge Road, London W13 8RA
Telephone	0181 840 5252
Fax	0181 840 6173

561	MARKETPOWER LTD
Title	**Catering Forecasts**
Coverage	Short-term forecasts for the UK catering industry based on research carried out amongst 700 caterers with trends given sector-by-sector.
Frequency	Annual
Availability	General
Cost	£395 + VAT
Comments	Also publishes various one-off and occasional reports on the catering market.
Address	84 Uxbridge Road, London W13 8RA
Telephone	0181 840 5252
Fax	0181 840 6173

562	MARKETPOWER LTD
Title	**Catering Express**
Coverage	A quarterly omnibus survey providing a detailed analysis of the UK catering market, including a separate analysis of ten sub-sectors of the market. Based on a sample of 750 caterers.
Frequency	Quarterly
Availability	General
Cost	On application
Comments	Also publishes various one-off and occasional reports on the catering market.
Address	84 Uxbridge Road, London W13 8RA
Telephone	0181 840 5252
Fax	0181 840 6173

563 MARKINTEL

Title	**Markintel Online**
Coverage	An online database with various files from market research publishers which are regularly updated. Included on the database are reports from Economist Intelligence Unit, Datamonitor, Euromonitor, Key Note, Leatherhead Food Research, Marketline, MSI, Verdict Research (see other entries).
Frequency	Continuous
Availability	General
Cost	On request
Comments	
Address	The Investext Group, Thomson Financial Services Ltd, 11 New Fetter Lane, London EC4A 1JN
Telephone	0171 815 38600
Fax	0171 353 2951

564 MARTIN-HAMBLIN RESEARCH

Title	**Food Attitude Monitor**
Coverage	A survey of the attitudes of around 1,500 housewives to food with an analysis of purchasing, behaviour, awareness etc. Based on research by the company.
Frequency	Annual
Availability	General
Cost	£695
Comments	
Address	Mulberry House, 36 Smith Square, London SW1P 3HL
Telephone	0171 222 8181
Fax	0171 222 3100

565 MARTIN-HAMBLIN RESEARCH

Title	**Sports Sponsorship Awareness**
Coverage	A survey of the awareness of sports sponsorship with an analysis of brands, products etc. Based on original research by the company.
Frequency	Annual
Availability	General
Cost	£120
Comments	
Address	Mulberry House, 36 Smith Square, London SW1P 3HL
Telephone	0171 222 8181
Fax	0171 222 3100

566

MASTER FOODS

Title **Wet Cooking Sauces Market Report**

Coverage A review of the market based on market research sources and some commissioned research. Includes a general review of the market plus sections on specific sauces – Italian, Indian, Oriental, Mexican, traditional and other sauces. Figures for the last five years are usually given. Further information on the leading brands, manufacturers, TV advertising, trade sectors, merchandising, and demographics.

Frequency Annual

Availability General

Cost Free

Comments

Address Hansa Road, Kings Lynn, Norfolk PE30 4JE

Telephone 01553 692222

Fax 01553 697920

567

McCARTHY INFORMATION LTD

Title **FT Stats Fiche**

Coverage Statistics from the Financial Times produced on fiche and including data on unit trusts, insurances, overseas and money funds, share prices, foreign exchanges, money markets, FT indices, world value of the £ etc.

Frequency Twice a week

Availability General

Cost £420, £795 combined subscription with Overseas Company fiche noted below

Comments Also produces an Overseas Company fiche.

Address Manor House, Ash Walk, Warminster, Wiltshire BA12 8PY

Telephone 01985 215151

Fax 01985 217479

568

MDS TRANSMODAL

Title **Overseas Trade Data**

Coverage Detailed product information for imports and exports plus details of trading partners and port of entry and exit. Appointed as an official agent of HM Customs and Excise.

Frequency Monthly

Availability General

Cost Depends on amount of information required

Comments Available in various machine readable formats.

Address 5-6 Hunters Walk, Canal Street, Chester CH1 4EB

Telephone 01244 348391

Fax 01244 348471

569

MEAT TRADES JOURNAL

Title | **Market Prices**

Coverage Wholesale and retail prices for different types of meat and livestock and the data usually refers to prices at the end of the previous week.

Frequency Weekly in a weekly journal

Availability General

Cost £45

Comments

Address EMAP Maclaren, Maclaren House, 19 Scarbrook Road, Croydon CR9 1QH

Telephone 0181 277 5222

Fax 0181 277 5230

570

MERCER, WILLIAM M

Title | **Professional Compliance Staff – Survey of Pay and Benefits**

Coverage A salary and benefits survey of professional compliance staff broken down by job type and grade.

Frequency Annual

Availability General

Cost £375, £275 for participants

Comments Also specialist surveys available to participants only.

Address Dexter House, 2 Royal Mint Court, London EC3N 4NA

Telephone 0171 488 4949

Fax 0171 480 6132

571

MERCER, WILLIAM M

Title | **City Personnel Group Salary and Benefits Survey**

Coverage A salary survey covering specialists in London banks based on a sample of personnel in the city.

Frequency Twice per annum

Availability General

Cost £400, £200 to participants

Comments Also specialist surveys available to participants only.

Address Dexter House, 2 Royal Mint Court, London EC3N 4WA

Telephone 0171 488 4949

Fax 0171 480 6132

572 MERCER, WILLIAM M

Title	**Pensions Scheme Managers and Administrators Survey**
Coverage	A salary and benefits survey of pension scheme managers and related staff based on over 540 specific jobs.
Frequency	Annual
Availability	General
Cost	£375, £275 for participants
Comments	Also specialist surveys available to participants only.
Address	Dexter House, 2 Royal Mint Court, London EC3N 4WA
Telephone	0171 488 4949
Fax	0171 480 6132

573 METAL BULLETIN BOOKS LTD

Title	**Metal Bulletin's Prices and Data**
Coverage	Prices of various metals, with latest price figures and trends over the recent period. Based on various sources.
Frequency	Annual
Availability	General
Cost	On request
Comments	
Address	Park House, Park Terrace, Worcester Park, Surrey KT4 7HY
Telephone	0171 827 9977
Fax	0171 337 8943

574 METAL PACKAGING MANUFACTURERS' ASSOCIATION

Title	**Annual Report**
Coverage	Includes a review of the year with statistics on sales of packaging materials, sales by end-user sector, sales by type of packaging, exports, and employees. Based mainly on data collected by the association.
Frequency	Annual
Availability	General
Cost	Free
Comments	
Address	19 Elmshott Lane, Cippenham, SL1 SL1 5QS
Telephone	01628 605203
Fax	01628 665597

575

METALWORKING PRODUCTION

Title **Survey of Machine Tools and Production Equipment**

Coverage Trends in sales and use of the various types of machine tools with a detailed breakdown by industrial sector and a regional analysis. Based on returns from over 4,000 companies. A detailed commentary introduces the statistics.

Frequency Every five years published separately from the journal

Availability General

Cost On request

Comments

Address Morgan Grampian, 30 Calderwood Street, Woolwich, London SE18 6QH

Telephone 0181 855 7777

Fax 0181 855 7913

576

MICHAEL LAURIE

Title **The ML-CIG Property Index**

Coverage An annual review of property investment performance broken down by types of property and location.

Frequency Annual

Availability General

Cost On request

Comments

Address Fitzroy House, 18-20 Grafton Street, London W1X 4DD

Telephone 0171 493 7050

Fax 0171 491 8998

577

MIL MOTORING RESEARCH

Title **MIL Motoring Telephone Omnibus**

Coverage An omnibus survey of a national representative sample of motorists in Great Britain. Based on a sample of 500 and the results include a wide range of motoring demographics plus consumer results.

Frequency Weekly

Availability General

Cost On application

Comments

Address 1-2 Berners Street, London W1P 3AG

Telephone 0171 612 0265

Fax 0171 612 0263

578	MILLS, ROWENA & ASSOCIATES LTD
Title	**Statistical and Economic Review of UK Packaging Industries**
Coverage	A detailed commentary plus a statistical analysis of the industry covering the last five years with data on production, imports, exports, industrial structure, consumption, prices. Also forecasts for the next few years. Based on official statistics and various non-official sources.
Frequency	Regular
Availability	General
Cost	£495 plus p+p
Comments	Published in association with Packaging Week.
Address	Peart Hall, Spaxton, Bridgewater, Somerset TA5 1DA
Telephone	01278 671343
Fax	01278 671209

579	MILPRO
Title	**Pharmaceutical Development Service**
Coverage	A monthly omnibus survey of 200 NHS general practitioners with data on prescribing trends for various products and therapeutic groups. Analysis available by regional health authority, practice size, date of qualification, practice type etc.
Frequency	Monthly
Availability	General
Cost	On request
Comments	
Address	NOP Research Group, Evelyn House, 62 Oxford Street, London W1N 9LD
Telephone	0171 612 0153
Fax	0171 612 0159

580	MINTEL
Title	**Leisure Subscription**
Coverage	A series of regular reports on the UK leisure sector with basic data updated regularly and analytical articles updated every few years.
Frequency	Regular
Availability	General
Cost	On request
Comments	Special reports, services covering specific markets, ad-hoc reports and analyses are also available. Mintel is available online and via CD-ROM.
Address	
Telephone	0171 606 6000
Fax	0171 606 5932

581	MINTEL
Title	**Finance Subscription**
Coverage	A series of regular reports on the UK financial services sector with basic data updated regularly and analytical articles updated every few years.
Frequency	Regular
Availability	General
Cost	On request
Comments	Special reports, services covering specific markets, ad-hoc reports and analyses are also available. Mintel is available online and via CD-ROM.
Address	18-19 Long Lane, London EC1A 9HE
Telephone	0171 606 6000
Fax	0171 606 5932

582	MINTEL
Title	**Retailing Subscription**
Coverage	A series of regular reports on the UK retailing sector with basic retailing data updated regularly and specific reports updated every few years.
Frequency	Regular
Availability	General
Cost	On request
Comments	Special reports, services covering specific markets, ad-hoc reports and analyses are also available. Mintel is available online and via CD-ROM.
Address	18-19 Long Lane, London EC1A 9HE
Telephone	0171 606 6000
Fax	0171 606 5932

583	MINTEL
Title	**MINTEL Monthly Digest**
Coverage	A range of reports in each monthly issue with commentary and statistics on various consumer products and services. Surveys are usually updated every few years.
Frequency	Monthly
Availability	General
Cost	On request
Comments	Special reports, services covering specific markets, ad-hoc reports and analyses are also available. Mintel reports are available online and via CD-ROM.
Address	18-19 Long Lane, London EC1A 9HE
Telephone	0171 606 6000
Fax	0171 606 5932

MONEYFACTS PUBLICATIONS

Title **Business Money Figures**

Coverage A range of economic and monetary statistics including retail prices, annual inflation rates, average earnings, base rates, tax and price index, finance house base rates, commercial rents, employment statistics, and house price data from the Halifax. Based on various official and non-official sources.

Frequency Regular

Availability General

Cost £59.80, £14.95 per issue

Comments

Address Laundry Lake, North Walsham, Norfolk NR28 0BD

Telephone 01692 500765

Fax 01692 500865

585

MONKS PARTNERSHIP

Title **Management Remuneration in UK**

Coverage Pay and benefits of directors and managers in various industries and sectors. Also details of incentives, company cars. Based on the company's own research.

Frequency Twice per annum

Availability General

Cost £300

Comments Usually published in March and October. Other reports available on remuneration in specific sectors.

Address The Mill House, Wendens Ambo, Saffron Walden CB11 4JX

Telephone 01799 54222

Fax 01799 541805

586

MONKS PARTNERSHIP

Title **Board Earnings UK**

Coverage Published in two volumes with the first covering earnings in UK quoted companies. The second has details of company incentive agreements. Based on a survey of around 1,200 companies.

Frequency Annual

Availability General

Cost £125 for each volume, or £225 combined

Comments Other reports available on remuneration in specific sectors.

Address The Mill House, Wendens Ambo, Saffron Walden CB11 4JX

Telephone 01799 54222

Fax 01799 541805

587	MONKS PARTNERSHIP
Title	**Board Earnings in FTSE 100 Companies**
Coverage	A survey of salary trends based on an analysis of company annual reports and other published data.
Frequency	Annual
Availability	General
Cost	£215
Comments	Other reports available on remuneration in specific sectors.
Address	The Mill House, Wendens Ambo, Saffron Walden CB11 4JX
Telephone	01799 54222
Fax	01799 541805

588	MONKS PARTNERSHIP
Title	**Survey of Non-Executive Director Practices and Fees**
Coverage	A survey of non-executive director salaries and benefits, and other issues, based on a survey by the company.
Frequency	Annual
Availability	Participants
Cost	£100
Comments	Other reports available on remuneration in specific sectors.
Address	The Mill House, Wendens Ambo, Saffron Walden CB11 4JX
Telephone	01799 54222
Fax	01799 541805

589	MONKS PARTNERSHIP
Title	**Board and Senior Management Remuneration in Smaller Companies**
Coverage	Pay and benefits of managers and board members in a sample of smaller companies. Based on original research by the company.
Frequency	Regular
Availability	General
Cost	£75
Comments	Other reports available on remuneration in specific sectors.
Address	The Mill House, Wendens Ambo, Saffron Walden CB11 4JX
Telephone	01799 54222
Fax	01799 541805

590 MONKS PARTNERSHIP

Title	**UK Company Car Policy**
Coverage	Details of policies, benefits, changes based on a survey by the company.
Frequency	Annual
Availability	General
Cost	£150
Comments	Other reports available on remuneration in specific sectors.
Address	The Mill House, Wendens Ambo, Saffron Walden CB11 4JX
Telephone	01799 54222
Fax	01799 541805

591 MORI

Title	**GB Omnibus**
Coverage	Face-to-face omnibus survey of 2,000 adults in the UK. Detailed analysis of results covering purchasing trends, consumer attitudes, consumer awareness etc.
Frequency	Fortnightly
Availability	General
Cost	On application
Comments	Various other research services available.
Address	95 Southwark Street, London SE1 0HX
Telephone	0171 928 5955
Fax	0171 955 0067

592 MORTGAGE FINANCE GAZETTE

Title	**Loans Figures and Figures/Indicators**
Coverage	Details of the number of mortgage loans by type of loan and other indicators of the housing market. Based on various sources.
Frequency	Monthly in a monthly journal
Availability	General
Cost	£45.50
Comments	Incorporates the previously published Building Societies Gazette.
Address	Francy & Co Ltd, South Quay Place, 183 Marsh Wall, London E14 9FS
Telephone	0171 538 5386
Fax	0171 538 8624

593   MOTOR CYCLE ASSOCIATION OF GREAT BRITAIN

Title	**Annual Report**
Coverage	The annual report contains some basic statistics on the motor cycle industry.
Frequency	Annual
Availability	General
Cost	On request
Comments	
Address	Starley House, Eaton Road, Coventry CV1 2FH
Telephone	01203 227427
Fax	01203 229175

594   MOTOR CYCLE INDUSTRY ASSOCIATION

Title	**In a Nutshell**
Coverage	Summary statistics on production, imports, exports, vehicles in use, and general sales. Based on a combination of the Association's own data and Central Government statistics.
Frequency	Annual
Availability	General
Cost	On application
Comments	
Address	Starley House, Eaton Road, Coventry CV1 2FH
Telephone	01203 227427
Fax	01203 229175

595   MOTOR CYCLE INDUSTRY ASSOCIATION

Title	**Statistical Booklet**
Coverage	A monthly review of registrations, imports, and exports with breakdowns by motor cycle type, model, and geographical area.
Frequency	Monthly
Availability	Members and bona-fide researchers
Cost	Free to members
Comments	
Address	Starley House, Eaton Road, Coventry CV1 2FH
Telephone	01203 227427
Fax	01203 229175

MOTOR TRANSPORT

Title	**199– Road Transport Market Survey**
Coverage	A survey of companies, vehicles, haulage trends in the road transport sector carried out for Motor Transport by NOP. The survey also includes comparative data for previous years.
Frequency	Annual in a weekly journal
Availability	General
Cost	£70
Comments	
Address	Reed Business Publishing, The Quadrant, Sutton, Surrey SM2 5AS
Telephone	0181 652 3500
Fax	0181 652 8957

MOTOR TRANSPORT

Title	**Market Intelligence**
Coverage	Summary statistics and news covering vehicles and road transport with data collected from various sources.
Frequency	Weekly in a weekly journal
Availability	General
Cost	£70
Comments	
Address	Reed Business Publishing, The Quadrant, Sutton, Surrey SM2 5AS
Telephone	0181 652 3500
Fax	0181 652 8957

MSL INTERNATIONAL

Title	**Survey of the Remuneration of Corporate Treasurers**
Coverage	A survey of average salaries for corporate treasurers analysed by turnover group, region, type of work etc. Based on a survey by the company.
Frequency	Annual
Availability	General
Cost	£20
Comments	
Address	32 Aybrook Street, London W1M 3JL
Telephone	0171 487 3000
Fax	

	MUSHROOM GROWERS ASSOCIATION
599	
Title	**Industry Survey**
Coverage	Production and manpower figures for the sector plus a cost analysis, methods of growing, and industry yield figures. Based on a survey of members, and accompanied by a commentary.
Frequency	Annual
Availability	Members
Cost	
Comments	
Address	Agriculture House, Knightsbridge, London SW1X 7NJ
Telephone	0171 806 6888
Fax	0171 806 6558

	MUSIC PUBLISHERS ASSOCIATION LTD
600	
Title	**Summary of Printed Music Sales**
Coverage	UK and overseas sales with data for the latest year and the previous year. Based on a survey by the Association with a small amount of supporting text. Published four to five months after the end of the year to which it relates.
Frequency	Bi-annual
Availability	General
Cost	Free
Comments	
Address	18-21 York Buildings, London WC2N 6JU
Telephone	0171 839 7779
Fax	0171 839 7776

	NATIONAL ASSOCIATION OF ESTATE AGENTS
601	
Title	**Market Trends**
Coverage	A review of trends in the housing market based on a survey of a sample of members, plus data from other sources.
Frequency	Monthly
Availability	General
Cost	On request
Comments	
Address	Arbon House, 21 Jury Street, Warwick CV34 4EH
Telephone	01926 496800
Fax	01926 403958

602 NATIONAL ASSOCIATION OF PENSION FUNDS LTD

Title **Annual Survey of Occupational Pension Schemes**

Coverage A survey of various schemes with data on income, expenditure, size of fund, the nature of the schemes, benefits provided. The data is collected via a postal survey to all members of the association. A supporting commentary is included with the statistics.

Frequency Annual

Availability General

Cost £48 to members, £96 to others

Comments

Address 12-18 Grosvenor Gardens, London SW1W 0DH

Telephone 0171 730 0588

Fax 0171 730 2595

603 NATIONAL CAVITY INSULATION ASSOCIATION

Title **Annual Statistics**

Coverage Details of trends in the cavity insulation sector based on a survey of members.

Frequency Annual

Availability Members

Cost

Comments

Address PO Box 12, Haslemere, Surrey GU27 3AN

Telephone 01428 654011

Fax 01428 651401

604 NATIONAL COMPUTING CENTRE LTD (NCC)

Title **Salaries and Staff Issues in Computing**

Coverage A survey of salaries and benefits for 34 IT job titles based on questionnaires sent to 12,000 individuals in 600 organisations.

Frequency Annual

Availability General

Cost On application

Comments Produced in association with Computer Weekly.

Address Oxford House, Oxford Road, Manchester M1 7ED

Telephone 0161 228 6333

Fax 0161 242 2345

605

NATIONAL COUNCIL OF BUILDING MATERIAL PRODUCERS

Title	**BMP Forecasts**
Coverage	Forecasts three years ahead for housing starts and completions, other new work and repair, maintenance and improvement. Based on BMP's own forecasts with a large amount of supporting commentary.
Frequency	3 issues per year
Availability	General
Cost	£250
Comments	
Address	26 Store Street, London WC1E 7BT
Telephone	0171 323 3770
Fax	0171 323 0307

606

NATIONAL COUNCIL OF BUILDING MATERIAL PRODUCERS

Title	**BMP Statistical Bulletin**
Coverage	Covers housebuilding starts and completions, renovations, prices, mortgages, value of new orders and output, capital expenditure, trade, and building materials. Based on a combination of Central Government data and non-official sources.
Frequency	Monthly
Availability	General
Cost	£250
Comments	
Address	26 Store Street, London WC1E 7BT
Telephone	0171 323 3770
Fax	0171 323 0307

607

NATIONAL HOUSE BUILDING COUNCIL

Title	**Private House Building Statistics**
Coverage	Covers dwelling starts and completions, prices, market share of timber frame, first time buyers' ability to buy, and some regional trends. Largely based on the Council's own survey plus some Central Government data. Usually published two to three weeks after the quarter to which it relates, and some historical data is included.
Frequency	Quarterly
Availability	General
Cost	On request
Comments	
Address	Chiltern Avenue, Amersham, Buckinghamshire HP6 5AP
Telephone	01494 434477
Fax	01494 434477

608

NATIONAL INSTITUTE OF ECONOMIC AND SOCIAL RESEARCH (NIESR)

Title	**National Institute Economic Review**
Coverage	General analysis of the UK and world economy with forecasts usually up to 18 months ahead. Special articles on relevant topics. A separate statistical section is included in each issue along with some tables in the text.
Frequency	Quarterly
Availability	General
Cost	£80
Comments	Macroeconomic analysis package available in machine-readable format.
Address	2 Dean Trench Street, Smith Square, London SW1P 3HE
Telephone	0171 222 7665
Fax	0171 222 1435

609

NATIONAL ON-LINE MANPOWER INFORMATION SYSTEM (NOMIS)

Title	**NOMIS**
Coverage	A database of approximately 19 billion monthly, quarterly, annual, and triennial population and labour statistics and, with the appropriate software, users can access the data, manipulate it, and produce graphs, charts etc. Based on data supplied by Central Government departments.
Frequency	Regular
Availability	A 'Public Domain' file is available generally but the complete file is only available to authorised users.
Cost	On request
Comments	
Address	Unit 3, Mountjoy Research Centre, Durham University, Durham DH1 3SW
Telephone	0191 374 2468
Fax	0191 374 3741

610 NATIONAL READERSHIP SURVEY

Title	**National Readership Survey**
Coverage	Statistics on the readership of national newspapers and various consumer magazines based on a stratified random sample of over 28,000 individuals. Results are published a few months after the survey. Some commentary supports the text.
Frequency	Annual
Availability	General
Cost	On request
Comments	
Address	Garden Studios, 11-15 Betterton Street, Covent Garden, London WC2H 9BP
Telephone	0171 379 0344
Fax	0171 240 4399

611 NATIONAL WESTMINSTER BANK/SMALL BUSINESS RESEARCH TRUST

Title	**Quarterly Survey of Small Business in Britain**
Coverage	A survey of small businesses in the UK, 95% of which employ less than 50 people. Information on turnover, employment, sales, exports, and business problems plus features on the sector.
Frequency	Quarterly
Availability	General
Cost	On request
Comments	
Address	UK Branch Business, 41 Lothbury, London EC2P 2BP
Telephone	0171 726 1119
Fax	

612 NATIONWIDE BUILDING SOCIETY

Title	**Housing Finance Review**
Coverage	A review of the UK housing market with commentary and statistics on house prices, types of houses purchased, mortgage lending, regional house prices, and house prices by type of house. Based on data collected and analysed by the building society.
Frequency	Quarterly
Availability	General
Cost	Free
Comments	Nationwide also has summary sheets of house price data available back to 1952 for national data and back to 1973 for regional data. A guide to the house price methodology used by Nationwide is available free from the address below.
Address	Nationwide House, Pipers Way, Swindon SN38 1NW
Telephone	01793 455198
Fax	01793 455903

613 NATIONWIDE BUILDING SOCIETY

Title House Price Bulletin

Coverage The bulletin monitors the changes in national house prices, based on data collected and analysed by the building society.

Frequency Monthly

Availability General

Cost Free

Comments Nationwide also has summary sheets of house price data available back to 1952 for national data and 1973 for regional data. A guide to the house price methodology used by Nationwide is available free from the address below.

Address Nationwide House, Pipers Way, Swindon SN38 1NW

Telephone 01793 455198

Fax 01793 455903

614 NDL INTERNATIONAL

Title NDL Lifestyle Data

Coverage The NDL database contains information on over 16 million consumers and the original sources used include the 1991 census, postcode address file, and electoral roll data.

Frequency Continuous

Availability General

Cost On application, and depending on the range and nature of the information required

Comments

Address Port House, Plantation Wharf, London SW1 3TY

Telephone 0171 738 0522

Fax 0171 738 0415

615 NESTLÉ (UK) LTD

Title Hot Beverages Report

Coverage A review of the hot beverages market with sections on tea, coffee, chocolate, and food drinks. Includes details of market value, brands, retailing, and new developments.

Frequency Annual

Availability General

Cost Free

Comments

Address St Georges House, Park Lane, Croydon CR9 1NR

Telephone 0181 686 3333

Fax 0181 686 6072

616

NIELSEN

Title **Off-Licence Liquor Trade Data**

Coverage A statistics and analysis service with reports and other packages covering retail sales of alcoholic drinks. Detailed product analysis available.

Frequency Regular

Availability General

Cost On request

Comments

Address Nielsen House, Headington, Oxford OX3 9RX

Telephone 01865 742742

Fax 01865 742222

617

NIELSEN

Title **The Nielsen Media-Line**

Coverage A telephone request service that can provide facts about products sold throughout Great Britain. Covers products in the grocery, health and beauty, confectionery, off-licence, toys sectors and has access to data from Homescan, Nielsen's consumer panel (see previous entry).

Frequency Continuous

Availability General

Cost Varies according to the information required

Comments The service aims to provide a report within 48 hours of receiving a request.

Address Nielsen House, Headington, Oxford OX3 9RX

Telephone 01865 742742

Fax 01865 742222

618

NIELSEN

Title **Toys Industry Data**

Coverage A statistical and analysis service with reports and other packages covering retail sales of toys. Detailed product analysis available.

Frequency Regular

Availability General

Cost On request

Comments

Address Nielsen House, Headington, Oxford OX3 9RX

Telephone 01865 742742

Fax 01865 742222

619	NIELSEN
Title	**Health and Beauty Industry Data**
Coverage	A statistics and analysis service providing reports and other packages covering sales of toiletries and medicines through grocers, chemists, and drugstores. Detailed product analysis available.
Frequency	Regular
Availability	General
Cost	On request
Comments	
Address	Nielsen House, Headington, Oxford OX3 9RX
Telephone	01865 742742
Fax	01865 742222

620	NIELSEN
Title	**Grocery Industry Market Development Report**
Coverage	A review of trends in the grocery market plus a detailed statistical analysis of the sector. Based on Nielsen's own research.
Frequency	Annual
Availability	General
Cost	£750
Comments	Various other reports on the retail sector are available.
Address	Nielsen House, Headington, Oxford OX3 9RX
Telephone	01865 742742
Fax	01865 742742

621	NIELSEN
Title	**Grocery Industry**
Coverage	Information and statistics on the grocery trade with details of shop numbers and turnover trends by type of outlet, region. Based on Nielsen's own research.
Frequency	Annual
Availability	General
Cost	£750
Comments	Various other reports on the retail sector are available.
Address	Nielsen House, Headington, Oxford OX3 9RX
Telephone	01865 742742
Fax	01865 742222

622   NIELSEN

Title	**Homescan**
Coverage	A consumer panel measuring in-home purchasing from a sample of 10,000 homes in Great Britain and 450 in Northern Ireland. Over 700 product categories are covered and demographic analysis is available for many products and brands.
Frequency	Continuous
Availability	General
Cost	On application
Comments	
Address	Nielsen House, Headington, Oxford OX3 9RX
Telephone	01865 742742
Fax	01865 742222

623   NIELSEN

Title	**Confectionery Industry Data**
Coverage	A statistics and analysis service providing reports and other packages covering sales of confectionery via various retail channels. Detailed product analysis is available.
Frequency	Regular
Availability	General
Cost	On request
Comments	
Address	Nielsen House, Headington, Oxford OX3 9RX
Telephone	01865 742742
Fax	01865 742222

624   NIKKO BANK (UK) PLC

Title	**UK Quarterly Outlook**
Coverage	A review of economic trends and forecasts for the key economic indicators in the UK.
Frequency	Quarterly
Availability	General
Cost	On application
Comments	
Address	17 Godliman Street, London EC4V 5BD
Telephone	0171 528 7070
Fax	0171 528 7077

625 NOP CONSUMER MARKET RESEARCH

Title	**Alcoholic Drinks Survey**
Coverage	The drinking habits of a sample of around 2,000 adults analysed by social class, age, sex, TV area. Also analysis of brand awareness, sources of purchases, frequency of drinking etc. Based on a sample of adults taken from the electoral register.
Frequency	Annual
Availability	General
Cost	£12,000, extracts and specific sections also available
Comments	
Address	Tower House, Southampton Street, London WC2E 7HN
Telephone	0171 612 0444
Fax	0171 612 0447

626 NOP CONSUMER MARKET RESEARCH

Title	**Random Omnibus Survey**
Coverage	A weekly omnibus survey covering 2,000 adults and based around face-to-face in-home interviews. Demographic and lifestyle analysis plus details of purchasing trends, consumer habits etc.
Frequency	Weekly
Availability	General
Cost	On application
Comments	
Address	Tower House, Southampton Street, London WC2E 7HN
Telephone	0171 612 0100
Fax	0171 612 0547

627 NOP CONSUMER MARKET RESEARCH

Title	**Telebus**
Coverage	A weekly omnibus survey of 1,000 adults based on telephone interviews. The data analysis follows the same breakdown as the Random Omnibus Survey (see previous entry).
Frequency	Weekly
Availability	General
Cost	On application
Comments	
Address	Tower House, Southampton Street, London WC2E 7HN
Telephone	0171 612 0100
Fax	0171 612 0547

628

NOP CORPORATE AND FINANCIAL

Title	**Office Equipment Dealer Omnibus**
Coverage	A survey of 300 office equipment dealers covering products such as copiers, computers, telecommunications equipment, office furniture and other office supplies.
Frequency	Regular
Availability	General
Cost	On application
Comments	
Address	1-2 Berners Street, London W1P 3AG
Telephone	0171 612 0181
Fax	0171 612 0397

629

NOP CORPORATE AND FINANCIAL

Title	**National Architects' Survey**
Coverage	A survey of a sample of architects with results covering journal readership, information sources used, etc.
Frequency	Six issues per year
Availability	General
Cost	On application
Comments	
Address	1-2 Berners Street, London W1P 3AG
Telephone	0171 612 0181
Fax	0171 612 0222

630

NOP CORPORATE AND FINANCIAL

Title	**NOP Financial Research Survey (FRS)**
Coverage	An omnibus survey monitoring trends in the personal finance sector based on a regular sample of 2,000 people. Analysis of customer bases, products, and cross holdings.
Frequency	32 surveys per year
Availability	General
Cost	On application
Comments	
Address	1-2 Berners Street, London W1P 3AG
Telephone	0171 612 0181
Fax	0171 612 0397

NOP CORPORATE AND FINANCIAL

Title	**New Business Start Up Omnibus**
Coverage	A syndicated quarterly survey of 1,000 new business start-ups. Concentrates on the financial issues in running a business.
Frequency	Quarterly
Availability	Participants
Cost	On application
Comments	
Address	1-2 Berners Street, London W1P 3AG
Telephone	0171 612 0181
Fax	0171 612 0397

632

NTC PUBLICATIONS LTD

Title	**Insurance Pocket Book**
Coverage	Basic data on the insurance sector including an overview and detailed sections on life insurance, general insurance, the London Insurance Market, corporate risk management, specialised insurance carriers and the international insurance market.
Frequency	Regular
Availability	General
Cost	£32
Comments	Published in association with Tillinghast, a Towers Perrin company.
Address	PO Box 69, Henley-on-Thames, Oxfordshire RG9 1EJ
Telephone	01491 411000
Fax	01491 571188

633

NTC PUBLICATIONS LTD

Title	**Geodemographic Pocket Book**
Coverage	A profile of Britain's towns, counties, products, and consumer spending patterns based primarily on data collected by CACI (see other entry).
Frequency	Annual
Availability	General
Cost	£32
Comments	Published in association with CACI.
Address	PO Box 69, Henley-on-Thames, Oxfordshire RG9 1GB
Telephone	01491 411000
Fax	01491 571188

	NTC PUBLICATIONS LTD
634	
Title	**The Drink Forecast**
Coverage	Data, analysis, and forecasts for the beer, wine, cider, spirits, and soft drinks markets of the UK. Based on a range of sources.
Frequency	Quarterly
Availability	General
Cost	£695
Comments	
Address	PO Box 69, Henley-on-Thames, Oxfordshire RG9 1EJ
Telephone	01491 411000
Fax	01491 571188

	NTC PUBLICATIONS LTD
635	
Title	**The Food Forecast**
Coverage	Information, analysis, and forecasts for the food markets of the UK. Analysis and commentary accompanies the data.
Frequency	Quarterly
Availability	General
Cost	£595
Comments	
Address	PO Box 69, Henley-on-Thames, Oxfordshire RG9 1EJ
Telephone	01491 411000
Fax	01491 571188

	NTC PUBLICATIONS LTD
636	
Title	**The Report on Business**
Coverage	Based on a monthly opinion survey of UK purchasing managers, it provides a series of monthly economic indicators of the health of the UK economy and industry.
Frequency	Monthly
Availability	General
Cost	£175, fax service available for £395
Comments	Published in association with the Chartered Institute of Purchasing and Supply whose members are surveyed every month.
Address	PO Box 69, Henley-on-Thames, Oxfordshire RG9 1EJ
Telephone	01491 411000
Fax	01491 571188

637

NTC PUBLICATIONS LTD

Title	**Pensions Pocket Book**
Coverage	Statistics on pension schemes, the legal background, and current pension issues.
Frequency	Regular
Availability	General
Cost	£17.50
Comments	Published in association with Bacon & Woodrow.
Address	PO Box 69, Henley-on-Thames, Oxfordshire RG9 1EJ
Telephone	01491 411000
Fax	01491 571188

638

NTC PUBLICATIONS LTD

Title	**Pay and Benefits Pocket Book**
Coverage	A compilation of pay and benefits data based on various sources.
Frequency	Regular
Availability	General
Cost	£19.95
Comments	Published in association with Bacon & Woodrow.
Address	PO Box 69, Henley-on-Thames, Oxfordshire RG9 1EJ
Telephone	01491 411000
Fax	01491 571188

639

NTC PUBLICATIONS LTD

Title	**Parliament and Government Pocket Book**
Coverage	Information on the UK and EU parliaments with data on their spending of public money and the public's attitude to them.
Frequency	Regular
Availability	General
Cost	£32
Comments	Published in association with the Hansard Society.
Address	PO Box 69, Henley-on-Thames, Oxfordshire RG9 1EJ
Telephone	01491 411000
Fax	01491 571188

640	
	NTC PUBLICATIONS LTD
Title	**Media Pocket Book**
Coverage	A statistical profile of British commercial media. Coverage includes advertising spending by media and product category, circulation and readership data, publisher information, titles, stations, audiences, viewing, reach, indices of media rates and cover prices.
Frequency	Regular
Availability	General
Cost	£24
Comments	
Address	PO Box 69, Henley-on-Thames, Oxfordshire RG9 1EJ
Telephone	01491 411000
Fax	01491 571188

641	
	NTC PUBLICATIONS LTD
Title	**Retail Pocket Book**
Coverage	Statistics on specific retail markets and the major retailers plus advertising trends and developments in retailing. A final section covers international retailing. Based on data collected from various sources.
Frequency	Annual
Availability	General
Cost	£28
Comments	Published in association with Nielsen.
Address	PO Box 69, Henley-on-Thames, Oxfordshire RG9 1GB
Telephone	01491 411000
Fax	01491 571188

642	
	NTC PUBLICATIONS LTD
Title	**Food Pocket Book**
Coverage	Basic data on the food market with a general overview followed by sections on specific foods, food retailing, food companies. Some European data. Based on various sources.
Frequency	Annual
Availability	General
Cost	£28
Comments	
Address	PO Box 69, Henley-on-Thames, Oxfordshire RG9 1GB
Telephone	01491 411000
Fax	01491 571188

NTC PUBLICATIONS LTD

643	
Title	**Drink Pocket Book**
Coverage	Basic data on the drinks sector including general statistics on the market followed by sections on specific drinks and drink outlets. Some international data is included. Based on various sources but a strong reliance on data from Stats MR.
Frequency	Annual
Availability	General
Cost	£32
Comments	Published in association with Stats MR.
Address	PO Box 69, Henley-on-Thames, Oxfordshire RG9 1GB
Telephone	01491 411000
Fax	01491 571188

NTC PUBLICATIONS LTD

644	
Title	**Marketing Pocket Book**
Coverage	A statistical profile of the marketing, distribution, and consumption of goods and services in the UK, with some additional data on Europe and other areas. Based on various sources, including official and market research publications.
Frequency	Annual
Availability	General
Cost	£16.95
Comments	Published in association with the Advertising Association. A companion volume, European Marketing Pocket Book, is also available.
Address	PO Box 69, Henley-on-Thames, Oxfordshire RG9 1GB
Telephone	01491 411000
Fax	01491 571188

NTC PUBLICATIONS LTD

645	
Title	**Lifestyle Pocket Book**
Coverage	Lifestyle data for the UK with sections on shopping habits, consumption patterns, leisure, holidays, media usage, personal finance, housing and households, transport, communications, employment, education, health, crime, economics, and demographics. A final section provides some summary data on the rest of Europe. Based on various official and non-official sources.
Frequency	Annual
Availability	General
Cost	£24
Comments	Published in association with the Advertising Association.
Address	PO Box 69, Henley-on-Thames, Oxfordshire RG9 1GB
Telephone	01491 411000
Fax	01491 571188

646

	NTC PUBLICATIONS LTD
Title	**Financial Marketing Pocket Book**
Coverage	Published in association with NOP Financial, a guide to the UK personal finance sector. Includes data from NOP research and covers personal incomes, wealth and savings, consumers' expenditure, personal investments, life assurance, general insurance, consumer credit, mortgages, banking, credit cards, and advertising.
Frequency	Regular
Availability	General
Cost	£32
Comments	
Address	PO Box 69, Henley-on-Thames, Oxfordshire RG9 1GB
Telephone	01491 411000
Fax	01491 571188

647

	NTC PUBLICATIONS LTD
Title	**Regional Marketing Pocket Book**
Coverage	Statistics on consumer spending, health, media use, leisure activities, personal finance, demographics, tourism, transport, communications, economic trends, crime, education by region. Based on various sources with some additional information on Europe's regions.
Frequency	Annual
Availability	General
Cost	£24
Comments	Published in association with the Advertising Association.
Address	PO Box 69, Henley-on-Thames, Oxfordshire RG9 1GB
Telephone	01491 411000
Fax	01491 571188

648

	NTC PUBLICATIONS LTD
Title	**The British Shopper**
Coverage	A pocket book of data on British shopping patterns, consumers, and consumer purchasing behaviour. Based on various sources but a strong reliance on Nielsen data.
Frequency	Annual
Availability	General
Cost	£22
Comments	Published in association with Nielsen.
Address	PO Box 69, Henley-on-Thames, Oxfordshire RG9 1GB
Telephone	01491 411000
Fax	01491 571188

649

	OPINION LEADER RESEARCH
Title	**Opinion Leader Panel**
Coverage	A panel survey of over 100 key opinion leaders such as directors in industry, politicians, media, trade unionists, city analysts etc.
Frequency	Regular
Availability	Participants
Cost	On application
Comments	
Address	Alliance House, 30-32 Grays Inn Road, London WC1X 8HR
Telephone	0171 242 2222
Fax	0171 404 7250

650

	OUTDOOR ADVERTISING ASSOCIATION
Title	**OSCAR**
Coverage	The Outdoor Site Classification and Audience Research (OSCAR) measures the effectiveness and awareness of poster advertising. Based on commissioned research.
Frequency	Regular
Availability	Detailed results only available to poster industry but summary results published.
Cost	On request
Comments	
Address	77 Newman Street, London W1A 1DX
Telephone	0171 298 8035
Fax	0171 298 8034

651

	OXFORD JOURNALS
Title	**Oxford Review of Economic Policy**
Coverage	Articles plus statistics on current economic trends and economic forecasts.
Frequency	Quarterly
Availability	General
Cost	£99
Comments	
Address	Walton Street, Oxford OX2 6DP
Telephone	01865 56767
Fax	01865 56646

652

P-E INTERNATIONAL

Title **UK Survey of Executive Salaries and Benefits**

Coverage A survey of salaries and benefits covering 56 executive job titles based in over 20 industrial groupings. Based on a survey carried out by the company.

Frequency Annual

Availability General

Cost £400, £150 to participants

Comments

Address Park House, Wick Road, Egham, Surrey TW20 0HW

Telephone 01784 434411

Fax 01784 437828

653

PA CONSULTING

Title **Survey of Graduate Salaries and Recruitment Trends**

Coverage Statistics and analysis of trends in the graduate labour market based on research by the company.

Frequency Annual

Availability General

Cost £445, £295 for participants

Comments

Address 123 Buckingham Palace Road, London SW1

Telephone 0171 730 9000

Fax 0171 333 5050

654

PA CONSULTING

Title **Telesales and Customer Services Sales Survey**

Coverage A survey of salaries in telesales and customer services based around 18 job categories. Based on a survey carried out by the company.

Frequency Annual

Availability General

Cost £375

Comments

Address 123 Buckingham Palace Road, London SW1W 9SR

Telephone 0171 730 9000

Fax 0171 333 5050

655	
	PACKAGING WEEK
Title	**Business Bulletin**
Coverage	General business trends and specific trends in the packaging sector with data for a number of previous months and/or quarters.
Frequency	Regular in a weekly journal
Availability	General
Cost	£76
Comments	
Address	Miller Freeman Publications Ltd, Sovereign Way, Tonbridge TN9 1RW
Telephone	01732 364422
Fax	01732 361534

656	
	PANNELL KERR FORSTER ASSOCIATES
Title	**Wales Hotel Occupancy Survey**
Coverage	A survey of occupancy levels in Wales based on a sample survey of Welsh hotels across various grades. Some supporting text.
Frequency	Annual
Availability	General
Cost	£50
Comments	Also publishes surveys of European and international trends.
Address	78 Hatton Garden, London EC1N 8JA
Telephone	0171 831 7393
Fax	0171 405 6736

657	
	PANNELL KERR FORSTER ASSOCIATES
Title	**Monthly UK Chain Profits and Loss Survey**
Coverage	A survey of profit and loss trends for the major UK hotel chains based on a survey of key hotel groups.
Frequency	Monthly
Availability	Contributors only
Cost	On request
Comments	Summary data from the survey may be available to others. Also publishes surveys on European and international trends and these are generally available. Also produces a monthly survey of chain hotels in UK cities.
Address	78 Hatton Garden, London EC1N 8JA
Telephone	0171 831 7393
Fax	0171 405 6736

658

PANNELL KERR FORSTER ASSOCIATES

Title **Outlook – UK Trends**

Coverage A review of the operating and financial characteristics of a sample of around 245 provincial hotels from AA 5-star to 2-star. Details of occupancy rates, revenues, costs and expenses with data for the latest year and the previous year. Some supporting text.

Frequency Annual

Availability General

Cost £250

Comments Also publishes surveys on European and international trends.

Address 78 Hatton Garden, London EC1N 8JA

Telephone 0171 831 7393

Fax 0171 405 6736

659

PANNELL KERR FORSTER ASSOCIATES

Title **Oulook – London Trends**

Coverage Summary of the performance of approximately 72 London hotels with details of occupancy levels, achieved room rate, sales, and the cost of sales of food and beverage departments. Some supporting text.

Frequency Annual

Availability General

Cost £100

Comments Also publishes surveys on European and international trends.

Address 78 Hatton Garden, London EC1N 8JA

Telephone 0171 831 7393

Fax 0171 405 6736

660

PANNELL KERR FORSTER ASSOCIATES

Title **Monthly Bulletin of UK Regional Trends**

Coverage Analysis of performance, in volume and value terms, based on a sample survey of hotels around the country.

Frequency Monthly

Availability Contributors only

Cost Free

Comments Summary data from the survey may be available to others. Also publishes surveys on European and international trends and these are generally available.

Address 78 Hatton Garden, London EC1N 8JA

Telephone 0171 831 7393

Fax 0171 405 6736

661	PANNELL KERR FORSTER ASSOCIATES
Title	**Monthly Bulletin of London Trends**
Coverage	Performance trends by volume and revenue based on a sample survey of London hotels from AA 5-star to 2-star.
Frequency	Monthly
Availability	Contributors only
Cost	Free
Comments	Summary data from the survey may be available to others. Also publishes surveys on European and international trends and these are generally available.
Address	78 Hatton Garden, London EC1N 8JA
Telephone	0171 831 7393
Fax	0171 405 6736

662	PAPER FACTS AND FIGURES
Title	**Paper and Board Indices**
Coverage	Indices of prices for various types of paper based on figures collected by the journal.
Frequency	Six times per annum in a journal published six times per annum
Availability	General
Cost	£68
Comments	
Address	M-G Information Services Ltd, Riverbank House, Angel Lane, Tonbridge TN9 1SE
Telephone	01732 362666
Fax	01732 367301

663	PAPER FEDERATION OF GREAT BRITAIN
Title	**Annual Survey of Energy Use and Costs**
Coverage	Analysis and statistics on energy use and costs in the paper and board sector.
Frequency	Annual
Availability	General
Cost	£150
Comments	Enquiry service can deal with ad hoc enquiries (minimum charge £15).
Address	Papermakers House, Rivenhall Road, Swindon SN5 7BD
Telephone	01793 886086
Fax	01793 886182

664

PAPER FEDERATION OF GREAT BRITAIN

Title **Fact Card**

Coverage Summary data on the paper and board industry based on the various statistics produced by the Federation.

Frequency Annual

Availability General

Cost £4 for paper edition, prices on request for transparencies, 35mm slides, electronic graphics file

Comments Enquiry service can deal with ad hoc enquiries (minimum charge £15).

Address Papermakers House, Rivenhall Road, Swindon SN5 7BD

Telephone 01793 886086

Fax 01793 886182

665

PAPER FEDERATION OF GREAT BRITAIN

Title **Waste Paper Consumption**

Coverage Monthly statistics on waste paper demand, stocks, and overseas trade based on various sources.

Frequency Monthly

Availability General

Cost £250

Comments Enquiry service can deal with ad hoc enquiries (minimum charge £15).

Address Papermakers House, Rivenhall Road, Swindon SN5 7BD

Telephone 01793 886086

Fax 01793 886182

666

PAPER FEDERATION OF GREAT BRITAIN

Title **Pulp Consumption**

Coverage Monthly statistics covering pulp demand, stocks, and trade based on various sources.

Frequency Monthly

Availability General

Cost £250

Comments Enquiry service can deal with ad hoc enquiries (minimum charge £15).

Address Papermakers House, Rivenhall Road, Swindon SN5 7BD

Telephone 01793 886086

Fax 01793 886182

667	PAPER FEDERATION OF GREAT BRITAIN
Title	**Paper and Board Imports**
Coverage	Detailed monthly import statistics for paper and board based on Central Government data.
Frequency	Monthly
Availability	General
Cost	£250
Comments	Enquiry service can deal with ad hoc enquiries (minimum charge £15).
Address	Papermakers House, Rivenhall Road, Swindon SN5 7BD
Telephone	01793 886086
Fax	01793 886182

668	PAPER FEDERATION OF GREAT BRITAIN
Title	**Paper and Board Consumption**
Coverage	Monthly statistics and commentary on paper and board consumption in the UK.
Frequency	Monthly
Availability	General
Cost	£125
Comments	Enquiry service can deal with ad hoc enquiries (minimum charge £15).
Address	Papermakers House, Rivenhall Road, Swindon SN5 7BD
Telephone	01793 886086
Fax	01793 886182

669	PAPER FEDERATION OF GREAT BRITAIN
Title	**Industry Key Figures**
Coverage	Key figures on production and consumption plus a commentary on trends.
Frequency	Monthly
Availability	General
Cost	£125
Comments	Enquiry service can deal with ad hoc enquiries (minimum charge £15).
Address	Papermakers House, Rivenhall Road, Swindon SN5 7BD
Telephone	01793 886086
Fax	01793 886182

	PAPER FEDERATION OF GREAT BRITAIN
670	
Title	**Annual Survey of Capacity**
Coverage	Historical data for the last few years and forecasts for three or four years ahead of capacity in the industry.
Frequency	Annual
Availability	General
Cost	£850
Comments	Enquiry service can deal with ad hoc enquiries (minimum charge £15).
Address	Papermakers House, Rivenhall Road, Swindon SN5 7BD
Telephone	01793 886086
Fax	01793 886182

	PAPER FEDERATION OF GREAT BRITAIN
671	
Title	**Reference Statistics**
Coverage	Ten-year series of tables and charts with data on production, consumption, sales, stocks, imports and exports of paper and board plus consumption, production, stocks, and imports of raw materials. Also data on employment, energy, and finance. Based on various sources.
Frequency	Annual
Availability	General
Cost	£100
Comments	Enquiry service can deal with ad hoc enquiries (minimum charge £15).
Address	Papermakers House, Rivenhall Road, Swindon SN5 7BD
Telephone	01793 886086
Fax	01793 886182

	PAPER FEDERATION OF GREAT BRITAIN
672	
Title	**Market Statistics**
Coverage	Detailed tables and charts on consumption, production, sales, stocks, imports, exports of paper and board plus consumption, production, stocks and imports of raw materials. Based on a combination of sources.
Frequency	Monthly
Availability	General
Cost	£900, £100 for individual copies, individual tables and sections can also be supplied on request
Comments	Enquiry service can deal with ad hoc enquiries (minimum charge £15).
Address	Papermakers House, Rivenhall Road, Swindon SN5 7BD
Telephone	01793 886086
Fax	01793 886182

PAPER FEDERATION OF GREAT BRITAIN

Title **Paper and Board Production**

Coverage Monthly data and analysis on production, sales, and stocks of paper and board.

Frequency Monthly

Availability General

Cost £250

Comments Enquiry service can deal with ad hoc enquiries (minimum charge £15).

Address Papermakers House, Rivenhall Road, Swindon SN5 7BD

Telephone 01793 886086

Fax 01793 886182

674

PAY AND WORKFORCE RESEARCH (PWR)

Title **Survey of Independent Healthcare Pay and Conditions**

Coverage A survey of salaries, benefits, and conditions in the independent healthcare sector based on a survey of a sample of relevant organisations.

Frequency Annual

Availability General

Cost £20, £15 to PWR clients

Comments

Address Clarendon House, 9 Victoria Avenue, Harrogate HE1 1DY

Telephone 01423 842684

Fax 01423 520272

675

PAY AND WORKFORCE RESEARCH (PWR)

Title **Terms and Conditions of Service for Healthcare Staff**

Coverage A survey of around 80 NHS organisations with data on salaries, terms, and conditions.

Frequency Annual

Availability General

Cost £250, free to participants and PWR clients

Comments

Address Clarendon House, 9 Victoria Avenue, Harrogate HE1 1DY

Telephone 01423 842684

Fax 01423 520272

676

PEARSON PROFESSIONAL LTD

Title **Unit Trust Yearbook**

Coverage Includes a market commentary plus a statistical section on sales, total funds, performance, income from unit trusts etc. The official yearbook of the Association of Unit Trusts and Investment Funds and many figures are taken from this source.

Frequency Annual

Availability General

Cost On request

Comments An FT Financial Publishing imprint.

Address Maple House, 149 Tottenham Court Road, London   W1P 9LL

Telephone 0171 896 2222

Fax 0171 896 2274

677

PEDDER ASSOCIATES

Title **Applications Usage by Industry Sector**

Coverage Statistics and analysis of applications usage by companies spending £15,000 or more on data processing. Usage is broken down into 31 areas. Based on research by the company.

Frequency Annual

Availability General

Cost £2,600

Comments

Address 34 Duncan Road, Richmond-upon-Thames, Surrey   TW9 2JD

Telephone 0181 940 4300

Fax 0181 948 1531

678

PEDDER ASSOCIATES

Title **Operating Systems Trends**

Coverage Statistics and analysis of the usage and installed base of operating systems for companies spending more than £15,000 on data processing. Based on research by the company.

Frequency Annual

Availability General

Cost £2,600

Comments

Address 34 Duncan Road, Richmond-upon-Thames, Surrey   TW9 2JD

Telephone 0181 940 4300

Fax 0181 948 1531

679 PEDDER ASSOCIATES

Title	**Software Package Trends**
Coverage	Statistics and analysis of expenditure on software by companies spending £15,000 or more on data processing. Based on research by the company.
Frequency	Annual
Availability	General
Cost	£2,600
Comments	
Address	34 Duncan Road, Richmond-upon-Thames, Surrey TW9 2JD
Telephone	0181 940 4300
Fax	0181 948 1531

680 PEDDER ASSOCIATES

Title	**DP Expenditure by Industry Sector**
Coverage	Statistics and analysis covering expenditure on hardware, software, and services for 20 industry sectors. Based on research by the company.
Frequency	Annual
Availability	General
Cost	£2,600
Comments	
Address	34 Duncan Road, Richmond-upon-Thames, Surrey TW9 2JD
Telephone	0181 940 4300
Fax	0181 948 1531

681 PEDDER ASSOCIATES

Title	**General Purpose Computer Systems**
Coverage	A report detailing the ten-year installed base of computers and shipments history, broken down model by model. Also includes five-year projections of the installed base. Based on research by the company.
Frequency	Annual
Availability	General
Cost	£7,500
Comments	
Address	34 Duncan Road, Richmond-upon-Thames, Surrey TW9 2JD
Telephone	0181 940 4300
Fax	0181 948 1531

682 PEDDER ASSOCIATES

Title	**Computer Usage by Geographical Region**
Coverage	Statistics and analysis of the use of computers in companies spending £15,000 or over on data processing, broken down by region. Based on research by the company.
Frequency	Annual
Availability	General
Cost	£2,600
Comments	
Address	34 Duncan Road, Richmond-upon-Thames, Surrey TW9 2JD
Telephone	0181 940 4300
Fax	0181 948 1531

683 PEDDER ASSOCIATES

Title	**Computer Usage by Industry Sector**
Coverage	Statistics and analysis of the use of computers by companies spending over £15,000 on data processing per year. Covers 20 SIC sectors and based on research by the company.
Frequency	Annual
Availability	General
Cost	£2,600
Comments	
Address	34 Duncan Road, Richmond-upon-Thames, Surrey TW9 2JD
Telephone	0181 940 4300
Fax	0181 94 8 1531

684 PERIODICAL PUBLISHERS' ASSOCIATION

Title	**Handbook of Statistics on the Magazine Industry**
Coverage	A compilation of data on the journal sector based on various sources.
Frequency	Regular
Availability	General
Cost	On request
Comments	Also publishes an Annual Review.
Address	15-19 Kingsway, London WC2B 6UN
Telephone	0171 379 6268
Fax	0171 379 5661

685 PET FOOD MANUFACTURERS' ASSOCIATION

Title **PFMA Profile**

Coverage Data on the market size and value for prepared pet foods plus some figures on pet ownership. Figures usually for the latest year and percentage change over the previous year. Based on the association's own survey with a general commentary on the figures.

Frequency Regular

Availability General

Cost On request

Comments

Address 6 Catherine Street, London WC2B 5JJ

Telephone 0171 836 2460

Fax 0171 836 0580

686 PETROLEUM ECONOMIST

Title **Markets**

Coverage Tables covering oil prices, world production, and tanker freight rates based on various sources.

Frequency Monthly in a monthly journal

Availability General

Cost £230

Comments Also publishes regular statistics on world oil trends.

Address 25-31 Ironmonger Row, London EC1V 3PN

Telephone 0171 251 3501

Fax 0171 253 1224

687 PETROLEUM ECONOMIST

Title **UK North Sea Survey**

Coverage Statistics on North Sea oil fields with data on reserves, ownership, production etc. Compiled from a variety of sources.

Frequency Annual in a monthly journal

Availability General

Cost £230

Comments Also contains regular statistics on world oil trends.

Address 25-31 Ironmonger Row, London EC1V 3PN

Telephone 0171 251 3501

Fax 0171 253 1224

688 PETROLEUM TIMES

Title	**Petroleum Times Energy Report**
Coverage	Provides pump prices for petrol in various towns and cities in the UK. Based on the journal's own survey with some supporting text.
Frequency	Monthly in a monthly journal
Availability	General
Cost	£154, combined subscription with Petroleum Times Business Review
Comments	
Address	Nexus Media Ltd, Nexus House, Azalea Drive, Swanley, Kent BR8 8HY
Telephone	01322 660070
Fax	01322 667633

689 PHARMACEUTICAL JOURNAL

Title	**Retail Sales Index for Chemists**
Coverage	General figures on the sales trends in total and for specific products sold in chemists. Based on Central Government data.
Frequency	Monthly in a weekly journal
Availability	General
Cost	£69, free to members of the Pharmaceutical Society
Comments	Other statistics published occasionally.
Address	1 Lambeth High Street, London SE1 7JN
Telephone	0171 735 9141
Fax	0171 735 7629

690 PHOTO MARKETING ASSOCIATION INTERNATIONAL (UK) LTD

Title	**PMA United Kingdom Consumer Photographic Survey**
Coverage	Survey of consumer photographic buying behaviour and equipment ownership and usage. Data on camera ownership, type of cameras used, distribution channels, films used, type of films, use of professional photographic and video services. Based on a panel of almost 1,000 households. Detailed commentary supports the data.
Frequency	Regular
Availability	General, but incorporated in the annual international publication PMA Industry Trends Report which reviews market trends around the world.
Cost	Free to members, £94 to others
Comments	The latest survey was carried out in 1994 and the previous survey was in 1989.
Address	Peel Place, 50 Carver Street, Hockley, Birmingham B1 3AS
Telephone	0121 212 0299
Fax	0121 212 0298

691 PIRA INTERNATIONAL

Title	**Paper and Packaging Analyst**
Coverage	A review of trends in the paper and packaging sectors with articles and statistics.
Frequency	Quarterly
Availability	General
Cost	£495, £140 for a single issue
Comments	Also publishes reviews of the European printing and packaging sectors.
Address	Randalls Road, Leatherhead, Surrey KT22 7RU
Telephone	01372 376161
Fax	01372 360104

692 PIRA INTERNATIONAL

Title	**UK Printing Industry Statistics**
Coverage	The report includes 120 statistical tables covering production, and trends in the key sectors such as book, periodicals, and newspaper publishing. The strategic issues facing the industry are examined and company profiles are also included.
Frequency	Annual
Availability	General
Cost	£195
Comments	Also publishes reviews of the European printing and packaging sectors.
Address	Randalls Road, Leatherhead, Surrey KT22 7RU
Telephone	01372 376161
Fax	01372 360104

693 PIZZA ASSOCIATION

Title	**Pizza and Pasta Statistics**
Coverage	General data and market statistics on the pizza and pasta sectors are available from the association.
Frequency	Regular
Availability	General
Cost	On request
Comments	Also publishes a regular journal, Pizza and Pasta Magazine.
Address	29 Market Place, Wantage, Oxfordshire
Telephone	01235 766339
Fax	01235 769044

694 PMSI UK LTD

Title	**Medical Research Omnibus**
Coverage	A monthly omnibus survey of 400 general medical practitioners with face-to-face interviews in surgeries.
Frequency	Monthly
Availability	General
Cost	On application
Comments	Also carries out media advertising recall surveys and specialist omnibus surveys in the health care area.
Address	Mallard House, Peregrine Business Park, Gomm Road, High Wycombe, Buckinghamshire HP13 7DL
Telephone	01494 450098
Fax	01494 521934

695 PRE-SCHOOL PLAY GROUP ASSOCIATION

Title	**Figures and Figures**
Coverage	Facts and figures on pre-school play based on data collected by the association and published sources.
Frequency	Regular
Availability	General
Cost	On request
Comments	Also publishes an annual report.
Address	61-63 Kings Cross Road, London WC1X 9LL
Telephone	0171 833 0991
Fax	0171 837 4442

696 PRICE WATERHOUSE

Title	**Price Waterhouse IT Review**
Coverage	A review of IT trends in the UK including data on expenditure, systems in place etc. Based on research by the company.
Frequency	Annual
Availability	General
Cost	Free
Comments	
Address	Southwark Towers, 32 London Bridge Street, London SE1 9SY
Telephone	0171 939 3000
Fax	0171 378 0647

697

PRICE WATERHOUSE

Title **UK Financial Services Information Technology**

Coverage Based on a survey of IT directors in leading financial service companies, the report includes statistics on IT staff numbers, budgets, technologies etc. A commentary supports the tables and graphs.

Frequency Regular

Availability General

Cost On request

Comments

Address Southwark Towers, 32 London Bridge Street, London SE1 9SY

Telephone 0171 939 3000

Fax 0171 378 0647

698

PRINTED CIRCUIT INTERCONNECTION FEDERATION (PCIF)

Title **UK PCB Report**

Coverage Statistics and analysis on production, imports, exports, UK market supply, employment, and a market breakdown. Based largely on original research supported by government import and export data.

Frequency Annual

Availability General

Cost Free to members, £250 to others

Comments

Address Romano House, 399-401 Strand, London WC2R 0LT

Telephone 0171 497 1090

Fax 0171 497 3594

699

PRINTED CIRCUIT INTERCONNECTION FEDERATION (PCIF)

Title **Quarterly Monitor**

Coverage Basic data on sales, orders, exports with percentage changes from the previous figures. Based largely on the federation's own research.

Frequency Quarterly

Availability General

Cost Free to members, £150 to others

Comments

Address Romano House, 399-401 Strand, London WC2R 0LT

Telephone 0171 497 1090

Fax 0171 497 3594

700 PROCESSING AND PACKAGING MACHINERY ASSOCIATION (PPMA)

Title	**UK Imports and Exports of Packaging Machinery**
Coverage	Brief commentary and graphs showing exports and imports over a three-year period. The figures are produced from Customs and Excise sources and separate intra-EU and extra-EU trade.
Frequency	Annual
Availability	
Cost	Free
Comments	
Address	Progress House, 404 Brighton Road, South Croydon, Surrey CR2 6AN
Telephone	0181 681 8226
Fax	0181 681 1641

701 PRODUCE STUDIES LTD

Title	**Omnifarm**
Coverage	An omnibus survey of 1,000 farmers in Great Britain with data on purchases, product awareness, general expenditure, readership etc.
Frequency	3 times per annum
Availability	General
Cost	On application
Comments	Various other research projects and reports produced.
Address	Northcroft House, West Street, Newbury, Berkshire RG13 1HD
Telephone	01635 46112
Fax	01635 43945

702 PROFESSIONAL PERSONNEL CONSULTANTS

Title	**Review of Directors' Remuneration and Benefits**
Coverage	A survey of directors' salaries and benefits in small- and medium-sized companies employing up to 400 staff. Based on data collected by the company.
Frequency	Annual
Availability	General
Cost	£65
Comments	
Address	Godwin House, George Street, Huntingdon PE18 6BU
Telephone	01480 411111
Fax	01480 411111

703	PROFESSIONAL PERSONNEL CONSULTANTS
Title	**PPC High Technology Salary Survey**
Coverage	A survey of salaries and benefits for staff in small high technology companies based on data collected by the company.
Frequency	Annual
Availability	General
Cost	£65
Comments	
Address	Godwin House, George Street, Huntingdon PE18 6BU
Telephone	01480 411111
Fax	01480 411111

704	PROFESSIONAL PERSONNEL CONSULTANTS
Title	**PPC Wage and Salary Survey**
Coverage	A salary and wages survey covering around 60 managerial, administrative, and manual jobs. Based on data collected by the company.
Frequency	Twice per annum
Availability	General
Cost	£75
Comments	
Address	Godwin House, George Street, Huntingdon PE18 6BU
Telephone	01480 411111
Fax	01480 411111

705	PROFESSIONAL PERSONNEL CONSULTANTS
Title	**Salary Survey for Hospitals and Nursing Homes**
Coverage	A survey of salaries and benefits covering 31 job functions in hospitals and nursing homes. Based on data collected by the company.
Frequency	Annual
Availability	General
Cost	£145, £75 for participants
Comments	
Address	Godwin House, George Street, Huntingdon PE18 6BU
Telephone	01480 411111
Fax	01480 411111

706	PROPERTY INTELLIGENCE PLC
Title	**UK Town and County Focus**
Coverage	A database, available online or on disc, of over 700 UK towns and cities, plus counties. For each town there is a statistical profile including demographic data, projections, employment trends, socio-economic profiles, rents, and unemployment data. Additional information on local plans, major retailers, proximity to other towns, and recent articles on the town. Based on various sources including the Population Census, geodemographic data, local information, and property consultants.
Frequency	Continuous
Availability	General
Cost	On request
Comments	Property Intelligence PLC offers various property, and related databases. Also operates a European Town Focus database. Information Research Network (see other entry) and Chas E. Goad act as agents for the UK town profile database.
Address	Ingram House, 13-15 John Adam Street, London WC2N 6LD
Telephone	0171 839 7684
Fax	0171 839 1060

707	PUBLISHERS ASSOCIATION
Title	**Book Trade Yearbook**
Coverage	Commentary followed by a statistical section covering publishers' sales, consumer expenditure, prices, exports, export prices. Statistics usually cover the last four or five years.
Frequency	Annual
Availability	General
Cost	£50 to non-members
Comments	Also published Book Industry Trends in 1990 as a one-off publication, priced £50.
Address	19 Bedford Square, London WC1B 3HJ
Telephone	0171 580 6321
Fax	0171 636 5375

708 PURCON CONSULTANTS LTD

Title	**The Purcon Index: A Salary Survey for the Purchasing Profession**
Coverage	A salary survey prepared from the Purcon Register which has records of over 10,000 candidates for jobs in purchasing.
Frequency	Twice per annum
Availability	General
Cost	£50
Comments	
Address	Ardenham Lane House, Aylesbury, Buckinghamshire HP19 3AA
Telephone	01926 393993
Fax	

709 QUANTIME LTD

Title	**UK Labour Force Surveys**
Coverage	Quantime is an agent for the UK government's labour force statistics and it can provide data for specific requests or produce regular packages for clients. The original data is based on a sample survey of 65,000 households.
Frequency	Regular
Availability	General
Cost	Varies according to information required
Comments	Available in various formats including a dial-up database, information sheets, discs, hard copy reports etc.
Address	Maygrove House, 67 Maygrove Road, London NW6 2EG
Telephone	0171 625 7111
Fax	0171 624 5293

710 REED INFORMATION SERVICES

Title	**Laxtons' Building Price Book**
Coverage	A listing of 250,000 price elements relevant in the development of small and large building works.
Frequency	Annual
Availability	General
Cost	£87.50
Comments	
Address	Windsor Court, East Grinstead House, East Grinstead, West Sussex RH19 1XA
Telephone	01342 326972
Fax	01342 335612

711	REED PERSONNEL SERVICES
Title	**Reed Employment Index**
Coverage	A review of trends in the jobs market with separate indices for temporary employment and permanent employment. Based on information obtained by the company.
Frequency	Monthly
Availability	General
Cost	On request
Comments	
Address	6th Floor, Tolworth Tower, Ewell Road, Tolworth, Surrey KT6 7EL
Telephone	0181 399 5221
Fax	0181 399 4930

712	REGISTER-MEAL
Title	**Quarterly Summary of Brands and Advertisers**
Coverage	Total advertising expenditure for all brands spending over £150,000 per annum. Data covers the latest quarter, a monthly breakdown within the quarter, and a moving annual total. Based on a monitoring of advertising in the press, television, satellite TV, radio, outdoor, and the cinema.
Frequency	Quarterly
Availability	General
Cost	£880
Comments	Also available online through Register-MEAL's own PC system Dataview, or through Donovan Data Services (see other entry).
Address	2 Fisher Street, London WC1R 4QA
Telephone	0171 833 1212
Fax	0171 831 7686

713	REGISTER-MEAL
Title	**Expenditure Summary**
Coverage	A report format showing advertising expenditure for press, TV, radio, cinema, and outdoor (or any combination), across time for brands, product groups, categories, or advertisers. The time periods can be shown monthly for up to 12 months or can be shown as 10 specified periods such as quarterly, six-monthly, or annual. Product groups, brands, advertisers can be combined.
Frequency	Regular
Availability	General
Cost	Varies according to the nature of the information required
Comments	Statistics also available online through Register-MEAL's own PC system Dataview, or through Donovan Data Services (see other entry).
Address	2 Fisher Street, London WC1R 4QA
Telephone	0171 833 1212
Fax	0171 831 7686

714	REGISTER-MEAL
Title	**Selected Media Report**
Coverage	A report showing expenditure or volume for brands, product groups, categories, advertisers or agencies for press, TV, radio, cinema, outdoor or any combination of these.
Frequency	Regular
Availability	General
Cost	Varies according to the nature of the information required
Comments	Statistics also available online through Register-MEAL's own PC system Dataview, or through Donovan Data Services (see other entry).
Address	2 Fisher Street, London WC1R 4QA
Telephone	0171 833 1212
Fax	0171 831 7686

715	REGISTER-MEAL
Title	**Adlisting**
Coverage	A detailed report providing a range of information by brand across all press titles and TV stations.
Frequency	Regular
Availability	General
Cost	Varies according to the nature of the information required
Comments	Statistics also available online through Register-MEAL's own PC system Dataview, or through Donovan Data Services (see other entry).
Address	2 Fisher Street, London WC1R 4QA
Telephone	0171 833 1212
Fax	0171 831 7686

716	REMUNERATION ECONOMICS
Title	**Survey of Pensions Managers**
Coverage	A salary survey of pensions managers and related jobs with data by company size, industry group, location, age etc. Based on the company's own survey with some supporting text.
Frequency	Annual
Availability	General
Cost	£340, £195 for participants
Comments	
Address	Survey House, 51 Portland Road, Kingston-upon-Thames KT1 2SH
Telephone	0181 549 8726
Fax	0181 541 5705

717

	REMUNERATION ECONOMICS
Title	**Survey of Actuaries and Actuarial Students**
Coverage	A salary survey of actuaries and students with data by levels of responsibility, company size, age, qualifications etc.
Frequency	Annual
Availability	General
Cost	£520, £260 to participants
Comments	Produced in association with the Institute of Actuaries.
Address	Survey House, 51 Portland Road, Kingston-upon-Thames KT1 2SH
Telephone	0181 549 8726
Fax	0181 541 5705

718

	REMUNERATION ECONOMICS
Title	**Survey of Personnel Functions**
Coverage	A salary survey covering various levels of responsibility by size of company, industry group, location, age, qualifications etc. Additional data on benefits and recruitment. Based on the company's own survey with some supporting text.
Frequency	Annual
Availability	General
Cost	£220, £115 for participants
Comments	
Address	Survey House, 51 Portland Road, Kingston-upon-Thames KT1 2SH
Telephone	0181 549 8726
Fax	0181 541 5705

719

	REMUNERATION ECONOMICS
Title	**National Management Salary Survey**
Coverage	A survey of managers to produce statistics on earnings, fringe benefits, and bonuses. Produced in three volumes: a general review of the survey, a detailed statistics volume, and a small business review.
Frequency	Annual
Availability	General
Cost	£380 for volumes 1 and 2 combined, £200 for the small business review. £470 for all three reports, discounts available to participants
Comments	Produced in association with the Institute of Management.
Address	Survey House, 51 Portland Road, Kingston-upon-Thames KT1 2SH
Telephone	0181 549 8726
Fax	0181 541 5705

720	REMUNERATION ECONOMICS
Title	**Survey of Engineering Functions**
Coverage	A survey of engineering salaries covering nine levels of responsibility, by company size, type of work, qualifications, location etc. Based on the company's own survey with some supporting text.
Frequency	Annual
Availability	General
Cost	£220, £115 for participants
Comments	
Address	Survey House, 51 Portland Road, Kingston-upon-Thames KT1 2SH
Telephone	0181 549 8726
Fax	0181 541 5705

721	REMUNERATION ECONOMICS
Title	**A Survey of Sales and Marketing Functions**
Coverage	A salary survey covering nine levels of responsibility and broken down into various sectors. Based on data collected by the company.
Frequency	Annual
Availability	General
Cost	£300, £150 for participants
Comments	
Address	Survey House, 51 Portland Road, Kingston-upon-Thames KT1 2SH
Telephone	0181 549 8726
Fax	0181 541 5705

722	REMUNERATION ECONOMICS
Title	**Directors' Survey**
Coverage	A survey of salaries and benefits for chief executives, directors, and senior executives.
Frequency	Annual
Availability	General
Cost	£600
Comments	Produced in association with Bacon & Woodrow.
Address	Survey House, 51 Portland Road, Kingston-upon-Thames KT1 2SH
Telephone	0181 549 8726
Fax	0181 541 5705

723

	REMUNERATION ECONOMICS
Title	**Survey of Financial Functions**
Coverage	A salary survey for various levels of responsibility by company size, industry group, location, age, qualifications etc. Additional data on benefits and recruitment. Based on the company's own survey with some supporting text.
Frequency	Annual
Availability	General
Cost	£220, £115 to participants
Comments	
Address	Survey House, 51 Portland Road, Kingston-upon-Thames KT1 2SH
Telephone	0181 549 8726
Fax	0181 541 5705

724

	RESEARCH AND AUDITING SERVICES LTD
Title	**National Business Omnibus**
Coverage	A regular omnibus survey of 2,000 businesses stratified by SIC code, UK region, and company size.
Frequency	Monthly
Availability	General
Cost	On application
Comments	
Address	Monarch House, Victoria Road, London NW3 6RZ
Telephone	0181 993 2220
Fax	0181 993 1114

725

	RESEARCH SURVEYS OF GREAT BRITAIN
Title	**Omnibus Survey**
Coverage	A weekly omnibus survey based on face-to-face interviews with 2,000 adults. Demographic analysis and socio-economic analysis using the ACORN and MOSAIC classifications.
Frequency	Weekly
Availability	General
Cost	On application
Comments	Various other consumer surveys carried out.
Address	AGB House, West Gate, London W5 1EL
Telephone	0181 566 3010
Fax	0181 967 4330

726 RESEARCH SURVEYS OF GREAT BRITAIN (RSGB)

Title	**Mailmonitor**
Coverage	A panel of 1,350 households is used to obtain data on the receipt of mail, including direct mail.
Frequency	Quarterly
Availability	General
Cost	On request
Comments	Various other consumer surveys carried out.
Address	AGB House, West Gate, London W5 1EL
Telephone	0181 566 3010
Fax	0181 967 4330

727 RESEARCH SURVEYS OF GREAT BRITAIN (RSGB)

Title	**Baby Omnibus**
Coverage	Purchasing trends for baby products plus frequency of purchase, price paid, source of purchase, brand share. Also data on advertising awareness, and attitudes to new and existing products and images of products, services, and companies. Based on a sample of 700 mothers and analysis by age, social group, and incidence of birth.
Frequency	Quarterly
Availability	General
Cost	On request
Comments	Various other consumer surveys carried out.
Address	AGB House, West Gate, London W5 1EL
Telephone	0181 566 3010
Fax	0181 967 4330

728 RETAIL JEWELLER

Title	**Precious Metal Prices**
Coverage	Selling, scrap and market prices; the prices are usually a week old.
Frequency	Weekly in a weekly journal
Availability	General
Cost	£45
Comments	
Address	Audit House, 260 Field End Road, Ruislip HA4 9BR
Telephone	0181 956 3017
Fax	0181 956 3023

729	REWARD GROUP
Title	**Charities Salary Survey**
Coverage	A survey of salaries in the charity sector with analysis by job and level of charity income for full-time employees. Based on research by the company.
Frequency	Annual
Availability	General
Cost	£195, £80 to participants
Comments	Published in November. Specific inquiries answered from Reward's Data Bank.
Address	Reward House, Diamond Way, Stone Business Park, Stone ST15 0SD
Telephone	01785 813566
Fax	01785 817007

730	REWARD GROUP
Title	**Distribution Rewards**
Coverage	Salary information on management, professional, technical, and commercial jobs in the distribution sector. Based on research by the company.
Frequency	Bi-annual
Availability	General
Cost	£440, £220 to participants
Comments	Specific inquiries answered by Reward's Data Bank.
Address	Reward House, Diamond Way, Stone Business Park, Stone ST15 0SD
Telephone	01785 813566
Fax	01785 817007

731	REWARD GROUP
Title	**Pay for Senior Managers in the NHS**
Coverage	A review of pay and conditions of service for senior managers in the NHS. Based on research by the company.
Frequency	Regular
Availability	General
Cost	£300
Comments	First published in March 1995. Produced in association with the Institute of Health Services Management. Specific inquiries answered from Reward's Data Bank.
Address	Reward House, Diamond Way, Stone Business Park, Stone ST15 0SD
Telephone	01785 813566
Fax	01785 817007

732	REWARD GROUP
Title	**Software and Electronics Specialists**
Coverage	Salary information on management, professional, technical, and commercial jobs in the software and electronics sector. Based on research by the company.
Frequency	Bi-annual
Availability	General
Cost	£420, £210 to participants
Comments	Specific inquiries answered from Reward's Data Bank.
Address	Reward House, Diamond Way, Stone Business Park, Stone ST15 0SD
Telephone	01785 813566
Fax	01785 817007

733	REWARD GROUP
Title	**Oilfield Services**
Coverage	Salary information on management, professional, technical, and commercial jobs in oilfield services. Based on research by the company.
Frequency	Annual
Availability	General
Cost	£720, £360 to participants
Comments	Specific inquiries answered from Reward's Data Bank.
Address	Reward House, Diamond Way, Stone Business Park, Stone ST15 0SD
Telephone	01785 813566
Fax	01785 817007

734	REWARD GROUP
Title	**Retail Rewards**
Coverage	Salary information for management, professional, technical, and commercial jobs in the retail sector. Based on the company's own research.
Frequency	Annual
Availability	General
Cost	£225, £110 to participants
Comments	Specific inquiries answered from Reward's Data Bank.
Address	Reward House, Diamond Way, Stone Business Park, Stone ST15 0SD
Telephone	01785 813566
Fax	01785 817007

735 REWARD GROUP

Title	**London Secretarial Survey**
Coverage	A salary survey of six types of secretarial jobs in the capital. Based on research by the company.
Frequency	Bi-annual
Availability	General
Cost	£225, £110 to participants
Comments	Published in January and August. Specific inquiries answered from Reward's Data Bank.
Address	Reward House, Diamond Way, Stone Business Park, Stone ST15 0SD
Telephone	01785 813566
Fax	01785 817007

736 REWARD GROUP

Title	**Local Authority Survey**
Coverage	A salary survey of local authority jobs, including many which are specific to local authorities. Based on research by the company.
Frequency	Bi-annual
Availability	General
Cost	£225, £110 to participants
Comments	Published in April and November. Specific inquiries answered from Reward's Data Bank.
Address	Reward House, Diamond Way, Stone Business Park, Stone ST15 0SD
Telephone	01785 813566
Fax	01785 817007

737 REWARD GROUP

Title	**Clerical and Operative Rewards**
Coverage	A review of all clerical and operative positions analysed by size of company, sector, and geographical area. Based on research by the company.
Frequency	Bi-annual
Availability	General
Cost	£310
Comments	Published in January and July. Specific inquiries answered from Reward's Data Bank.
Address	Reward House, Diamond Way, Stone Business Park, Stone ST15 0SD
Telephone	01785 813566
Fax	01785 817007

738	REWARD GROUP
Title	**Personnel Rewards**
Coverage	An annual report with details of basic and total pay, company cars and other benefits. Based on research by the company.
Frequency	Annual
Availability	General
Cost	£230, £190 to IPD members (see below)
Comments	Produced in association with the Institute of Personnel and Development (IPD). Published in October. Specific inquiries answered from Reward's Data Bank.
Address	Reward House, Diamond Way, Stone Business Park, Stone ST15 0SD
Telephone	01785 813566
Fax	01785 817007

739	REWARD GROUP
Title	**Sales and Marketing Rewards**
Coverage	An annual review of salaries, bonuses, commission, company cars and other benefits. Based on research by the company.
Frequency	Annual
Availability	General
Cost	£230, £190 to CIM members (see below)
Comments	Produced in association with the Chartered Institute of Marketing (CIM). Published in October. Specific inquiries answered from Reward's Data Bank.
Address	Reward House, Diamond Way, Stone Business Park, Stone ST15 0SD
Telephone	01785 813566
Fax	01785 817007

740	REWARD GROUP
Title	**Directors' Rewards**
Coverage	Detailed information of salaries and benefits for chairman, managing director, and a wide range of functional directors posts, analysed by company turnover and number of employees. Based on the company's own research.
Frequency	Annual
Availability	General
Cost	£395
Comments	Produced in association with the Institute of Directors. Published in November. Specific inquiries answered from Reward's Data Bank.
Address	Reward House, Diamond Way, Stone Business Park, Stone ST15 0SD
Telephone	01785 813566
Fax	01785 817007

741	REWARD GROUP
Title	**Reward – The Management Salary Survey**
Coverage	A management salary report covering over 115 jobs and including advice, forecasts, and comments on salary movements. Based on the company's own research.
Frequency	Bi-annual
Availability	General
Cost	£390
Comments	Published in March and September. Specific inquiries answered from Reward's Data Bank.
Address	Reward House, Diamond Way, Stone Business Park, Stone ST15 0SD
Telephone	01785 813566
Fax	01785 817007

742	REWARD GROUP
Title	**Regional Salary and Wage Survey**
Coverage	Twice-yearly surveys covering 17 local areas with salaries and conditions given for all grades of employees. Based on annual research.
Frequency	Bi-annual
Availability	General
Cost	£225, £90 to participants
Comments	Specific inquiries answered by Reward's Data Bank.
Address	Reward House, Diamond Way, Stone Business Park, Stone ST15 0SD
Telephone	01785 813566
Fax	01785 817007

743	REWARD GROUP
Title	**Regional Comparisons**
Coverage	Cost of living comparisons for the main regions of the UK covering various products and services, income levels, and lifestyles. Based on Reward's own survey in key centres. Historical data back to 1973.
Frequency	Bi-annual
Availability	General
Cost	£290
Comments	Reports published in March and September. Specific inquiries answered from Reward's Data Bank.
Address	Reward House, Diamond Way, Stone Business Park, Stone ST15 0SD
Telephone	01785 813566
Fax	01785 817007

744

Title	**Research and Development Salary Survey**
Coverage	An annual report covering basic salaries, total remuneration, and benefits in the R&D field. Based on research by the company.
Frequency	Annual
Availability	General
Cost	£225, £110 to participants
Comments	Published in May. Specific inquiries answered from Reward's Data Bank.
Address	Reward House, Diamond Way, Stone Business Park, Stone ST15 0SD
Telephone	01785 813566
Fax	01785 817007

REWARD GROUP

745

RICHARD HOLWAY LTD

Title	**Holway Report**
Coverage	A 2-volume report on the software and computing services industry. Volume 1 contains general market data and analysis, including projections for the next 4 years. Volume 2 has profiles of 800 leading companies. Based largely on research by the company.
Frequency	Annual
Availability	General
Cost	£1,600
Comments	
Address	18 Great Austins, Farnham GU9 8JQ
Telephone	01252 724584
Fax	01252 725800

746

RICHARD HOLWAY LTD

Title	**System House**
Coverage	A monthly review of the financial performance of the UK computing service industry.
Frequency	Monthly
Availability	General
Cost	£295
Comments	
Address	18 Great Austins, Farnham GU9 8JQ
Telephone	01252 724584
Fax	01252 725800

747	
	RMIF LTD
Title	**Monthly Statistics**
Coverage	Monthly figures for new car sales, in units, with a breakdown between total cars and company cars.
Frequency	Monthly
Availability	Primarily members but other requests considered..
Cost	Free
Comments	RMIF is the Retail Motor Industry Federation.
Address	201 Great Portland Street, London W1N 6AB
Telephone	0171 580 9122
Fax	0171 580 6376

748	
	RMIF LTD
Title	**New Car Sales by County**
Coverage	A regional and county breakdown of new car sales, in units, for the latest year with the percentage change over the previous year. Sales are broken down into total cars and company cars.
Frequency	Annual
Availability	Primarily members but other requests considered.
Cost	Free
Comments	RMIF is the Retail Motor Industry Federation.
Address	201 Great Portland Street, London W1N 6AB
Telephone	0171 580 9122
Fax	0171 580 6376

749	
	ROSS YOUNG'S HOLDINGS LTD
Title	**Frozen Food Retail Market Report**
Coverage	Commentary and statistics on retail sales, market trends, brands, distribution channels, and current issues.
Frequency	Regular
Availability	General
Cost	On request
Comments	
Address	Ross House, Wickham Road, Grimsby, South Humberside DN31 3SW
Telephone	01472 359111
Fax	01472 240640

	ROYAL BANK OF SCOTLAND PLC
750	
Title	**Royal Bank/Radio Scotland Oil Index**
Coverage	Data on production from North Sea oil fields and the average daily value of oil production based on a telephone survey of oil field operators. An analysis of the statistics is also included.
Frequency	Monthly
Availability	General
Cost	Free
Comments	
Address	42 St Andrew Square, Edinburgh EH2 2YE
Telephone	0131 556 8555
Fax	0131 556 8555

	ROYAL BANK OF SCOTLAND PLC
751	
Title	**Quarterly Survey of Exports**
Coverage	A survey of export trends and prospects in Scotland based on returns from Scottish exporters. Includes a commentary and analysis of the data.
Frequency	Quarterly
Availability	General
Cost	Free
Comments	
Address	42 St Andrew Square, Edinburgh EH2 2YE
Telephone	0131 556 8555
Fax	0131 556 8555

	ROYAL BANK OF SCOTLAND PLC
752	
Title	**Summary of UK Business Conditions**
Coverage	Covers production, employment, overseas transactions, prices, wages, industrial investment, banking, short-term money rates and the Stock Exchange. Based on a mixture of bank statistics, Central Government data, and non-official sources. Approximately 50% of the report is text.
Frequency	Monthly
Availability	General
Cost	Free
Comments	
Address	42 St Andrew Square, Edinburgh EH2 2YE
Telephone	0131 556 8555
Fax	0131 556 8555

753

ROYAL INSTITUTION OF CHARTERED SURVEYORS

Title **Housing Market Survey**

Coverage National figures and regional data each month for various types and ages of property. Shows the trends in prices over the previous 3 months and includes comments on the market situation from estate agents.

Frequency Monthly

Availability General

Cost £10

Comments

Address 12 Great George Street, Parliament Square, London SW1P 3AD

Telephone 0171 222 7000

Fax 0171 222 9430

754

ROYAL INSTITUTION OF CHARTERED SURVEYORS

Title **RICS Workload Statistics**

Coverage A regular survey of architects' workload based on a sample survey of RICS members. Includes an opinion survey covering the short term outlook for the sector.

Frequency Quarterly

Availability General

Cost £50

Comments

Address 12 Great George Street, Parliament Square, London SW1P 3AD

Telephone 0171 222 7000

Fax 0171 222 9430

755

ROYAL INSTITUTION OF CHARTERED SURVEYORS, BUILDING COST INFORMATION SERVICE

Title **BCIS Quarterly Review of Building Prices**

Coverage Prices by type of building and by region based on a survey of subscribers to BICS.

Frequency Quarterly

Availability General

Cost £175, or £55 for a single issue

Comments

Address 85-87 Clarence Street, Kingston-upon-Thames KT1 1RB

Telephone 0181 546 7554

Fax 0181 547 1238

257

756

ROYAL INSTITUTION OF CHARTERED SURVEYORS, BUILDING COST INFORMATION SERVICE

Title	**Building Cost Information Service**
Coverage	An annual subscription service covering tenders, labour, and materials and based on information supplied by members of BICS.
Frequency	Monthly
Availability	General
Cost	£315, £250 to members
Comments	
Address	85-87 Clarence Street, Kingston-upon-Thames KT1 1RB
Telephone	0181 546 7554
Fax	0181 547 1238

757

ROYAL INSTITUTION OF CHARTERED SURVEYORS, BUILDING COST INFORMATION SERVICE

Title	**Construction Tender Price Index**
Coverage	Price indices for various building materials based on information supplied by BICS members.
Frequency	Quarterly
Availability	General
Cost	£50
Comments	
Address	85-87 Clarence Street, Kingston-upon-Thames KT1 1RB
Telephone	0181 546 7554
Fax	0181 547 1238

758

ROYAL INSTITUTION OF CHARTERED SURVEYORS, BUILDING COST INFORMATION SERVICE

Title	**Guide to House Rebuilding Costs for Insurance Valuation**
Coverage	Data on housebuilding costs by area and condition and type of building. Based on original research by BCIS.
Frequency	Annual
Availability	General
Cost	£26
Comments	
Address	85-87 Clarence Street, Kingston-upon-Thames KT1 1RB
Telephone	0181 546 7554
Fax	0181 547 1238

759

	RSL – RESEARCH SERVICES LTD
Title	**Capibus**
Coverage	A weekly omnibus survey of 2,000 adults based on face-to-face interviews in the home.
Frequency	Weekly
Availability	General
Cost	On application
Comments	Capibus was the UK's first computer assisted face-to-face omnibus, launched in 1992. RSL also publish the British Business Survey for the Business Media Research Committee (see other entry).
Address	Research Services House, Elmgrove Road, Harrow, Middlesex HA1 2QG
Telephone	0181 861 6000
Fax	0181 861 5515

760

	RSL – RESEARCH SERVICES LTD
Title	**Flexifarm Livestock Omnibus**
Coverage	An omnibus survey of 800 cattle farmers, 500 sheep farmers, and 400 pig farmers based on telephone and face-to-face interviews.
Frequency	Annual and bi-annual
Availability	General
Cost	On application
Comments	RSL also publish the British Business Survey for the Business Media Research Committee (see other entry).
Address	Research Services House, Elmgrove Road, Harrow, Middlesex HA1 2QG
Telephone	0181 861 6000
Fax	0181 861 5515

761

	RSL – RESEARCH SERVICES LTD
Title	**Signpost**
Coverage	A monthly monitor of the effectiveness of outdoor advertising posters based on a consumer survey by the company.
Frequency	Monthly
Availability	General
Cost	On application
Comments	RSL also publish the British Business Survey for the Business Media Research Committee (see other entry).
Address	Research Services House, Elmgrove Road, Harrow, Middlesex HA1 2QG
Telephone	0181 861 6000
Fax	0181 861 5515

762

RYDEN PROPERTY CONSULTANTS AND CHARTERED SURVEYORS

Title	**Scottish Industrial & Commercial Property Review**
Coverage	A review of economic trends in Scotland, with forecasts, is followed by a commentary on the Scottish property market covering Edinburgh, Glasgow, Aberdeen, and Dundee. Specific sections on shops, and industrial and warehouse property. Based primarily on data from the company.
Frequency	Bi-annual
Availability	General
Cost	Free
Comments	
Address	46 Castle Street, Edinburgh EH2 3BN
Telephone	0131 225 6612
Fax	0131 225 5766

763

SALARY SURVEY PUBLICATIONS

Title	**Survey of Appointments' Data and Trends**
Coverage	A survey of salaries and appointments trends in the IT sector based on an analysis of IT advertisements in the press and actual salary data.
Frequency	Quarterly
Availability	General
Cost	£325
Comments	Produced in association with Computer Weekly.
Address	10 Gwyn's Place, Lambourn RG17 8YZ
Telephone	01488 72705
Fax	

764

SAMPLE SURVEYS LTD

Title	**Omnicar**
Coverage	A monthly motoring omnibus survey based on a sample of 1,000 motorists. Analysis of purchases, services, DIY, insurance, number of cars in household, engine size, make, model etc.
Frequency	Monthly
Availability	General
Cost	On application
Comments	
Address	Abbey Court, Boarley Lane, Sandling, Maidstone, Kent ME14 3AL
Telephone	01622 690318
Fax	01622 690530

SAMPLE SURVEYS LTD

Title	**The Great British Motorist**
Coverage	A detailed report on the state of British motoring with nine main sections covering the motorist, car ownership, car purchasing, the cost of motoring, motorist behaviour, ownership of motoring items, motoring issues, regional profiles, and an executive summary. Based on original research by the company and some published sources.
Frequency	Regular
Availability	General
Cost	£175
Comments	Produced in association with the Automobile Association (AA).
Address	Abbey Court, Boarley Lane, Sandling, Maidstone, Kent ME14 3AL
Telephone	01622 690318
Fax	01622 690530

SCOTCH WHISKY ASSOCIATION

Title	**Statistical Report**
Coverage	Figures on the activities of the industry including production, exports, stocks, and duty paid. Figures for some previous years also given. Based mainly on Central Government statistics with a small amount of original data.
Frequency	Annual
Availability	General
Cost	Free
Comments	
Address	17 Half Moon Street, London W1Y 7RB
Telephone	0171 629 4384
Fax	0171 493 1398

SCOTTISH COUNCIL DEVELOPMENT AND INDUSTRY

Title	**Survey of Scottish Manufactured Exports**
Coverage	Estimates of the value and volume of Scottish exports in aggregate terms and by industry. Also includes an analysis of export prospects. Based on a sample of Scottish exporters with a commentary supporting the text.
Frequency	Annual
Availability	General
Cost	£25
Comments	
Address	23 Chester Street, Edinburgh EH3 3TG
Telephone	0131 225 7911
Fax	0131 220 2116

768	SCOTTISH COUNCIL DEVELOPMENT AND INDUSTRY
Title	**Quarterly Export Index**
Coverage	An index measuring the performance of Scottish exports, based on a survey by the Scottish Council.
Frequency	Quarterly
Availability	General
Cost	
Comments	Various other reports on Scottish economic and business trends also produced.
Address	23 Chester Street, Edinburgh EH3 3TG
Telephone	0131 225 7911
Fax	0131 220 2116

769	SCREEN PRINTING ASSOCIATION (UK) LTD
Title	**Survey of Trends**
Coverage	Pay survey of the sector based on returns from members, with additional information on holidays, conditions of employment, union involvement. Respondents are also asked by approximately what percentage do they expect wages to increase in the next pay review.
Frequency	Quarterly
Availability	Members
Cost	Free to participating members
Comments	
Address	7a West Street, Reigate, Surrey RH2 9BL
Telephone	01737 240792
Fax	01737 240770

770	SCREEN PRINTING ASSOCIATION (UK) LTD
Title	**Survey of Trends**
Coverage	A survey of trends in the previous three months and likely trends in the coming three months based on returns from members. Includes data on costs, sales, orders, margins on sales, capital expenditure, employment, and prices.
Frequency	Quarterly
Availability	Members
Cost	Free to participating members
Comments	
Address	7A West Street, Reigate, Surrey RH2 9BL
Telephone	01737 240792
Fax	01737 240770

SEA FISH INDUSTRY AUTHORITY

Title **Trade Bulletin**

Coverage Quantity and value of imports and exports of fish intended for human consumption. The latest month's figures with the year to date and comparative figures for the previous year. Based on Central Government data.

Frequency Monthly

Availability General

Cost On request

Comments Also publishes the European Supplies Bulletin with statistics on specific European countries.

Address 18 Logie Mill, Logie Green Road, Edinburgh EH7 4HG

Telephone 0131 558 3331

Fax 0131 558 1442

SEA FISH INDUSTRY AUTHORITY

Title **Key Indicators**

Coverage Key statistics on supplies, household consumption, prices, international trade etc. Based mainly on Central Government sources.

Frequency Quarterly

Availability General

Cost On request

Comments Also publishes a European Supplies Bulletin with statistics on specific European countries.

Address 18 Logie Mill, Logie Green Road, Edinburgh EH7 4HG

Telephone 0131 558 3331

Fax 0131 558 1442

SEA FISH INDUSTRY AUTHORITY

Title **Household Fish Consumption in Great Britain**

Coverage Analysis of sales by species for household consumption, split into fresh/chilled and frozen sales. The statistics are taken from a sample survey of households and comparable data for the previous year is given. Some text supports the data.

Frequency Quarterly

Availability General

Cost On request

Comments Also publishes a regular European Supplies Bulletin with statistics on specific European countries.

Address 18 Logie Mill, Logie Green Road, Edinburgh EH7 4HG

Telephone 0131 558 3331

Fax 0131 558 1442

774

SEVEN SEAS LTD

Title	**A Healthy Focus**
Coverage	A regular report on the foods supplement market with commentary and statistics on total sales, product shares, brand shares, and new developments. Based on research commissioned by the company.
Frequency	Regular
Availability	General
Cost	Free
Comments	
Address	Hedon Road, Marfleet, Hull HU9 5NJ
Telephone	01482 75234
Fax	

775

SHARWOOD & CO LTD

Title	**Ethnic Foods Market Review**
Coverage	An analysis of trends in the ethnic foods market with data on total sales, sales by market sector (eg Chinese, Indian etc), sales by type of product, household penetration, and brand shares. Based on research commissioned by the company.
Frequency	Annual
Availability	General
Cost	Free
Comments	
Address	J A Sharwood & Co Ltd, Egham, Surrey TW20 9QG
Telephone	01784 473000
Fax	

776

SHAWS' PRICE GUIDES LTD

Title	**Shaws' Retail Price Guide**
Coverage	Fair selling prices, recommended by the manufacturers or by the editors, for 13,000 products divided into various categories, eg groceries, household, medicines, tobacco,etc. Based on regular surveys carried out by the company.
Frequency	Monthly
Availability	General
Cost	£18.50
Comments	
Address	Baden House, 7 St Peters Place, Brighton, East Sussex BN1 6TB
Telephone	01273 680041
Fax	01273 606588

777	SHOWERINGS
Title	**Cider Survey**
Coverage	A market review of the cider market with data on market size, brands, outlets etc. Based mainly on commissioned research.
Frequency	Regular
Availability	General
Cost	Free
Comments	
Address	King Street, Shepton Mallet BA4 5ND
Telephone	01749 3333
Fax	01749 5653

778	SILK ASSOCIATION OF GREAT BRITAIN
Title	**Serica**
Coverage	Mainly news and comment on the silk industry but it includes some statistics, mainly imports and exports.
Frequency	Six issues per year
Availability	General
Cost	On application
Comments	
Address	Morley Road, Tonbridge TN9 1RN
Telephone	01732 351357
Fax	01732 770217

779	SILVER FERN RESEARCH
Title	**Silver Fern Omnibus**
Coverage	Regular omnibus survey of general practitioners with a sample size of 50 in 12 areas. Concentrates on prescribing behaviour.
Frequency	Fortnightly
Availability	General
Cost	On application
Comments	
Address	Gartside House, Harris Way, Windmill Road, Sunbury, Middlesex TW16 7EL
Telephone	01932 765751
Fax	01932 783403

780	SMART CARD CLUB
Title	**The Status of the UK Smart Card Marketplace**
Coverage	A review of the market broken down by applications plus a forecast of card penetration levels for the year 2000. Also includes details of suppliers, the history of the smart card, and technological issues. Mainly text with two main statistical tables.
Frequency	Regular
Availability	General
Cost	
Comments	The first report was produced in 1994 but there are plans for regular updates.
Address	8-9 Bridge Street, Cambridge CB2 1UA
Telephone	01223 329900
Fax	01223 358222

781	SOAP AND DETERGENT INDUSTRY ASSOCIATION
Title	**Fact Sheet on the Market**
Coverage	Summary statistics on market trends with data on production, imports, exports.
Frequency	Regular
Availability	General
Cost	Free
Comments	More detailed statistics for members.
Address	PO Box 9, Hayes Gate House, Hayes UB4 0JD
Telephone	0181 573 7992
Fax	0181 561 5077

782	SOCIETY OF BUSINESS ECONOMISTS
Title	**Business Economists' Salary Survey**
Coverage	Basic salaries and benefits by employment type, age, and sex. Based on a sample of society members. A commentary supports the data.
Frequency	Annual
Availability	General
Cost	£12.50
Comments	Published in the June issue of the Society's journal, The Business Economist.
Address	11 Baytree Walk, Watford WD1 3RX
Telephone	01923 237287
Fax	

783

SOCIETY OF COUNTY TREASURERS

Title	**Standard Spending Indicators**
Coverage	Statistics on spending on particular services by local authorities in England. Based on returns from the local authorities.
Frequency	Annual
Availability	General
Cost	£15, free to members
Comments	Produced in association with the Society of Metropolitan Treasurers and the Association of District Council Treasurers.
Address	RSG Team, Finance Department, Kent County Council, County Hall, Maidstone, Kent ME14 1XE
Telephone	01622 694557
Fax	01622 694690

784

SOCIETY OF MOTOR MANUFACTURERS' AND TRADERS (SMMT)

Title	**SMMT Monthly Statistical Review**
Coverage	Production and registrations of motor vehicles by manufacturer and model plus imports and exports of products of the motor industry. Less frequent special tables such as forecasts and the annual motor vehicle census. Based on a combination of Central Government data and the society's own survey.
Frequency	Monthly
Availability	General
Cost	£119, £93 members
Comments	Also publishes monthly and annual statistics for European countries and the world market.
Address	Automotive Data Services, Forbes House, Halkin Street, London SW1X 7DS
Telephone	0171 235 7000
Fax	0171 235 7112

785

SOCIETY OF MOTOR MANUFACTURERS' AND TRADERS (SMMT)

Title	**MVRIS – Motor Vehicle Registration Information System**
Coverage	Monthly statistics plus individual tailored reports on vehicle registrations. Data available by model, manufacturer, location etc.
Frequency	Regular
Availability	General
Cost	Price depends on the nature of the information required
Comments	Also publishes monthly and annual statistics for other European countries and the world market.
Address	Automotive Data Services, Forbes House, Halkin Street, London SW1X 7DS
Telephone	0171 235 7000
Fax	0171 235 7112

786

SOCIETY OF MOTOR MANUFACTURERS' AND TRADERS (SMMT)

Title	**MPSS – Motorparc Statistics Service**
Coverage	A service based on the annual census of motor vehicles carried out by the government agency, DVLA.
Frequency	Regular
Availability	General
Cost	Price depends on the nature of the information required
Comments	Also publishes monthly and annual statistics for other European countries and the world market.
Address	Automotive Data Services, Forbes House, Halkin Street, London SW1X 7DS
Telephone	0171 235 7000
Fax	0171 235 7112

787

SOCIETY OF MOTOR MANUFACTURERS' AND TRADERS (SMMT)

Title	**SMMT Economic and Market Reports**
Coverage	UK and international editions covering economic trends and the impact of these trends on the motor vehicle market. Commentary and statistics.
Frequency	Quarterly
Availability	General
Cost	£230, £160 for members
Comments	Also publishes monthly and annual statistics on other European countries and the world market.
Address	Automotive Data Services, Forbes House, Halkin Street, London SW1X 7DS
Telephone	0171 235 7000
Fax	0171 235 7112

788

SOCIETY OF PRACTITIONERS IN INSOLVENCY

Title	**Personal Insolvency in the UK**
Coverage	An analysis of personal insolvency trends over the last year based on returns from members. The latest issue is based on over 1,200 individual cases.
Frequency	Annual
Availability	General
Cost	£50
Comments	
Address	18-19 Long Lane, London EC1 9HE
Telephone	0171 600 3375
Fax	0171 600 3602

789

SOCIETY OF PRACTITIONERS IN INSOLVENCY

Title	**Company Insolvency in the UK**
Coverage	Based on returns from members, this report shows the trends in company insolvencies over the last twelve months. The report analyses the reasons for failure and the characteristics of failed companies. Based on almost 3,000 individual cases.
Frequency	Annual
Availability	General
Cost	£100
Comments	
Address	18-19 Long Lane, London EC1 9HE
Telephone	0171 600 3375
Fax	0171 600 3602

790	SPA MARKETING SYSTEMS LTD
Title	**Mosaic**
Coverage	Specialising primarily in the retail sector, SPA provides various geodemographic services based on various sources including the 1991 census, postcode address file, Target Group Index, and the Financial Research Survey (FRS).
Frequency	Continuous
Availability	General
Cost	On application, and depending on the range and nature of the information required.
Comments	
Address	1 Warwick Street, Leamington Spa, Warwickshire
Telephone	01926 451199
Fax	01926 450592

791	SPON, E & FN
Title	**Spon's Contractors' Handbook: Painting and Decorating**
Coverage	Annual cost information on painting and decorating. Based on Spon's own survey.
Frequency	Annual
Availability	General
Cost	£15.95
Comments	Usually published in September.
Address	2-6 Boundary Row, London SE1 8HN
Telephone	0171 865 0066
Fax	0171 522 9623

792	SPON, E & FN
Title	**Spon's Contractors' Handbook: Minor Works**
Coverage	Annual building cost information for small contractors. Based on Spon's own surveys.
Frequency	Annual
Availability	General
Cost	£16.95
Comments	Usually published in September.
Address	2-6 Boundary Row, London SE1 8HN
Telephone	0171 865 0066
Fax	0171 522 9623

793	SPON, E & FN
Title	**Spon's Plant and Equipment Price Guide**
Coverage	New and second hand prices and specifications for nearly 5,000 models of construction plant. Based on Spon's own surveys.
Frequency	Monthly
Availability	General
Cost	£110
Comments	
Address	2-6 Boundary Row, London SE1 8HN
Telephone	0171 865 0066
Fax	0171 522 9623

794	SPON, E & FN
Title	**Spon's Mechanical and Electrical Services Price Book**
Coverage	Prices and costs of heating, lighting, ventilation, air conditioning, and other service items in industrial and commercial property. Based on Spon's own surveys plus other non-official sources.
Frequency	Annual
Availability	General
Cost	£45
Comments	Usually published in August.
Address	2-6 Boundary Row, London SE1 8HN
Telephone	0171 865 0066
Fax	0171 522 9623

795	SPON, E & FN
Title	**Spon's Landscape and External Works Price Book**
Coverage	Prices and costs covering hard and soft landscapes and external works generally. Based on Spon's own surveys and some other non-official data.
Frequency	Annual
Availability	General
Cost	£39.50
Comments	Usually published in August.
Address	2-6 Boundary Row, London SE1 8HN
Telephone	0171 865 0066
Fax	0171 522 9623

796	SPON, E & FN
Title	**Spon's Civil Engineering Price Book**
Coverage	Prices and costs of building, services, engineering, external work, landscaping etc. Based on Spon's own surveys and other non-official sources.
Frequency	Annual
Availability	General
Cost	£49.50
Comments	Usually published in March.
Address	2-6 Boundary Row, London SE1 8HN
Telephone	0171 865 0066
Fax	0171 522 9623

797	SPON, E & FN
Title	**Spon's Architects' and Builders' Price Book**
Coverage	Prices of materials, prices for measured work and rates of wages. Based mainly on Spon's own surveys with additional data from other non-official sources.
Frequency	Annual
Availability	General
Cost	£45
Comments	Usually published in August.
Address	2-6 Boundary Row, London SE1 8HN
Telephone	0171 865 0066
Fax	0171 522 9623

798	SPON, E & FN
Title	**Spon's Price Book Update**
Coverage	A quarterly update available to the purchasers of the annual price books.
Frequency	Quarterly
Availability	Subscribers to annual publications.
Cost	Free
Comments	
Address	206 Boundary Row, London SE1 8HN
Telephone	0171 865 0066
Fax	0171 522 9623

799	
Title	**SPORTS COUNCIL** **Digest of Sports Statistics**
Coverage	Compendium of statistics about organized and casual sports participation during a ten-year period. Additional information on the facilities and purchase of equipment and magazines. General section and section on specific sports. Data mainly taken from sports organizations.
Frequency	Every few years
Availability	General
Cost	On request
Comments	
Address	16 Upper Woburn Place, London WC1H 0QP
Telephone	0171 388 1277
Fax	0171 383 5740

800	
Title	**SPORTS MARKETING SURVEYS** **Racket Sports Survey**
Coverage	A monthly survey of 2,500 tennis, squash, and badminton players interviewed during the playing season. Purchases and ownership of rackets, footwear, and other equipment.
Frequency	Monthly
Availability	Participants
Cost	On application
Comments	
Address	Byfleet Business Centre, Chertsey Road, Byfleet, Surrey KT14 7AN
Telephone	01932 350600
Fax	01932 350375

801	
Title	**SPORTS MARKETING SURVEYS** **Golf Survey**
Coverage	1,000 golfers are interviewed at golf courses every month with approximately 50 golf clubs covered each month.
Frequency	Monthly
Availability	Participants
Cost	On application
Comments	
Address	Byfleet Business Centre, Chertsey Road, Byfleet, Surrey KT14 7AN
Telephone	01932 350600
Fax	01932 350375

802

	SPORTS MARKETING SURVEYS
Title	**Football Survey**
Coverage	A survey of amateur footballers with a sample of 1,200 interviewed at 80 clubs around the UK. Ownership and purchasing of football boots and other equipment.
Frequency	Regular
Availability	Participants
Cost	On application
Comments	
Address	Byfleet Business Centre, Chertsey Road, Byfleet, Surrey KT14 7AN
Telephone	01932 350600
Fax	01932 350375

803

	STANDING CONFERENCE OF NATIONAL AND UNIVERSITY LIBRARIES (SCONUL)
Title	**Sconul Statistics: Expenditure**
Coverage	Expenditure trends based on the annual returns from SCONUL libraries. A small amount of text is included.
Frequency	Annual
Availability	General
Cost	£16.50, £27.50 combined purchase with SCONUL Statistics: Library Operations (see next entry)
Comments	
Address	102 Euston Street, London NW1 2HA
Telephone	0171 387 0317
Fax	

804

	STANDING CONFERENCE OF NATIONAL AND UNIVERSITY LIBRARIES (SCONUL)
Title	**Sconul Statistics: Library Operations**
Coverage	Annual statistics on library operations based on returns from SCONUL member libraries.
Frequency	Annual
Availability	General
Cost	£16.50, £27.50 combined subscription with SCONUL Statistics: Expenditure (see previous entry)
Comments	
Address	102 Euston Street, London NW1 2HA
Telephone	0171 387 0317
Fax	

805	
Title	**STATIONERY TRADE REVIEW** **Reference Book and Buyers Guide**
Coverage	The annual handbook for the stationery industry which includes an overview of the market and trends in the previous year. Includes market information on business machines, social stationery, and office products. Based on the journal's regular survey of manufacturers.
Frequency	Annual
Availability	General
Cost	£45
Comments	
Address	Nexus Media Ltd, Warwick House, Azalea Drive, Swanley, Kent BR8 8HY
Telephone	01322 660070
Fax	01322 667633

806	
Title	**SURVEY RESEARCH ASSOCIATES** **SRA Omnibus Survey**
Coverage	A multi-client survey covering various topics and based on a sample size of 1,500 adults. Interviews are carried out in the home.
Frequency	Fortnightly
Availability	General
Cost	On application
Comments	
Address	Tower House, Southampton Street, London WC2E 7HN
Telephone	0171 612 0369
Fax	0171 612 0361

807	
Title	**SUTHERLAND & PARTNERS (EDINBURGH) LTD** **Scotch Whisky Industry Review**
Coverage	A detailed analysis of the sector with data on home and export prices, costs and profit margins, sales, distillers, market shares, brand and company information, exports, and forecasts of future trends. Based on various sources.
Frequency	Annual
Availability	General
Cost	£295
Comments	
Address	20 Castle Terrace, Edinburgh EH1 2EY
Telephone	0131 228 5333
Fax	0131 459 0493

808	SYSTEM THREE SCOTLAND
Title	**Scottish Opinion Survey**
Coverage	A regular survey monitoring opinion, marketing, and advertising activity in Scotland. Based on a sample of 1,000 adults.
Frequency	Monthly
Availability	General
Cost	On application
Comments	
Address	6 Hill Street, Edinburgh EH2 3JZ
Telephone	0131 220 1178
Fax	0131 220 1181

809	TABS LTD
Title	**Tracking Advertising and Brand Strength**
Coverage	A service specialising in continuous advertising tracking based on a sample of over 1,000 adults. Monitors brand goodwill, advertising awareness, price image, brand awareness, claimed levels of buying/usage etc.
Frequency	Monthly
Availability	General
Cost	On application
Comments	
Address	Mulliner House, Flanders Road, London W4 1NN
Telephone	0181 994 9177
Fax	0181 994 2115

810	TAS PARTNERSHIP LTD
Title	**Public Transport Monitors**
Coverage	An analysis of trends in three transport sectors – bus industry, rapid transport, and the rail industry – based on various sources.
Frequency	Annual with quarterly updates
Availability	General
Cost	£149.50 each for bus and rail reports, £125 for rapid transit
Comments	
Address	Britannic House, 1A Chapel Street, Preston PR1 8BU
Telephone	01729 840268
Fax	01729 840705

811	TAYLOR NELSON AGB PUBLICATIONS
Title	**UK Markets**
Coverage	A series of 91 annual reports and 34 quarterly reports providing market data on around 4,800 products in the UK. Reports include statistics on production, imports, exports, average prices, and UK net supply. Value and volume figures are given, where available. Based on data collected by the CSO.
Frequency	Quarterly and annual
Availability	General
Cost	Annual reports are priced between £65 and £150 each, quarterly reports are available on an annual subscription of between £65 and £225, complete report set – £4,950
Comments	Also available on CD-ROM and via fax (see the next two entries). UK Markets replaced the Business Monitor - Manufacturers Sales series previously produced by CSO and distributed by HMSO. The above reports are also distributed by HMSO. Also publishes various one-off reports on consumer markets.
Address	14-17 St John's Square, London EC1M 4HE
Telephone	0171 608 0072
Fax	0171 490 1550

812	TAYLOR NELSON AGB PUBLICATIONS
Title	**UK Market CD-ROM**
Coverage	A CD-ROM version of the market reports noted in the previous entry. Available in two formats. The Inter-Active edition allows full manipulation of the data with downloading of data onto spreadsheets. The Library Edition is not inter-active and allows Read and Print only.
Frequency	Quarterly and annual
Availability	General
Cost	£6,250 + VAT for the inter-active edition, £3,950 + VAT for the library edition, the inter-active version can also be purchased by broad industry category at less cost
Comments	Also publishes various one-off reports on consumer markets.
Address	14-17 St John's Square, London EC1M 4HE
Telephone	0171 608 0072
Fax	0171 490 1550

813   TAYLOR NELSON AGB PUBLICATIONS

Title	**UK Markets I-Fax**
Coverage	UK Markets data can also be accessed using the I-FAX information retrieval system. The system delivers any of the 4,800 individual tables.
Frequency	Continuous
Availability	General, from any fax machine 24 hours a day.
Cost	£5 a table
Comments	Also publishes various one-off reports on consumer markets.
Address	14-17 St John's Square, London EC1M 4HE
Telephone	0171 608 0072
Fax	0171 490 1550

814   TAYLOR NELSON AGB PUBLICATIONS

Title	**The AGB Television Yearbook**
Coverage	A report containing monthly BARB data on viewing for terrestial television, monthly viewing figures and audience profiles for the top 30 programmes, top programmes by channel and type, advertising spending and impact, demographic analysis, regional breakdowns, and company profiles.
Frequency	Annual
Availability	General
Cost	£395, £590 combined purchase with AGB Cable and Satellite Yearbook (see next entry)
Comments	Also publishes various one-off reports on consumer markets.
Address	14-17 St John's Square, London EC1M 4HE
Telephone	0171 608 0072
Fax	0171 490 1550

815   TAYLOR NELSON AGB PUBLICATIONS

Title	**The AGB Cable and Satellite Yearbook**
Coverage	The report includes an overview of the industry as a whole, data on the cable-active and non-terrestrial viewing populations including household penetration by cable and DTH, general viewing trends, average daily hours of viewing per month, advertising data, programming information, and profiles of satellite companies and cable providers.
Frequency	Annual
Availability	General
Cost	£295, £590 combined purchase with AGB Television Yearbook (see previous entry)
Comments	Also publishes various one-off reports on consumer markets.
Address	14-17 St John's Square, London EC1M 4HE
Telephone	0171 608 0072
Fax	0171 490 1550

816 TAYLOR NELSON AGB PUBLICATIONS

Title | **The Household Expenditure Survey Reports**

Coverage | A series of five reports analysing the detailed results of the government's Family Expenditure Survey by age, wealth, occupation, lifestage, and region. Each report contains data on 300 product categories.

Frequency | Annual

Availability | General

Cost | On application

Comments | Also publishes various one-off reports on consumer markets.

Address | 14-17 St John's Square, London EC1M 4HE

Telephone | 0171 608 0072

Fax | 0171 490 1550

817 TEA BROKERS ASSOCIATION OF LONDON

Title | **Tea Market Report**

Coverage | Statistics on the prices obtained for tea in the London auctions. Based on the association's own survey.

Frequency | Weekly

Availability | General

Cost | £35.50

Comments | Published every Friday.

Address | Sir John Lyon House, Upper Thames Street, London EC4V 3LA

Telephone | 0171 236 3368

Fax |

818 TECHECON

Title | **Heavy Load Ships Register**

Coverage | Data on heavy load ships in the UK based on registrations of vessels.

Frequency | Regular

Availability | General

Cost | £115

Comments | Produced at regular intervals and reports available on overseas areas as well as UK.

Address | Glen House, 125 Old Brompton Road, London SW7 3RP

Telephone | 01483 750728

Fax |

019 TELMAR COMMUNICATIONS LTD

Title	**Telmar Databases**
Coverage	Telmar has access to various media and consumer databases containing statistics, including the British Business Survey (see other entry).
Frequency	Continuous
Availability	General
Cost	On request, and depending on the nature and range of information required
Comments	
Address	21 Ivor Place, London NW1
Telephone	0171 224 9992
Fax	0171 723 5265

820 TFPL LTD

Title	**Business Information Salary Survey**
Coverage	Analyses the salaries and fringe benefits of over 500 business information specialists and librarians primarily in service sectors such as banking and finance, advertising and marketing, accountancy and management consultancy, insurance and actuarial services, legal, and professional bodies. Based on a survey carried out by TFPL.
Frequency	Annual
Availability	General
Cost	£75, £25 to participants
Comments	
Address	17-18 Britton Street, London EC1M 5NQ
Telephone	0171 251 5522
Fax	0171 251 8318

821 TIMBER TRADES JOURNAL

Title	**Markets**
Coverage	Various statistics on timber and wood consumption, trade, prices etc. Different statistics appear each week and based on various sources.
Frequency	Weekly in a weekly journal
Availability	General
Cost	£98
Comments	
Address	Miller Freeman Publications Ltd, Sovereign Way, Tonbridge TN9 1RW
Telephone	01732 364422
Fax	01732 361534

822	TIN INTERNATIONAL
Title	**LME Prices/Stocks/Turnover**
Coverage	Prices, stocks, and turnover of tin on the London Metal Exchange plus a general market report.
Frequency	Monthly in a monthly journal
Availability	General
Cost	£120
Comments	
Address	MIIDA Ltd, PO Box 224, Redhill, Surrey RH1 5YS
Telephone	01342 844988
Fax	01342 844988

823	TMS PARTNERSHIP
Title	**Clothesline**
Coverage	An omnibus survey based on a sample of 3,000 adults aged between 15 and 75. Information on attitudes to fashion, and recent clothing and footwear shopping behaviour.
Frequency	Monthly
Availability	General
Cost	On application
Comments	
Address	Cambridge House, 180 Upper Richmond Road, Putney, London SW15 2SH
Telephone	0181 785 2302
Fax	0181 788 2293

824	TMS PARTNERSHIP
Title	**Homehelp**
Coverage	A quarterly survey of 3,000 adults concentrating on their recent shopping behaviour in the house furnishing market.
Frequency	Quarterly
Availability	General
Cost	On application
Comments	
Address	Cambridge House, 180 Upper Richmond Road, Putney, London SW15 2SH
Telephone	0181 785 2302
Fax	0181 788 2293

825   TOBACCO MANUFACTURERS' ASSOCIATION

Title	**Tobacco Figures**
Coverage	Statistics and commentary on the tobacco industry with tables covering the market, taxes, employment, sponsorship, and advertising. Based on various sources.
Frequency	Regular
Availability	General
Cost	Free
Comments	
Address	Glen House, Stag Place, London SW1E 5AE
Telephone	0171 828 2041
Fax	0171 630 9638

826   TOP FLIGHT RESEARCH LTD

Title	**Exporter Omnibus**
Coverage	A regular telephone survey of exporting companies in manufacturing and services aimed at companies offering services to exporters.
Frequency	Regular
Availability	General
Cost	On application
Comments	
Address	Weir House, Hurst Road, Hampton Court, Surrey KT8 9AQ
Telephone	0181 941 2505
Fax	0181 941 2149

827   TOP FLIGHT RESEARCH LTD

Title	**International and Express Users Panel**
Coverage	A regular survey of users of freight and express parcel services, carried out by the above company.
Frequency	Regular
Availability	General
Cost	On request
Comments	
Address	Weir House, Hurst Road, Hampton Court KTA 9AQ
Telephone	0181 941 2505
Fax	0181 941 2149

828	TOY TRADER
Title	**Market Surveys**
Coverage	Each issue contains a survey of a specific toy market, eg electronic toys, board games, dolls, educational toys etc, with commentary and statistics on trends in the market.
Frequency	Regular in a monthly journal
Availability	General
Cost	£52
Comments	
Address	Turret Group PLC, Turret House, 171 High Street, Rickmansworth WD3 1SN
Telephone	01923 777000
Fax	01923 771297

829	TRADE INDEMNITY
Title	**Quarterly Financial Survey**
Coverage	Financial review of major sectors with details of late payments. Based on data collected by the company.
Frequency	Quarterly
Availability	General
Cost	Free
Comments	
Address	12-34 Great Eastern Street, London EC2A 3AX
Telephone	0171 739 4311
Fax	0171 729 7682

830	TRADE INDEMNITY
Title	**Quarterly Business Review**
Coverage	The UK economy and industrial performance by major sectors followed by annual and quarterly statistics on bad debtors and business failures by trade category. Based on debtors and failures notified to Trade Indemnity by its policy holders. Some Central Government statistics are included and there is a supporting commentary.
Frequency	Quarterly
Availability	General
Cost	Free
Comments	Also publishes a regular press release on business failures.
Address	12-34 Great Eastern Street, London EC2A 3AX
Telephone	0171 739 4311
Fax	0171 729 7682

831 TRANSPORT 2000 TRUST

Title	**Vital Travel Statistics**
Coverage	Details of demand for car, motorcycle, cycle, rail, and pedestrian travel based on the National Travel Survey.
Frequency	Regular
Availability	General
Cost	£3
Comments	
Address	Walkden House, 10 Melton Street, London NW1 2EJ
Telephone	0171 388 8386
Fax	

832 TRAVEL AND TOURISM RESEARCH LTD

Title	**Travel Agents' Omnibus Survey**
Coverage	A survey of travel agency staff with a sample of approximately 200 for each survey.
Frequency	Bi-monthly
Availability	General
Cost	On application
Comments	
Address	39c Highbury Place, London N5 1QP
Telephone	0171 354 3391
Fax	0171 359 4043

833 TRAVEL AND TOURISM RESEARCH LTD

Title	**UK Airlines Travel Trade Image Survey**
Coverage	Examines travel agents' images of the main international airlines. Annual report compare latest annual results with some previous years.
Frequency	Annual
Availability	General
Cost	£5,000
Comments	
Address	39c Highbury Place, London N5 1QP
Telephone	0171 354 3391
Fax	0171 359 4043

834

ULSTER MARKETING SURVEYS

Title	**UMS Northern Ireland Omnibus**
Coverage	A regular survey of 1,100 adults in Northern Ireland based on face-to-face interviews in the home. Covers consumer markets for both products and services.
Frequency	Monthly
Availability	General
Cost	On application
Comments	Also carries out specialist surveys of the Northern Ireland motoring market.
Address	115 University Street, Belfast BT7 1HP
Telephone	01232 231060
Fax	01232 243887

835

UNIT FOR RETAIL PLANNING INFORMATION (URPI)

Title	**Consumer Retail Expenditure Estimates**
Coverage	Expenditure estimates for small areas in Great Britain categorised by type of consumer goods.
Frequency	Continuous
Availability	General
Cost	On request
Comments	Also produces various other reports and packages including demographic profiles, local shopping surveys, floorspace data etc.
Address	7 Southern Court, Reading RG1 4QS
Telephone	01734 588181
Fax	01734 597637

836

UNIT FOR RETAIL PLANNING INFORMATION (URPI)

Title	**199– Register of UK Hypermarkets and Supermarkets**
Coverage	Includes aggregate data on the number of hypermarkets and supermarkets broken down by region.
Frequency	Annual
Availability	General
Cost	On request
Comments	Also produces various other reports and packages including demographic profiles, local shopping surveys, floorspace data.
Address	7 Southern Court, Reading RG1 4QS
Telephone	01734 588181
Fax	01734 597637

837

UNITED KINGDOM AGRICULTURAL SUPPLY TRADE ASSOCIATION LTD (UKASTA)

Title	**Feed Figures**
Coverage	Livestock numbers, output of compounds, compound production by region, use of raw materials, prices etc. Also some European data. Based on a combination of official and non-official sources.
Frequency	Annual
Availability	General
Cost	Free
Comments	
Address	3 Whitehall Court, London SW1A 2EQ
Telephone	0171 930 3611
Fax	0171 930 3952

838

UNITED KINGDOM IRON AND STEEL STATISTICS BUREAU

Title	**UK Iron and Steel Industry: Annual Statistics**
Coverage	Figures on production, consumption, trade of iron and steel products. Also details of raw materials consumed, cokemaking, iron foundries, and manpower. Historical figures given in most tables and based almost entirely on the Bureau's own data.
Frequency	Annual
Availability	General
Cost	£75
Comments	Also publishes regular statistics on steel in specific countries.
Address	Canterbury House, 2 Syndenham Road, Croydon CR9 2LZ
Telephone	01686 9050
Fax	01680 8616

839

UNIVERSITIES AND COLLEGES ADMISSION SERVICE (UCAS)

Title	**UCAS Annual Report**
Coverage	Contains statistics on university applications and acceptances with various breakdowns of the data. Based on data collected by UCAS.
Frequency	Annual
Availability	General
Cost	£12
Comments	UCAS was formed through the merger of UCCA and PCAS, and both organisations previously collected and published statistics.
Address	Fulton House, Jessop Avenue, Cheltenham GL50 3SH
Telephone	01242 222444
Fax	01242 221622

840

UNIVERSITY OF DURHAM BUSINESS SCHOOL

Title	**Small Business Trends**
Coverage	Detailed analysis and statistics on SMEs with sections on general trends, SMEs by industrial and service sector, and future trends. Based on an analysis of various sources.
Frequency	Every two years
Availability	General
Cost	On request
Comments	
Address	Mill Hill Lane, Durham DH1 3LB
Telephone	0191 374 2211
Fax	0191 374 3748

841

UNIVERSITY OF READING, DEPARTMENT OF AGRICULTURAL ECONOMICS AND MANAGEMENT

Title	**Farm Business Data**
Coverage	Based partly on a survey carried out by the University and summaries of other surveys, the report analyses performance trends in the farming sector.
Frequency	Annual
Availability	General
Cost	£7
Comments	
Address	4 Earley Gate, Whiteknights Road, Reading RG6 2AR
Telephone	01734 875123
Fax	01734 756467

842

UNIVERSITY OF READING, DEPARTMENT OF AGRICULTURAL ECONOMICS AND MANAGEMENT

Title	**Horticultural Business Data**
Coverage	Analysis and statistics for three business groups – glasshouse holdings, vegetable and mixed horticultural holdings, and fruit holdings. Based largely on the University's survey supplemented by some Central Government data.
Frequency	Annual
Availability	General
Cost	£7
Comments	
Address	4 Earley Gate, Whiteknights Road, Reading RG6 2AR
Telephone	01734 875123
Fax	01734 756467

843

UNIVERSITY OF WARWICK, CENTRE FOR RESEARCH IN ETHNIC RELATIONS

Title **National Ethnic Minority Data Archive**

Coverage A database of statistics on the UK's ethnic minority population, largely based on the 1991 Population Census. Various reports are published from the database on specific topics, eg economic activity, age/sex characteristics, households, demographic distribution etc.

Frequency Continuous

Availability General

Cost On request

Comments

Address University of Warwick, Gibbett Hill Road, Coventry CV4 7AL

Telephone 01203 523607

Fax 01203 524324

844

UNIVERSITY OF WARWICK, INSTITUTE FOR EMPLOYMENT RESEARCH

Title **Review of the Economy and Employment**

Coverage A regular report on labour market trends and general economic trends with features on specific aspects of the labour market. Includes regional, sector data and some forecasts of employment trends. Specific issues cover specific topics.

Frequency Regular

Availability General

Cost On request

Comments

Address University of Warwick, Gibbett Hill Road, Coventry CV4 7AL

Telephone 01203 523523

Fax

845

VENTURE CAPITAL REPORTS

Title **The Venture Capital Report Guide to Venture Capital in the UK and Europe**

Coverage General review of the venture capital sector with statistics on total trends and details of specific companies.

Frequency Annual

Availability General

Cost £106

Comments

Address Boston Road, Henley-on-Thames RG9 1DY

Telephone 01491 579999

Fax 01491 579825

288

846

	VERDICT RESEARCH
Title	**Clothing Retailers**
Coverage	Analysis and statistics on market trends and value, consumer spending, key players, and the issues affecting the sector. Based on a combination of published data and original research.
Frequency	Annual
Availability	General
Cost	£795
Comments	Also publishes monthly newsletters on retailing in the UK, USA, and Europe.
Address	112 High Holborn, London WC1V 6JS
Telephone	0171 404 5042
Fax	0171 430 0059

847

	VERDICT RESEARCH LTD
Title	**Electrical Retailers**
Coverage	Analysis and statistics on market trends and value, consumer spending, key players, and the issues affecting the sector. Based on a combination of published data and original research.
Frequency	Annual
Availability	General
Cost	£795
Comments	Also publishes monthly newsletters on retailing in the UK, USA, and Europe.
Address	112 High Holborn, London WC1V 6JS
Telephone	0171 404 5042
Fax	0171 430 0059

848

	VERDICT RESEARCH LTD
Title	**Home Shopping**
Coverage	Analysis and statistics on market trends and value, consumer spending, key players, and the issues affecting the sector. Based on a combination of published data and original research.
Frequency	Annual
Availability	General
Cost	£795
Comments	Also publishes monthly newsletters on retailing in the UK, USA, and Europe.
Address	112 High Holborn, London WC1V 6JS
Telephone	0171 404 5042
Fax	0171 430 0059

849

VERDICT RESEARCH LTD

Title	**Department and Variety Stores**
Coverage	Analysis and statistics on market trends and value, consumer spending, key players and the issues affecting the sector. Based on a combination of published data and original research.
Frequency	Annual
Availability	General
Cost	£795
Comments	Also publishes monthly newsletters on retailing in the UK, USA, and Europe.
Address	112 High Holborn, London WC1V 6JS
Telephone	0171 404 5042
Fax	0171 430 0059

850

VERDICT RESEARCH LTD

Title	**Footwear Retailers**
Coverage	Analysis and statistics on market trends and value, consumer spending, key players, and the issues affecting the sector. Based on a combination of published data and original research.
Frequency	Annual
Availability	General
Cost	£795
Comments	Also publishes monthly newsletters on retailing in the UK, USA, and Europe.
Address	112 High Holborn, London WC1V 6JS
Telephone	0171 404 5042
Fax	0171 430 0059

851

VERDICT RESEARCH LTD

Title	**Discounters – Non-Food**
Coverage	Analysis and statistics on market trends and value, consumer spending, key players, and the issues affecting the sector. Based on a combination of published data and original research.
Frequency	Annual
Availability	General
Cost	£890
Comments	Also publishes monthly newsletters on retailing in the UK, USA, and Europe.
Address	112 High Holborn, London WC1V 6JS
Telephone	0171 404 5042
Fax	0171 430 0059

852

Title **Grocers and Supermarkets**

VERDICT RESEARCH LTD

Coverage Analysis and statistics on market trends and value, consumer spending, key players, and the issues affecting the sector. Based on a combination of published data and original research.

Frequency Annual

Availability General

Cost £795

Comments Also publishes monthly newsletters on retailing trends in the UK, USA, and Europe.

Address 112 High Holborn, London WC1V 6JS

Telephone 0171 404 5042

Fax 0171 430 0059

853

VERDICT RESEARCH LTD

Title **DIY Retailers**

Coverage Analysis and statistics on market trends and value, consumer spending, key players, and the issues affecting the sector. Based on a combination of published data and original research.

Frequency Annual

Availability General

Cost £795

Comments Also publishes monthly newsletters on retailing in the UK, USA, and Europe.

Address 112 High Holborn, London WC1V 6JS

Telephone 0171 404 5042

Fax 0171 430 0059

854

VERDICT RESEARCH LTD

Title **Food Discounters**

Coverage Analysis and statistics on market trends and value, consumer spending, key players, and the issues affecting the sector. Based on a combination of published data and original research.

Frequency Annual

Availability General

Cost £795

Comments Also publishes monthly newsletters on retailing trends in the UK, USA, and Europe.

Address 112 High Holborn, London WC1V 6JS

Telephone 0171 404 5042

Fax 0171 430 0059

855	VERDICT RESEARCH LTD
Title	**Out of Town Retailing**
Coverage	Analysis and statistics on sector trends and value, consumer spending, key players, and the issues affecting the sector. Based on a combination of published data and original research.
Frequency	Annual
Availability	General
Cost	£890
Comments	Also publishes monthly newsletters on retailing in the UK, USA, and Europe.
Address	112 High Holborn, London WC1V 6JS
Telephone	0171 404 5042
Fax	0171 430 0059

856	VERDICT RESEARCH LTD
Title	**Neighbourhood Retailing**
Coverage	Analysis and statistics on market trends and value, consumer spending, key players, and the key issues affecting the sector. Based on a combination of published data and original research.
Frequency	Annual
Availability	General
Cost	£890
Comments	Also publishes monthly newsletters on retailing in the UK, USA, and Europe.
Address	112 High Holborn, London WC1V 6JS
Telephone	0171 404 5042
Fax	0171 430 0059

857	VERDICT RESEARCH LTD
Title	**CTNs**
Coverage	Analysis and statistics on market trends and value, consumer spending, key players, and the issues affecting the sector. Based on a combination of published data and original research.
Frequency	Annual
Availability	General
Cost	£795
Comments	Also publishes a monthly newsletter on retailing in the UK, USA, and Europe.
Address	112 High Holborn, London WC1V 6JS
Telephone	0171 404 5042
Fax	0171 430 0059

VERDICT RESEARCH LTD

Title **Chemists and Drugstores**

Coverage Analysis and statistics on market trends and value, consumer spending, key players, and the issues affecting the sector. Based on a combination of published data and original research.

Frequency Annual

Availability General

Cost £795

Comments Also publishes a monthly newsletter on retailing in the UK, USA, and Europe.

Address 112 High Holborn, London WC1V 6JS

Telephone 0171 404 5042

Fax 0171 430 0059

VERDICT RESEARCH LTD

Title **Food Pricing Survey**

Coverage A regular price survey of around 40 major grocery items around the country. Based on research carried out by the company.

Frequency Quarterly

Availability General

Cost £395

Comments Also publishes monthly newsletters on retailing in the UK, USA, and Europe.

Address 112 High Holborn, London WC1V 6JS

Telephone 0171 404 5042

Fax 0171 430 0059

VERDICT RESEARCH LTD

Title **Furniture and Carpets**

Coverage Analysis and statistics on market trends and value, consumer spending, key players, and the issues affecting the sector. Based on a combination of published data and original research.

Frequency Annual

Availability General

Cost £795

Comments Also publishes monthly newsletters on retailing in the UK, USA, and Europe.

Address 112 High Holborn, London WC1V 6JS

Telephone 0171 404 5042

Fax 0171 430 0059

861 WALLCOVERING MANUFACTURERS' ASSOCIATION OF GREAT BRITAIN

Title	**Members' Statistics**
Coverage	Data on the UK wallcoverings sector based on an analysis of returns from member companies.
Frequency	Regular
Availability	Members
Cost	Free
Comments	
Address	Alembic House, 93 Albert Embankment, London SE1 7TY
Telephone	0171 582 1185
Fax	0171 735 0616

862 WEATHERALL GREEN AND SMITH

Title	**Regional Office Rent Survey**
Coverage	Details of rates for prime offices in the main regional town centres and business parks. Based on data collected by the company.
Frequency	Twice per annum
Availability	General
Cost	Free
Comments	
Address	22 Chancery Lane, London WC2A 1LT
Telephone	0171 405 6944
Fax	0171 430 2628

863 WEATHERALL GREEN AND SMITH

Title	**London Offices**
Coverage	Details of rates for premium offices in areas of London. Based on data collected by the company.
Frequency	Quarterly
Availability	General
Cost	Free
Comments	
Address	22 Chancery Lane, London WC2A 1LT
Telephone	0171 405 6944
Fax	0171 430 2628

864 WEFA LTD

Title	**Economic Indicators: Forecasts for Company Planning**
Coverage	A forecast summary is followed by commentary and statistics on UK demand and output and UK costs and prices. Forecasts are given for four to five years ahead.
Frequency	Annual
Availability	General
Cost	On request
Comments	Staniland Hall Associates, the originator of the above report, is now a wholly owned subsidiary of WEFA Ltd. WEFA Ltd also has a range of databases and packages providing international economic statistics and forecasts.
Address	Mappin House, 3rd Floor, 4 Winsley Street, London W1N 7AR
Telephone	0171 631 0757
Fax	0171 631 0754

865 WHITBREAD BEER COMPANY

Title	**Whitbread Take-Home Report**
Coverage	Commentary and statistics on the take-home market for alcoholic drinks with data on market size, brands, outlets, and current trends. Based primarily on commissioned research.
Frequency	Annual
Availability	General
Cost	Free
Comments	
Address	Porter Tun House, Capability Green, Luton LU1 3LW
Telephone	01582 391166
Fax	01582 397397

866 WILLIAMS DE BROE

Title	**Weekly Economic Indicators**
Coverage	Weekly data on UK economic trends with regular forecasts for the main economic indicators.
Frequency	Weekly
Availability	General
Cost	On request
Comments	
Address	6 Broadgate, London EC2M 2RP
Telephone	0171 588 7511
Fax	0171 588 8860

867	WOOL DEVELOPMENT INTERNATIONAL LTD
Title	**Wool Figures**
Coverage	Statistics covering raw fibres, net domestic availability, the manufacturing process, end products, and consumption. Historical data in most tables and based on various sources.
Frequency	Annual
Availability	General
Cost	£20
Comments	
Address	Development Centre, Valley Drive, Ilkley, West Yorkshire LS29 8PB
Telephone	01943 603376
Fax	

868	WOOL RECORD
Title	**The Wool Market**
Coverage	Statistics on the prices of wool based on data collected by the journal.
Frequency	Monthly in a monthly journal
Availability	General
Cost	£68
Comments	
Address	World Textile Publications Ltd, 76 Kirkgate, Bradford BD1 1TB
Telephone	01274 731907
Fax	01274 735045

869	WOOL RECORD
Title	**Weekly Market Report**
Coverage	A weekly summary of prices and news relating to the wool market.
Frequency	Weekly
Availability	General
Cost	£118
Comments	Published every Thursday.
Address	World Textile Publications Ltd, 76 Kirkgate, Bradford BD1 1TB
Telephone	01274 731907
Fax	01274 735045

WOOL RECORD

Title	**Weekly Market Fax Report**
Coverage	A summary of prices and news on the wool industry transmitted by fax to a client's fax machine.
Frequency	Weekly
Availability	General
Cost	£165
Comments	
Address	World Textile Publications Ltd, 76 Kirkgate, Bradford BD1 1TB
Telephone	01274 731907
Fax	01274 735045

Part II

Title Index

All the specific titles covered in this directory are listed alphabetically here. Titles beginning with numbers such as '31' are listed at the beginning of the sequence. Annual reports are listed individually under 'Annual Reports' followed by the name of the organization publishing a particular annual report. The numbers given are entry numbers, not pages.

Part III

Subject Index

A

Accountants - Salaries 3, 414
Actuaries - Salaries 722
Adhesives 71
Advertising 7, 8, 10, 638, 809
  Cinemas 267
  Complaints 12
  Costs 337
  Employment 482
  Expenditure 11, 712, 713, 714,
    715
  Forecasts 9
  Media 337
  Outdoor 650, 761
  Poster 650, 761
Aerosols 72, 549
Aggregates 73
Agricultural Machinery 74
  Overseas Trade 14
Agriculture 233, 701, 841
  Feed 837
  Investment 496
  Land 354
  Omnibus Surveys 760
Agrochemicals 75
Airlines 270, 833
  Punctuality 268, 271
Airports 46, 47, 48, 216, 228, 269
Alcoholic Drinks 68, 396, 620,
    627, 766, 777, 807, 865
Alternative Investment Market
    492, 508
Aluminium 16
Architects 19, 20, 629
  Opinion Surveys 754
Archives 229
Audio Equipment 129, 137
Audio Software 128, 129
Automatic Vending 45
Automotives 747, 748
  Company Cars 586
  Prices 274

B

Baby Foods 309
Baby Products - Omnibus
    Surveys 727
Bakery Products 358
Banking Staff - Salaries 3, 570

Bankruptcies 44, 329, 789, 829
Banks 49, 50, 52, 54, 55, 79, 81
  Clearings 22, 23, 527
  Computers 535
  Corporate Sector 54
  Lending 82, 375
  Mortgages 80
Barley 69
Beer 68
Benefits Housing 254
Betting 184
Biscuits 63, 64
Board 164, 663, 664, 667, 671,
    672
  Energy Use 669
  Overseas Trade 666
  Prices 662
Boating 120
Books 65, 66, 91, 707
  Prices 66, 518
Bottled Water 272
  Glass 112
Bread 370
Bricks 70
Brown Goods 136, 137, 138,
    139, 140, 217
Budgets - Libraries 517
  Public Libraries 517
Builders Merchants 171
Building 59, 70, 170, 171, 173,
    176, 178, 180, 605, 607
  Builders Merchants 171
  Contracts 289, 290
  Costs 175, 177, 755, 758
  Employment 172
  Forecasts 192, 286, 287, 606
  Opinion Surveys 179, 360
  Prices 710, 756, 757, 792, 793,
    795, 796, 797
  Share Prices 174
  Wages 797
Building Materials 73
Building Plant - Prices 791
Building Services 180
  Prices 794
Building Societies - Computers
    536
  Mortgages 181
Business Conditions 87, 207,
    279, 280, 584, 632, 750, 829,
    830